Kenrick and Lundberg-Kenrick have written a mind-opening and captivating book about what it means to be human. What can we learn from our ancestors and from the science of evolutionary and positive psychology to bring out the better angels of our nature? Full of little gems of revealing stories, research studies, insights, and practical advice, their book will help you understand your own motivation and behavior and become wiser, happier, and more successful in your everyday life.

The Kenricks' recommendations for how to live well are classic and wise, but they are also fresh. By embedding their advice in psychological research, this thoughtful father-and-son team appeals to a generation disaffected with traditional rationales. *Solving Modern Problems With a Stone-Age Brain* offers a well-informed recipe for an enlightened social life.

This book redesigns Maslow's classic pyramid of human needs and flips the script on every life advice book you've ever read. Its revolutionary insights show how to be more effective in the seven arenas of your life that really matter.

A terrific volume and a lively read. Evolutionary psychology has matured as a science with important real-world applications for improving the quality of life; the book captures these with the best scientific evidence and superbly engaging stories of real lives. It's a must-read.

I loved this book! *Solving Modern Problems With a Stone-Age Brain* is one part textbook, one part self-help manual. It addresses some of the most important questions facing people in our modern world with humor, compassion, and (most importantly!) solid science. I recommend this book to anyone who is looking to better understand themselves and why it can be so hard to be happy. Filled with an abundance of research-backed solutions for avoiding the pitfalls of contemporary living, this book will make you look at yourself differently.

This book is a great introduction to evolutionary psychology, a handy and useful handbook of practical advice, and a delightfully touching father-and-son collaborative tale.

Kenrick and Lundberg-Kenrick provide a truly new and unique vantage point—through the science of evolutionary psychology—to better understand what makes people do the things they do in the workplace and beyond, and how you can do them more effectively yourself.
—NOAH GOLDSTEIN, PHD, UNIVERSITY OF CALIFORNIA, LOS ANGELES ANDERSON SCHOOL OF MANAGEMENT, LOS ANGELES, CA, UNITED STATES; COAUTHOR OF *YES! 50 SCIENTIFICALLY PROVEN WAYS TO BE PERSUASIVE*

Doug Kenrick is no ordinary professor, and this is no ordinary book. Blending the hard-won lessons of a misspent youth and a brilliant career in the lab, Kenrick and his polymath progeny have written the book that Darwin and Maslow would have dreamed up had they only met. Great fun and hugely insightful!
—WILLIAM VON HIPPEL, PHD, UNIVERSITY OF QUEENSLAND, ST. LUCIA, QUEENSLAND, AUSTRALIA; AUTHOR OF *THE SOCIAL LEAP: THE NEW EVOLUTIONARY SCIENCE OF WHO WE ARE, WHERE WE COME FROM, AND WHAT MAKES US HAPPY*

Solving Modern
Problems with a
STONE-AGE
BRAIN

Nancy's Friend,

   Nancy read this
book and then gave it
to you!

              -Dave L-K

                    Doug Kenrick

Douglas T. Kenrick, PhD, and David E. Lundberg-Kenrick

Solving Modern Problems with a STONE-AGE BRAIN

Human Evolution and the Seven Fundamental Motives

 AMERICAN PSYCHOLOGICAL ASSOCIATION

Published by
APA LifeTools
750 First Street, NE
Washington, DC 20002
https://www.apa.org

Order Department
https://www.apa.org/pubs/books
order@apa.org

In the U.K., Europe, Africa, and the Middle East, copies may be ordered from Eurospan
https://www.eurospanbookstore.com/apa
info@eurospangroup.com

Typeset in Sabon by Circle Graphics, Inc., Reisterstown, MD

Printer: Gasch Printing, Odenton, MD
Cover Designer: Mark Karis

Library of Congress Cataloging-in-Publication Data

Names: Kenrick, Douglas T., author. | Lundberg-Kenrick, David E., author. | American Psychological Association.
Title: Solving modern problems with a stone-age brain : human evolution and the seven fundamental motives / by Douglas T. Kenrick and David E. Lundberg-Kenrick.
Description: Washington, DC : American Psychological Association, [2022] | Includes bibliographical references and index. | Summary: "This book uses stories and advice rooted in the science of evolutionary psychology to present a systematic new way to thrive in the modern world"-- Provided by publisher.
Identifiers: LCCN 2021047288 (print) | LCCN 2021047289 (ebook) | ISBN 9781433834783 (paperback) | ISBN 9781433834790 (ebook)
Subjects: LCSH: Evolutionary psychology. | Self-actualization (Psychology)
Classification: LCC BF698.95 .K47 2022 (print) | LCC BF698.95 (ebook) | DDC 155.7--dc23/eng/20211210
LC record available at https://lccn.loc.gov/2021047288
LC ebook record available at https://lccn.loc.gov/2021047289

https://doi.org/10.1037/0000286-000

Printed in the United States of America

10 9 8 7 6 5 4 3 2 1

For Greta, Fin, and Liam.
May this book help you conquer the world.

CONTENTS

ACKNOWLEDGMENTS

We owe a great debt to our friends and colleagues who read through the whole book and provided invaluable feedback: Jill M. Sundie, Cari M. Pick, Bob Luce, and Liam Kenrick. Bob Cialdini, Jean Luce, and Michael Barlev gave helpful feedback on early chapter drafts. Steve Neuberg, Mark Schaller, Rich Keefe, Ed Sadalla, John Alcock, Vaughn Becker, and Steve Friedlander provided decades of intellectual inspiration and thought-provoking conversations about the topics and research presented in this book. Several of our anthropological colleagues provided resources on life in traditional societies, including Kim Hill, Elizabeth Cashdan, Barry Hewlett, and Ed Hagen. Joan Silk, Randy Nesse, Rob Boyd, Kim Hill, Bob Cialdini, Jay Braun, Steve Neuberg, Vaughn Becker, Athena Aktipis, Michael Varnum, Clive Wynne, Greg Stone, Art Glenberg, and Sam McClure shared their wisdom with Doug for his seminar on *The Discovery of Human Nature* and provided some of the inspiration for many of the ideas discussed here. Finally, Susan Herman of the American Psychological Association did an outstanding job editing an earlier draft of the book, providing invaluable feedback about ways to get the message across more effectively.

Solving Modern
Problems with a
STONE-AGE
BRAIN

EVOLUTIONARY PSYCHOLOGY AS A GUIDE TO SELF-ACTUALIZATION

How do you win friends, influence people, achieve success at work, get in shape, and, meanwhile, find true love, lasting happiness, and meaning in life? Should one of these life challenges take priority over the others?

Hordes of motivational speakers tell you how you can "win" the game of life: by expanding your network of friends, by earning the most money, by attracting lots of romantic partners, or by acquiring the most status. But pursuing those goals as ends in themselves may not solve your problems and might not make you very happy. Even trying too hard to be happy all the time may take you down the wrong path. Research suggests that doing everything you can to make yourself happy can sometimes paradoxically make you unhappy. Occasionally, you may even *want* to do things that aren't immediately pleasurable—for example, you will often benefit by leaving the comfort of a nice, warm bed to help your friends, coworkers, or family members with an unpleasant task.

Indeed, we aren't naturally designed to ever sit back and feel like we've "won" in a general sense. After we solve one problem on Monday, we wake up on Tuesday and find a new problem to solve. Ditto for Wednesday.

Most of us have at least one or two areas of our lives in which there are problems we would really like to solve. You could run down to the local bookstore, where you would find dozens of advice books about how to win friends, get ahead, find love, and reach fulfillment. Those books, are, for the most part, full of common sense. But, alas, much of that common sense is either wrong, or is only right for some of the people some of the time, or is only applicable at some phases of your life as opposed to others (the rules for making a new friend when you're a teenager are quite different from the rules for finding a romantic partner, and you need a whole new set of rules to hold onto a romantic partner).

One important point we make in this book is this: We don't *win* at life; we just solve problems. But as we discuss, solving problems is something human beings are designed to do, and every problem is also an opportunity. Indeed, the very process of meeting life's fundamental challenges is the secret to a truly fulfilling life.

EVOLUTIONARY POSITIVE PSYCHOLOGY AND THE SEVEN FUNDAMENTAL MOTIVES

The past few decades have seen major advances in our understanding of human nature. A lot of those advances were made in the pursuit of purely scientific goals: to answer theoretical questions about the links between *Homo sapiens* and other animals, to figure out how the human brain processes information or experiences emotion, or to gauge the differences and similarities between human beings living in widely dispersed cultures from the Brazilian jungle to Outer Mongolia. Along the way, though, the basic science has, almost serendipitously, uncovered precious nuggets of practical wisdom. Those nuggets are often scattered about, sometimes hidden in obscure scientific articles accessible only to those who have a multilingual mastery of arcane jargons found in biology, anthropology, and experimental psychology journals. And a collection of all the practical wisdom from all those decades of interdisciplinary research and theorizing might simply make for an updated and more complicated laundry list—101 random scientific factoids about this, that, or some other thing.

But after years of delving into all this research, we came to a surprising realization: A lot of that emerging wisdom can be organized into a simple and easy-to-visualize scheme—a seven-step pyramid of fundamental human motives (see Figure 1). Understanding how those seven motives operate can help you make

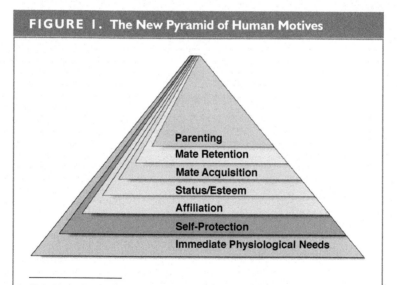

FIGURE 1. The New Pyramid of Human Motives

Parenting
Mate Retention
Mate Acquisition
Status/Esteem
Affiliation
Self-Protection
Immediate Physiological Needs

Note. Many of our everyday problems in the modern world are linked to these seven fundamental motives. These motives are linked to recurring problems and opportunities faced by our ancestors, but as we discuss throughout this book, they can present novel problems today. From "Renovating the Pyramid of Needs: Contemporary Extensions Built Upon Ancient Foundations," by D. T. Kenrick, V. Griskevicius, S. L. Neuberg, and M. Schaller, 2010, *Perspectives on Psychological Science, 5*(3), p. 293 (https://doi.org/10.1177/1745691610369469). Copyright 2010 by D. T. Kenrick. Adapted with permission.

more thoughtful choices and ultimately result in a more satisfying and fulfilling life.

You might be familiar with Abraham Maslow's hierarchy of needs, which has often been depicted in books on psychology and business as a similar-looking pyramid (see Figure 2). Maslow's view was that we all begin life trying to satisfy physiological and social motives (the lower four steps in the classic pyramid), which he viewed as *deficiency needs*. If you satisfy all those deficiency needs, you are free to move on to growth needs; the highest level

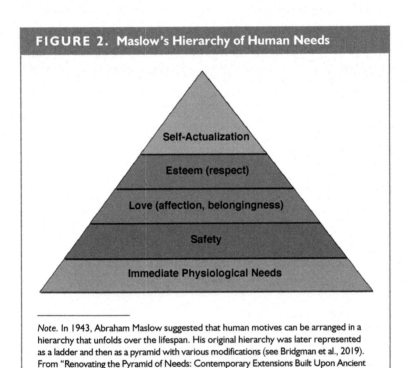

FIGURE 2. Maslow's Hierarchy of Human Needs

Note. In 1943, Abraham Maslow suggested that human motives can be arranged in a hierarchy that unfolds over the lifespan. His original hierarchy was later represented as a ladder and then as a pyramid with various modifications (see Bridgman et al., 2019). From "Renovating the Pyramid of Needs: Contemporary Extensions Built Upon Ancient Foundations," by D. T. Kenrick, V. Griskevicius, S. L. Neuberg, and M. Schaller, 2010, *Perspectives on Psychological Science, 5*(3), p. 293 (https://doi.org/10.1177/1745691610369469). Copyright 2010 by D. T. Kenrick. Adapted with permission.

is *self-actualization*, or the desire to become all you can become. Maslow's favorite examples of self-actualization were a musician playing music, a poet writing poetry, or an artist painting—not for the praise of others but solely for the satisfaction of expressing their own self-potential.

Maslow proposed his hierarchy of needs as an alternative to the then-prevailing behaviorist blank slate model of human nature. According to the old view, social motives—such as the desire for love or friendship or respect from others—are not part of our nature but are built on more basic physiological needs like hunger and thirst. From that traditional perspective, we only crave love and affection because we associate those social rewards with the milk we received from our mothers. Since Maslow's time, developments in cognitive neuroscience, developmental psychology, and evolutionary biology have lent support to his alternative view—that the human mind comes pre-equipped with several different social motives and that those separate motives are not simply secondary add-ons to a general hunger-based motivational system.

Another of Maslow's contributions was to help turn the field of psychology away from an exclusive focus on the negative—the miserably neurotic and aggressive side of humanity—and toward the study of healthy people. Indeed, Maslow did an intensive study of a number of people he regarded as shining exemplars of healthy and productive human functioning, including public figures, such as Eleanor Roosevelt, Abraham Lincoln, Albert Einstein, and John Muir, as well as several of his own colleagues and mentors, including the influential anthropologist Ruth Benedict. As such, Maslow set the stage for more recent developments in *positive psychology*, which scientifically delves into the causes and consequences of human virtues and well-being as opposed to simply dwelling on our vices and agonies.

Maslow's approach had a lot going for it, but it also had a couple of problems. First, Maslow's theory was, in the style of American society in the 1950s and 1960s, a bit self-centered. He believed that the highest level of human achievement—self-actualization—was a state removed from, and above, the lower social motives, which he saw as based on deficiencies. In contrasting normal people with those self-actualized role models, his favorite examples were artsy poets and musicians pursuing their crafts for themselves, completely independent of the opinions of others. Second, Maslow's focus on self-actualization was quite elitist, so much so that most normal people had little hope of making the grade. In his 1954 book, *Motivation and Personality*, he observed that of 3,000 college students he and his colleagues interviewed, only one of them qualified as psychologically healthy. One!

Another problem is that Maslow's work was done before the modern integration of evolutionary biology and psychology, so he gave no attention to the central Darwinian themes of reproduction. For Maslow, sexual desire was just another one of those physiological deficiencies at the bottom of the pyramid, which presumably could be dispensed with by masturbation, to free one to move up to higher needs. Even the desire for love was something Maslow viewed as based on a deficiency.

THE CLASSIC PYRAMID GETS AN UPDATE

After studying the evolutionary psychology of human motives for almost 2 decades, I (Doug) and several colleagues decided to renovate the pyramid of needs to reflect developments in the behavioral and biological sciences during the half century since Maslow originally proposed his hierarchy.

Two important things have changed in the new pyramid. First, self-actualization has been removed from its hallowed place at the top. Why? For one thing, it would make little sense for natural selection to have shaped an organism whose crowning achievement would be to forsake biological and social payoffs and go off to play classical guitar by themselves. More importantly, though, it turns out that there are real social payoffs for artistic and intellectual achievements: Other people respect you, and it may even win you mates (think of Frida Kahlo and Diego Rivera). Indeed, artistic and intellectual performances advertise a highly functioning brain and, in the parlance of evolutionary biology, good genes.

It's not that people don't experience fulfillment from music and intellectual achievements, it's just that those fulfillments are not outside biology, and they are hardly disconnected from the lower social motives. Instead, those higher pursuits are intimately tied to the satisfaction of other less grand motives. Research from our team suggests that regular people associate self-actualization primarily with achieving status and secondarily with affiliating with their friends. If you have young children, parenting motives become increasingly linked to your sense of self-actualization and meaning in life.

Speaking of young children, the new pyramid addresses the missing goal that is paramount from a Darwinian perspective: reproduction. If our ancestors managed to feed themselves, win friends and respect, and then wander off on their own to seek nothing beyond the sheer personal pleasure of drawing pictures on the cave walls, we would not be here to talk about it. Instead, once they were well fed and had accumulated a sufficient bank account of social capital, our progenitors cashed it in to attract a mate. And because humans are mammals, we do not just lay a bunch of eggs and then wander off—as many fish, amphibians, and insects do, for example. All mammals, including our ancestors, have been designed to invest a great deal of resources in their offspring. Among mammals, humans invest more time in parenting than almost any other species (with the possible exception of elephants, which also spend more than a decade raising their calves).

But there's one other important way humans stand out from elephants and from 95% of other mammals: In our species, it's not just the mothers who are involved in parenting; fathers also typically invest heavily in their offspring. So, the new pyramid adds three more layers associated with reproduction: finding mates, maintaining relationships with those mates (which involves a distinct set of skills from finding them, as some of us have learned), and parenting.

Another change is that the motives are not stacked on top of one another but are shown as overlapping. Psychologists no longer view motives as falling into a linear hierarchy in which the lower motives are left behind in favor of the higher motives. Maslow himself did not arrange the motives into the familiar pyramid shape, but he did describe them as a hierarchy and often distinguished "basic needs" from "higher needs." This has led to a couple of problems. First, it makes it seem as though we can simply forget about one need as we move on to the next one in line. Second, it is an easy mistake to look at the classic pyramid and think, "I should really focus on self-actualization." When some people have looked at the new pyramid, they ask, "Does this imply that I should forget self-actualization and run out and have 50 kids?" As we describe, that's not how it works. You do not "win" by jumping up to the "top."

The overlapping motives in the revised pyramid also explicitly represent the assumption that none of the motives is any more important than any other. We have evolved separate motivational systems for each of the seven motives, and those systems don't go away as we develop. Instead, they click into action as needed (to get food, keep us safe, attend to our friends, and protect our reputations whenever the need arises).

THE NEW PYRAMID CONNECTS WITH A VERY OLD SET OF HUMAN PROBLEMS

We believe the new pyramid provides a perfect structure for organizing the essential tasks of human life. Rather than a nearly inaccessible peak experience for the chosen few, the potential for growth and self-actualization can be found at every step of the pyramid and in accomplishing the humblest goals of everyday life.

Each of the seven steps in the new motivational pyramid represents one of the core problems that unfolds over the life course: surviving, protecting ourselves from the bad guys, forming friendships, winning respect, attracting mates, hanging onto those mates, and caring for our families. These are the same problems our ancestors needed to solve, and they are also the problems you, me, and your Aunt Mildred in Cleveland need to solve today.

Our biggest problems in the modern world are the same problems our great-great grandparents had to solve back in their old-world ancestral village. But despite all the technological advances designed to make life easy in the modern world, there is an ironic twist: The perennial human problems are, in some important ways, even more difficult to solve today. Two big factors combine to make the old problems so difficult to solve in today's world. First, the default solutions—the psychological reactions we inherited because they helped our ancestors survive in the ancient world—are not always well matched to our modern circumstances. So, we can't just "act naturally" anymore. The second problem is this: The very strength of our ancestral desires has opened us up to a whole new set of technological parasites in the modern world.

A ROUGH MAP OF THE TERRAIN WE COVER

In the first chapter of this book, we look at a to-do list for a proto-typical human ancestor, someone living in a small group of hunter-gatherers in the preagricultural world. Then we compare the ancestral to-do list with a to-do list for someone living in the modern world. In other words, what did our human ancestors need to accomplish to survive and thrive in human groups, and what can we surmise about their motivations in life? And how do the powerful motivations we inherited from those ancestors help or hinder our attainment of fulfilling lives in today's world?

In each chapter that follows, we introduce someone with a uniquely modern problem—like Walter Hudson, a young suburbanite who ate his way up to a weight of 1,197 pounds and couldn't even fit through the doorway to leave his bedroom, or William Bulger, a successful university president who had to decide whether to help the FBI track down his brother, a mob boss responsible for more than a dozen murders. We then visit a traditional society—like the Maisin from coastal New Guinea or the Aché living deep inside the Paraguayan jungle. We delve into the day-to-day problems these traditional people face in trying to survive, avoid the bad guys, make friends, get ahead, find mates, hang onto those mates, and care for their families. After that, we consider how those same problems unfold for people trying to make it in the more luxurious circumstances of the modern world, with Siri, Alexa, and a thousand YouTube videos standing ready to help out. Each chapter then taps into research at the interface of evolutionary biology and positive psychology to derive a handful of practical tips about how to solve those perennial problems while simultaneously avoiding the newly evolved microplunderers and roboparasites that exploit the latest technologies to prey on our powerful ancestral motivations.

In the last chapter, we try to extract the most important lessons we've learned. We then come up with a plan to put ourselves, and you, into the picture.

THE NATURALISTIC FALLACY: OSCEOLA McCARTY VERSUS GENGHIS KHAN

Understanding our ancestral motivations can be helpful if we want to achieve fulfilment in the modern world, but that does not mean that the path to self-realization is to follow the dictates of "genetically determined" ancestral motivations. Indeed, we believe the role model for a personally fulfilling life is not Genghis Khan, who was successful in passing on his genes, but a woman named Osceola McCarty, who never had any offspring.

Osceola McCarty was an African American woman born in Mississippi in 1908. She dropped out of school in the sixth grade to help an ailing aunt. Osceola never returned to her education but went to work washing other people's clothes. She owned a washing machine for a time, but she felt it didn't do a thorough job, so she preferred the old-fashioned method: boiling a pot of water over a fire and washing clothes by hand with a scrubbing board.

Although washing clothes might not be everyone's idea of a dream job, Osceola took joy in her occupation: "I loved the work. The bright fire. Wrenching the wet, clean cloth. White shirts shinin' on the line." She stuck with it for 75 years, until, at age 86, her arthritis forced her to retire.

Osceola never owned a car, and she had to walk a mile with a shopping cart to get groceries at the local supermarket in Hattiesburg, Mississippi. She did not subscribe to a newspaper, which she considered too expensive. Her sole extravagance was occasionally watching a small black-and-white television set. The center of her social life was attending services at the Friendship Baptist Church.

Although Osceola's income was meager, she saved most of what she earned, and at age 87 had a bank account of $280,000. This is equivalent to $499,179 in 2021 dollars, a substantial sum for someone with essentially no bills to pay. When the trust officer at Osceola's bank asked her how she intended to invest all that money, she gave a surprising answer: She wanted to give it to other people.

True to her word, she donated $150,000 (more than half of her assets) to the University of Southern Mississippi, requesting that it be used to help poor Black students go to college.

When President Bill Clinton presented Osceola with the Presidential Citizens Medal for her noteworthy self-sacrifice, she was interviewed by the press. Although proud that her hard-earned money would be used to help young people, she said she regretted she did not have more to give. Her generosity inspired other donors to double her contribution to the scholarship fund and moved the wealthy Ted Turner to give away a billion dollars. In the face of all the attention, though, she was a model of humility:

> People tell me now that I am a hero . . . I am nobody special. I am a plain, common person . . . no better than anybody else . . . I don't want to be put up on a pedestal; I want to stay right here on the ground.

Although you might personally choose someone like the Nobel Prize–winning Jennifer Doudna or the Pulitzer Prize–winning Samantha Power as a role model, we explain in the final chapter why we think that the humble Osceola McCarty had figured out one of the main secrets to a satisfying and meaningful life.

There is a common misconception that an evolutionary perspective on human behavior would imply that your ideal role model should not be Osceola McCarty but, rather, someone like Genghis Khan, who successfully got his genes into future generations. By one estimate, Genghis Khan has 16 million descendants, roughly one out of every 200 people living on earth today. If the name of the evolutionary game is to replicate your genes, then shouldn't you act like Genghis Khan and lead a life of pillage, murder, and rape, or whatever it takes?

The notion that we modern people might want to imitate our most "genetically successful" ancestors is an example of what evolutionary psychologists and biologists call the *naturalistic fallacy*, the idea that what is natural is somehow "good." The problem with the natural-equals-good equation should become clear if you consider some of the natural ways in which various organisms replicate their genes: wasps that paralyze caterpillars and lay their eggs inside their bodies, cuckoos who trick other birds into raising the cuckoos' young, and viruses that deceive their hosts' immune systems. So, although people often advise you to "do what feels right for you" when deciding on the next step you should take in a love relationship or in your career path, it is often precisely the wrong advice to use the rule "do what comes naturally."

Should we instead do as some social scientists have suggested and just ignore biology? Forget how evolution designed your ancestors, and just imagine yourself as you want to be? That might sound lovely, but, unfortunately, all the biological baggage can pose real obstacles to becoming all that you imagine you can be. We imagine ourselves not eating up all the chocolate ice cream, at least not on the first day we bring it home from the store. But that dream can't come true until we learn a psychological trick to defeat our powerful evolved desires for sugar and fat, cravings that were quite adaptive for ancestral humans (as we discuss in Chapter 1). Rather than emulating Genghis Khan and giving free rein to our ancestral selfish desires to kill, rape, plunder, and otherwise self-indulge, we instead need to understand our inner Genghis Khan to help him settle down and enjoy a more civilized life.

Besides whatever barbaric genes we inherited from Genghis Khan, human beings also inherited some universally pleasant characteristics, such as the capacity for love, charity, and lifelong family bonds. So, when people equate a biological perspective with the Hobbesian view that human nature is inherently vicious and selfish, that's a mistake—but so is the Rousseauian view that we are, by nature, angelic. We all have the capacity for gluttony or self-control, xenophobia or samaritanism, cooperation or distrust, bullying or mentoring, lifelong love or infidelity, and brotherly love or sibling rivalry. Understanding what triggers those different inclinations can help each of us live a more fulfilling life and, in turn, improve the lives of the friends, lovers, and family members whose lives are tied to ours. As we describe, research at the interface of psychology, anthropology, economics, and evolutionary biology has begun to reveal some of those triggers. This book delves beneath those discoveries to uncover suggestions for how we can all be more like Osceola McCarty.

CHAPTER 1

MODERN PROBLEMS MEET
ANCIENT HUMAN MOTIVES

Are we obsessing over nothing these days?

The term "first-world problem" is often used to poke fun at the seemingly trivial issues that concern people living in the modern world: lost wireless earbuds, slow internet connections, or baristas forgetting to put a design in the foam on top of our double espresso latte.

Just look at all the signs of progress in the world most of us now live in: near universal rates of literacy, longer lifespans, antibiotics, heart transplants, air travel, supermarkets richly stocked with organic decaffeinated coffee beans, and fresh blueberries and kiwis from South America and New Zealand. And how about the amazing panoply of everyday technological devices: self-driving cars and digital wristwatches that allow you to take phone calls, send text messages, play your favorite tunes, remember a doctor's appointment, check today's weather in Seattle and New York at the same time, and even self-administer an electrocardiogram, all without having to lift your rear end off your double-padded vibrating massage chair with the built-in drink holder for your ginger turmeric kombucha.

These amazing advances in technology can be found not only in the sleek urban districts of Singapore and London but in most parts of the globe today. Whether you're living in a million-dollar high-rise in Bahrain or a small village in a rural part of Paraguay, there's a decent chance you have some pretty nifty modern conveniences, such as a television or a cell phone that brings you into contact with the rest of the modern world.

So, should you just relax? Chill out? Stop whining like a spoiled toddler and realize that whatever you've been obsessing about this week is no more significant than a bad Wi-Fi connection or a temporary shortage of your favorite double chocolate brownie at the local hipster coffee house?

It's easy to imagine that if any one of our ancestors were resurrected into modern London, Madrid, Sydney, Singapore, Buenos Aires, or Cape Town, their first impression would be that they had landed in paradise. They would mock the local residents for complaining about their trivial everyday problems.

But your resurrected ancestor might want to take a closer look because first impressions of the modern world can be deceiving. If you actually delve more deeply into the problems that concern us in the modern world today, they are not such a joke at all. On the contrary, we folks living in the latte-sipping, smartphone-connected, postmodern, postindustrial world are still dealing with all the same problems that our hunter–gatherer ancestors faced on the grasslands of North Africa. And in some ways, we have it worse than they did.

Can't decide between Häagen-Dazs's gluten-free butter pecan versus Ben & Jerry's low-fat Blackberry Cobbler ice cream? Of course, while you're standing there trying to decide, you're also weighing the question of whether you should be having any dessert at all. Our ancestral brains were designed to gobble high-calorie foods whenever they were available, but now we live in a world in which foods rich in fats and sugars are overabundant, and our naturally selected ancestral desires can bring serious costs. Overeating can lead to health problems, dating problems, and even career problems. And that amazing Apple watch that pairs with your late-generation iPhone to send texts and monitor your heartbeat? That nifty little setup comes with a hefty price tag and a recurring subscription cost that might push an already strained budget to the breaking point.

The modern world is filled with a whole new set of parasites that prey on our ancestral instincts, and it's populated by life coaches, religious figures, and fitness gurus taking more of our money to help us suppress those instincts.

Should we do what comes naturally, or not? There are times when our instincts serve us well and times they get us in trouble. In this book, we break down the seven fundamental motives that underlie all our best and worst decisions, and we provide a few scientifically validated tips for fulfilling each of those central human motives in ways that should help you live a happier, more fulfilling life. But first let's talk about how the ancestral solutions that evolved to deal with problems in the prehistoric world set the stage for a whole new set of problems today.

ANCESTRAL PROBLEMS

What are the fundamental problems of human existence? Together with a large team of researchers at more than 30 universities on five continents, we have been investigating the universal motivations faced by human beings around the globe. As part of our broader research program, and as described in the Introduction, we rebuilt Abraham Maslow's classic pyramid of human needs to reflect a half century of research from the fields of biology, anthropology, and evolutionary psychology.

Each of the motivations in the new pyramid (see Figure 1 in the book's Introduction) is associated with a different set of problems and opportunities that our ancestors confronted in the days before psychotherapy, televangelists, and online dating apps. We are all alive today because our progenitors managed to successfully work their way up the pyramid with a to-do list that would have looked something like this:

1. *Survive.* Meeting one's basic physiological needs—for food, water, and shelter from the elements—was a serious problem in the ancestral world. There were no supermarkets, no running water, and no thermostat-controlled air-conditioning systems to keep our ancestors' huts at 68 degrees all year round. Many early humans starved, died of thirst, or froze to death. If they did so before they reproduced, they were not our ancestors (your line descends from an unbroken chain of survivors).

2. *Protect yourself from attackers and plunderers.* Given the scarcity of resources and the ever-present possibility of starvation, there was a lot of competition among different groups for the precious real estate down in the fertile river valleys. Archeological criminologists and anthropologists have taken a hard look at the fossil record and at the circumstances faced by surviving hunter–gatherers living in the style our ancestors were accustomed to. Those historical detectives have discovered something shocking: Life in the good old days could be quite nasty and brutish, with stunningly high rates of homicide. Indeed, our ancestors suffered violent crime rates comparable with those faced today by drug dealers or people living in a war zone.

3. *Make and keep friends.* Our ancestors were not rugged individualists. They needed to band together not only to protect themselves from bands of marauding bad guys but also to accomplish most of the tasks of everyday life. Anthropologists Kim Hill and Magdalena Hurtado carefully tracked the daily calories brought in by members of the Aché, a group of people living deep in the jungles of South America. Most Aché families went through periods during which they would have starved if they had to depend only on their own proceeds from hunting and gathering. But rather than starving, the Aché solved the problem elegantly. Each family pooled

their risks with those of other families: Sometimes, one family captured a wild pig—too much to consume on its own in a world without refrigerators and deep freezers—so they shared with their neighbors. When they had less luck, their neighbors returned the favor. Over the long haul, their alliances have allowed them to survive the inevitable spells of bad luck.

4. *Get some respect.* Some people in the ancient world were more resourceful and clever than others: better at fishing or hunting or building weather-resistant huts, for example. And some were more willing to bravely defend their groups against armed marauders coming over the hill. Those resourceful and courageous individuals won higher status. A better position in the ancient social hierarchy not only had direct payoffs for survival but also helped indirectly with reproduction—status that translated into attractiveness as a mate, especially for our male ancestors. The male/female difference in the status/sexiness equation stems from a trait humans share with all other mammals: Females carry the young inside their bodies and nurse them afterward. That female mammals pay a higher cost to reproduce leads them to be more selective about choosing mates. This, in turn, leads to male mammals competing to show off their superior characteristics: Pick me! Pick me!

5. *Find a mate.* From the perspective of evolution by natural selection, this step was essential. Every one of our ancestors managed to attract at least one person who wanted to mate with them. Not everybody in the ancient world got to reproduce, though, and a reasonable percentage of men went unmated. On the other side, women can only have a small number of children. Because it takes immense resources to carry a fetus inside one's body and then nurse it through infancy, female mammals—our female ancestors included—have been inclined to choose their mates with special care. Female mammals, including our great-great grandmothers, preferred males who had demonstrated they were superior to their competitors. Thus, men at the top of the hierarchy often managed to attract more than one partner.

Human mate choice wasn't all about social status, though. Both women and men placed a high value on cooperativeness in a mate; an agreeable spouse could help with the task of making and keeping friends as well as make everyday life easier in multiple ways. Besides cooperativeness, health and physical fitness were also valued highly by both sexes; any child who inherited traits that helped them stay healthier and more physically fit would have been better equipped to survive.

6. *Hang on to that mate.* Humans are unusual among mammals in that the male often makes substantial contributions to raising the offspring. That was important to human evolution because, unlike hoofed animals whose young can start running along with the herd within a couple of hours after birth, human offspring are completely helpless and dependent. Members of our sapient species are born prematurely because of the combination of their oversized skulls and the limitations that upright posture put on the female's birth canal. Studies of children living in hunter–gatherer groups indicate that kids with two parents as opposed to a solo parent were much more likely to survive. Contrary to the rumors that human love was invented in the Middle Ages, anthropologists have discovered that powerful emotional attachments between parents, completely absent in most other mammals, are universal across human societies. Because our ancestors also lived in small groups and their choices of age-appropriate mates were somewhat limited, if they could find a mate, they were strongly inclined to do what they could to keep that mate.

7. *Care for your family members.* When it comes to reproduction, humans play what biologists call a *slow reproductive strategy.* Some small mammals start churning out offspring at a fast and furious rate, producing litters of babies a few months after birth, but our human ancestors waited many years to begin reproducing and, even then, had few offspring and made a relatively high investment in each one. Not only did the father pitch in but so did the grandmother and grandfather.

Other research on hunter–gatherer societies has found that a child living under ancestral circumstances did not generate enough calories via hunting or gathering to cover their own needs until they were nearly 20 years old. And without the inputs from grandparents and other relatives, the average young couple could not produce enough calories to feed themselves and their children.

So, even under the best of circumstances, our ancestors faced numerous and daunting challenges at every step of life's pyramid. You might think that we, as the descendants of such resourceful individuals, who have inherited whatever traits allowed them to transcend so many obstacles, would be overqualified to make it in the modern world—engineered with so many conveniences and absent all of our natural threats. Shouldn't we all be giggling with happiness all day and all of the night?

MODERN PROBLEMS

Let's compare and contrast our ancestors' to-do list with that of a typical modern hominid dwelling in a typical modern habitat:

1. *Survive.* Unlike the ancestral world, the threat of starvation is not a big problem in the modern world. Although starvation and malnutrition still exist, even in countries with developed economies, the likelihood of starving has dropped dramatically over modern history in most of the world. Many people in wealthier countries now have the opposite problem. The rate of obesity in Europe has tripled in the past 20 years, with 23% of women and 20% of men qualifying as obese. On the other side of the Atlantic, the Centers for Disease Control and Prevention estimates that fully 42% of American adults are obese. It has reached the point at which the World Health Organization estimates

that more people around the globe now die of problems related to obesity than of malnutrition or starvation. Being overweight is linked to diabetes, cardiovascular problems, degenerative bone diseases, and several types of cancer. And, paradoxically, in developed countries, obesity is higher in poorer people than well-off people. Poorer people in developed countries have access to sufficient calories, but because of many factors, such as the relatively low cost of processed foods, they tend to eat foods lacking in other nutrients that would have been a natural part of ancestral diets.

Why the modern epidemic of obesity? The World Health Organization points to the increased consumption of high-calorie foods combined with a decrease in activity. People used to work in the fields and get exercise; now they sit in offices. People used to live in the country and had to walk everywhere; now they live in the suburbs and drive to work, or they live in the city and take the bus or train.

Assuming we're able to buy fresh food and have the skills, tools, and time to prepare it, why do we have such a hard time resisting those energy-dense foods, and why are we so willing to sit around on our rear ends all day? The answer is that our minds were not designed for modern times but for much harsher circumstances. Our ancestors had a hard time finding foods with enough calories to keep them going, and they didn't have refrigerators, so whenever they found a rich supply of berries or caught a fish, they ate as much as they could. And when they did have a full belly, they didn't burn up those precious calories by working any harder than they needed to. If they were near a flowering berry bush and a stream full of fish, they settled in until they really needed to move on.

Ironically, the very inclinations that helped our ancestors stay alive are now killing us. This points to one of the key problems we talk about in this book, which is called *evolutionary mismatch.* Our ancestors survived by doing what comes naturally. They had inherited genetic traits from their own ancestors who lived under similarly harsh circumstances, so they ate when they could and took it as easy as possible under those rough circumstances. We have inherited those same traits, but they are not always well matched to the conditions of modern life. That mismatch is what leads to the "Elvis Presley problem": When you can have all your needs met instantly, eat whatever you want, whenever you want, and get unlimited access to drugs that stimulate the brain's pleasure-producing reward centers (without first doing what our ancestors had to do to earn those rewards), it's hard to stay fit.

Despite the hyperabundance of easy-to-access calories in the modern world, however, we moderns are actually working more hours per day than our ancestors worked. One researcher mined the data from more than 200 studies, and estimated that foragers worked between 6 and 7 hours a day. According to a Gallup Poll, though, Americans now work more than 9 hours per day, not counting housework and cooking. Why put in so many hours when calories are so easy to find? Well, in the modern developed world, we pay an immense amount for shelter (for example, mortgage payments, heating and air-conditioning bills), and we also pay a lot not to have to walk around (car payments, gasoline, insurance, monthly bus passes, and so on). If those 9 hours of work involved hunting and gathering, which would mean a lot of walking around, we'd be in great shape. But when they involve sitting on our rumps at a desk in front of a computer with a handy bag of munchies and a triple chocolate mocha within easy reach, we don't do so well. Psychologists have discovered a solution to the Elvis Presley mismatch problem, and we talk about it in Chapter 2 on "stayin' alive."

2. *Protect yourself from the bad guys.* On a day-to-day basis, we are a lot safer from violence than our ancestors were. Steven Pinker reviewed a massive amount of literature on homicide rates in various groups throughout human history and discovered that the odds of being killed by another person in the most peaceful traditional societies, such as the

Eskimos and the Bushmen, were comparable to the most violent of modern societies. And if we compare ourselves with the more typical traditional groups, which were several magnitudes more violent than the Bushmen, we are many times safer. It turns out that having police forces and the rule of law make a big difference.

Why don't we feel safer, then? Well, our brain's threat detectors get thrown off because we have access to information our ancestors weren't privy to: about murders happening far outside their own local area. We moderns get to hear relentless stories about murders committed not only by our neighbors but also in other towns, distant states, and even faraway countries. All that scary news makes it hard to avoid the perception that these are the most violent of times.

Two things worsen our tendency to overestimate the threat of violence in the modern world. One is an inherited tendency to be selectively attentive to potential threats. That was a good thing in the past because our ancestors did not want to ignore information about anyone nearby who might pose a threat to them. In the modern world, though, we get no benefit from hearing about murders in Chicago, Paris, or Barcelona, unless we happen to live in one of those cities' more dangerous neighborhoods. But there's another mismatch there: Our brains were designed to process information in a world in which we only got news about people who were likely to be actual threats. They didn't know what was happening on the other side of the mountain or a hundred miles downriver, much less in a different tribe a thousand miles away.

And our natural curiosity about dangerous people opens us up to another problem. Because we are so hungry for news about threats, the media can make good money by feeding us stories about the most horrifying dangers everywhere in the world. We've seen evidence of this in our own experience writing blogs for *Psychology Today*: The bad news generates more clicks than the good news, and more clicks translate into more royalties (because they generate more money from the advertisers). An analysis of 20 years of news surveys found that five of the top six most popular categories were bad news, with war and terrorism at the top followed by bad weather, human-created disasters, natural disasters, and crime and social violence. Bad news sells, so the media delivers us a nonstop diet. One consequence is that we overestimate the likelihood of negative events, which makes us more nervous, which makes us even more hungry for news about potential threats.

The connection between news profits and natural fears is linked to another key concept we talk about throughout this book: *technologically enhanced parasitism.* In the natural world, any strong tendency for one organism to accumulate or invest resources will attract parasites wanting to take a share. An antelope spends years eating grass to accumulate enough calories to build sufficient body mass to reproduce. To a tiger, a nicely fattened antelope is just a fancy dinner. If the tiger brings down an antelope, the hyenas and vultures are next on the scene, eager to take their cut. Tigers are full-out predators, but many living organisms are parasites that only eat a small portion of their prey. Mosquitos, for example, drink a tiny drop of your blood but don't intentionally kill you (unless the mosquitos are themselves hosting smaller parasites, such as the tiny protozoans that cause malaria).

That we are willing to invest time and resources in keeping ourselves safe opens up the door to all kinds of technologically enhanced human parasitism not only by the news agencies but by lots of others lurking like hyenas and mosquitos. Political groups generate billions of dollars in contributions by feeding the fears of their particular constituents: "Alert! Those nasty characters on the other side are about to [insert your most feared outcome here]!!!" And every bit of scary news is accompanied by a button you can press to "contribute now to help us stop this threat!" All major credit cards are accepted.

The bad guys didn't always prey on our ancestors with physical violence; sometimes they just stole things from them.

In the modern world, there is less pillaging and plundering, but we are still prey for burglars, pickpockets, and muggers. Those small-time thieves account for only a small portion of financial parasitism today, however. The average person in the modern world probably loses more to institutionalized theft at various levels: Predatory lenders exploit the people least able to afford it, for example, and after scaring us into parting with our money, elected politicians rig the laws to make it relatively easy for white-collar criminals (their biggest contributors) to get away with big-ticket pocket-picking. In Chapter 3, we talk about some psychological techniques for protecting ourselves from physical and financial predation in the modern world.

3. *Make and keep friends.* When it comes to making and keeping friends, we almost certainly have it worse than our ancestors. In the old world, our ancestors were virtually always surrounded by people to whom they were closely linked— either by virtue of being close relatives or more distant kin with whom they shared daily activities, such as hunting, gathering, and tool-making. But in wealthier countries, an increasing number of people live completely on their own. Indeed, the U.S. Census has found a dramatic increase in the number of people living by themselves over time.

Modern mobility compounds the problem. Our ancestors never moved far from their families, but modern job opportunities now entice us to move thousands of miles away. In Florida and most of the states in the American West, more than 60% of residents were born elsewhere, and in Nevada, it's more than 80%. One third of the residents of Sydney are not native Australians but were born in a completely different country.

More and more people in the modern world also live in giant metropolitan areas like Mexico City or Beijing versus small towns or rural areas. Despite the crowds, urban life is associated with increases in loneliness. Numerous studies have also documented that people in the modern world are increasingly unlikely to join social groups or get together socially with friends because they are spending more hours working and commuting to work and then sitting exhausted in front of their video screens watching reruns of *Friends*. One could certainly go out of one's way to make new friends in the big city, but you can't count on an unrelated friend to lend you money for a down payment on a new car or house, or to care for you if you come down with a chronic illness.

Julianne Holt-Lunstad is a psychologist who has investigated what she calls the "epidemic of loneliness." Besides noting that the psychological experience of loneliness has been increasing in recent years, she also has reviewed data from hundreds of studies to suggest that being alone is actually harmful to our health. Not having social connections seems to increase our mortality risk as much as being obese or smoking 15 cigarettes a day.

You might think that the availability of social media could provide a technological solution to the problem of loneliness. But social psychologist Jean Twenge has documented that the more hours young people spend on social media and the fewer they spend in face-to-face contact with other people, the more depressed and anxious they are. In Chapter 4, we offer suggestions about how to make real friends and avoid some of the modern-world traps that undermine and exploit our natural sociability.

4. *Get some respect.* According to anthropologist Eric Alden Smith and his colleagues, our hunter–gatherer ancestors did not live in a completely classless society, but their level of inequality was similar to that in modern-day Denmark. Economists use the Gini coefficient, named after the Italian statistician Corrado Gini, as a measure of the wealth inequality in a country. The least egalitarian societies in the world have Gini coefficients over 55 (these include Brazil and South Africa). The most egalitarian societies, which include Denmark, Sweden, Norway, and Finland, have Gini coefficients of around 25. In the 40 to 45 range, the United States is a little closer to Brazil than to Denmark. Because the U.S.

economy is so much larger than that of Brazil, being at the top means having a whole lot more than those at the bottom. The richest 1% of Americans own almost 40% of the country's wealth. The next richest 9% own another third of the wealth. The remaining 90% of the population has to divide the leftover—28%—among themselves. Even within the leftover 90%, there's a lot of inequality. In dollar amounts, about a quarter of U.S. families have less than $10,000 to their names at a time when the average new automobile costs about $40,000 and the average new home costs about $400,000.

If our ancestors engaged in social comparison, they might measure themselves next to the local headman, who may have been a better fisherman but might also be willing to teach them some of what he knew. But we now compare ourselves with Elon Musk, Oprah Winfrey, Bill Gates, or Yang Huiyan, who live in a completely different, and much lusher, universe in which there are private planes, personal chefs, and architect-designed mansions filled with collections of fine art.

Psychologist Tim Kasser, who has studied the psychology of materialism, points out that more time spent watching television and more time being on social media are both associated with increasing materialism. Becoming more materialistic leads people to feel more competitive and to act more selfishly, with the ironic consequence that materialistic people are not more self-fulfilled. Rather, they are more depressed, more anxious, and more dissatisfied with their own lives.

There's even worse news, though. Martin Daly has collected abundant data to suggest that economic inequality is not merely harmful for your mental health but is also physically dangerous. Places with more inequality have higher homicide rates, owing in large part to the fact that males at the bottom of the social hierarchy, who can't win respect by showing off their Teslas and stock portfolios, are inclined to get physically violent when someone publicly insults them in a way that causes them to lose face. And economists Anne Case and Angus Deaton have documented another fatal consequence of increasing economic inequality in the United States, what they call "deaths of despair." Americans at the bottom of the social ladder—those without college degrees—have in recent years experienced an increasing level of self-destruction with soaring death rates from alcoholism, drugs, and suicide. In Chapter 5, we discuss research-based techniques for getting some respect in the modern world by choosing a career that matches your talents, doing well in that career, and avoiding roboparasites in the workplace.

5. *Find a mate.* Our ancestors' mate choices were rather limited to distant cousins of around their age living in the next village up or down the river—maybe three or four possible options, take it or leave it. Later, in traditional agrarian societies, marriages were often arranged, so your parents could narrow the field of possibilities. In the modern world, we are, on the other hand, bombarded with possible choices, both real and illusory. Men are continually showered in images of Jennifer Lawrence, Bella Hadid, and Rihanna. Women get to lust after Liam Hemsworth, Idris Elba, and Lionel Messi. And dating apps create an illusion of unlimited choice (allowing every mundane woman to hold out for a neurosurgeon who looks like George Clooney, and every mundane man to keep on hoping that the 10,000th swipe will connect him with a woman who looks like Jennifer Lopez but will only have eyes for him, and if she's a neurosurgeon, too, so much the better).

All those choices don't seem to be helping. Fewer Americans are getting married today, and those who do marry are doing so at a later age. In 2018, more than half of 18- to 34-year-olds had no steady partner. Compounded by economic inequality, the drop in marriage rates has been especially pronounced for Americans without college degrees. The same trend is occurring in many countries around the world, including Australia, the United Kingdom, Italy, Argentina, Bolivia, and South Korea.

Trends for the future don't look particularly promising in this regard. American teens are increasingly less likely to date. In 1976, 15% of 12th graders had never dated; in 2018, that percentage had risen to almost 50%. Jean Twenge attributes the decrease in dating to modern technology because teenagers on their cell phones are increasingly likely to stay home rather than to go out and hang out with real people. In Chapter 6, we mine the scientific research for a few tips about how to shop in the mating market, where you're sometimes the consumer and sometimes the merchandise.

6. *Hang on to that mate.* At the same time as marriage rates in the United States have been decreasing, divorce rates have been increasing. Although divorce rates are lower than they were in the 1980s and 1990s (at around 42%–45% in 2020), the general trend over the past 150 years has been a gradual increase (with noticeable peaks after World War II and the Vietnam War). Divorce rates in almost all European countries have also been increasing. Again, divorce compounds with social class, and in both Europe and the United States, divorce rates are higher in couples who are poor and working class as compared with middle and upper class.

The modern environment provides threats to marital fidelity that our ancestors didn't have to deal with. Whereas they lived in small villages surrounded by relatives and in-laws who kept them under surveillance, people in the modern world commute to work in environments in which they are typically around people who are not related to them but who may also be attractive potential partners. And technology doesn't help. Social media and email allow us easy contact with former and current flirtations and ready access to websites like Ashley Madison make it easy to connect with other people interested in infidelity. When we clicked on the Ashley Madison webpage, it featured a beautiful young woman holding a pretty finger in front of her full red lips (in a "shhh" gesture); that image was accompanied by the simple message: "Life is short. Have an affair." There's also a temptingly pink button you can click to "see your matches."

Although long-term relationships can be challenging, abundant evidence indicates that divorce is bad for your mental and physical health. In Chapter 7, we talk about psychological research on how to keep your relationship together in a world full of an increasing number of temptations.

7. *Care for my family members.* In the ancestral environment, we were around our closest relatives just about every minute of every day, and we could rely on a network of family members to help us with child care. Children could run out of the hut to play with their cousins under the watching eyes of aunts, uncles, grandparents, and older siblings. Today, one third of children under the age of 5 are cared for by a nonrelative, usually in a child care facility that is geographically disconnected from their home. And after age 5, virtually all children are shipped off to schools, where they are surrounded by people unrelated to them. Meanwhile, parents are commuting to work and spending longer hours away from the home. If an American family spends more than 37 minutes of "quality time" together every day, they are above average in connectedness. Australian parents spend a little more quality time—50 minutes per day, on average—teaching, reading, or playing with their children, and Ireland and Austria also score better than the United States in this regard, although only slightly. In a study of 21 countries, Korean parents spent the least time with their children, perhaps a by-product of that country's rapid economic development in recent decades.

Even when parents and children are in the home at the same time, the children are likely to be in an attentional black hole, wearing earphones and playing a computer game on their cell phone or tablet, which provide handy babysitting services while the parents are themselves looking at their own devices, reading the latest headlines about terrorism and violent crimes, or sneaking a peek at Ashley Madison. In Chapter 8, we consider the benefits of keeping your kin close and the dangers of modern parasites that prey on our familial instincts.

WHY WE WROTE THIS BOOK

Although parents and children often worked side by side in the ancestral world, and plenty of family businesses still exist in the modern world, there are not a lot of father–son or mother–daughter author teams. Over the past 2 decades, the two of us have been fortunate to be able to work together on a psychology textbook and to film interviews with prominent psychologists from around the world. The father part of our little team (Doug) is a social psychology professor, and the son part (Dave) is director of a media outreach program called Psych for Life.

Together and separately, we have spent thousands of hours digging into the research literature related to this book. While biking around the Arizona desert, we have had numerous conversations about how all those research findings could help us to solve our own personal problems and what we should teach our children about how to climb the pyramid of life. We've also interviewed some of the people we know who have lived incredibly fulfilling lives, many of them successful psychologists, anthropologists, and biologists, asking for their best advice to pass on to our students and to our own children. Along the way, we've learned that incredibly powerful, scientifically validated principles can really help solve the fundamental problems of human existence. We've also learned that the advice in the most popular "self-help" books, although often based on commonsense intuition, is often not useful, is usually oversimplified, and sometimes is actually counterproductive.

Although the framework for the book's organization is based on an evolutionary model of human motivation, the advice we offer is meant not just for fathers and sons or mothers and daughters intent on perpetuating their genes but for people of all reproductive persuasions, for those who choose not to reproduce, and for all sexual orientations and gender identities. As we explain at several points throughout the book, understanding our evolutionary past does not counsel that we repeat it. Far from it, equating "natural" with "good"—the *naturalistic fallacy*—is a logical mistake we noted in the Introduction and return to in later chapters. Doing what came naturally to our ancestors, as we will see, is not a formula for happiness, fulfillment, or a meaningful life in the modern world. However, understanding the past can help us overcome mindless biases that interfere with making effective choices in the present and living more fulfilling lives in the future.

HOW TO CLIMB THE PYRAMID OF LIFE

So, here's the plan for this book: In the chapters that follow, we describe each of the seven fundamental goals and how it operated in the past, and we lay out practical pointers that follow from understanding how each goal plays out in the modern world. We also talk about the obstacles that arise from people's own short-sighted selfish impulses and from other people trying to parasitize our natural impulses or trick us into acting in ways that serve their interests rather than ours.

The next chapter begins at the bottom of the pyramid, offering advice about basic survival. When our grandmother-in-law, Ruth Jaquette, was asked how she managed to live to 100, she offered a simple answer: "Don't drink, don't smoke, don't die." Sounds simple, but as we'll see, things get a bit more complicated.

CHAPTER 2

THE PSYCHOLOGY
OF BASIC SURVIVAL

In August 1962, Helen Klaben was 21 years old and wanted an adventure. She left Brooklyn, New York, to join her friend, Sue Beehler, on a road trip to Alaska (which was a lot less accessible back then). After 17 days on the road, during which she observed, "We met no robbers, sex maniacs, murderers, or con men, as we had been assured was practically inevitable," the duo arrived safely in Fairbanks. Helen landed a job with the Bureau of Land Management, where she worked until February, when she decided it was awfully cold and she needed another adventure—but perhaps in a more tropical milieu. Helen's original plan was to take a commercial flight to San Francisco, where she would meet up with a group of people heading for sunny Mexico. She discovered that Ray Flores was flying his private plane to San Francisco, and when he offered to take her along for half the price of a commercial flight, she jumped at the opportunity. Flores had no instrument flight training, could not work the plane's radio, and didn't have much in the way of navigational training, but his idea was to simply follow the Alaska Highway South. Sounded like a reasonable plan.

Along the way, though, they got lost in thick clouds and couldn't see the road below. After flying around aimlessly above the frozen Yukon wilderness, the small plane ran out of gas and crashed into the side of a mountain. Helen was knocked unconscious by the impact.

When she woke up, she discovered that her left arm was broken and that her foot was half crushed between the side of the plane and the seat. She saw Flores crumpled against the instrument panel, covered in blood. Although he had a broken jaw and several broken ribs, he was still alive. The injured duo managed to get out of the plane and into the frigid Yukon air—minus 48 degrees, according to the plane's thermometer. They realized quickly that they were completely lost and that their supplies were quite limited: a few cans of sardines and tuna fish, two cans of mixed fruit salad, two tablespoons of Tang, a few pieces of chocolate, and some protein pills.

Even with careful rationing, their meager food supply ran out after 10 days. Meanwhile, Helen's injured foot began to develop gangrene. During the first week, they saw a few search planes in the distance but were unable to draw their attention, and soon the planes stopped coming. After 49 days, just before a huge snowstorm that would likely have buried their campsite and spelled their doom, they were finally spotted. Helen had to be carried out on the back of one of the guys in the rescue party. She was surprised he was able to carry her so easily, but on arriving at the hospital, discovered she had dropped 40 pounds.

Most amazingly, Helen had retained an upbeat and positive attitude during the whole ordeal. As she was being carried into the Whitehorse hospital by her rescuers, she was besieged by news photographers. Despite being malnourished and frostbitten, she flashed them a wide smile and humorously recommended to them that getting lost in the wilderness is a great way to diet. When interviewed years later by *People* magazine, she described her harrowing experience not as negative but as positive: an opportunity to discover herself and to learn that she was able to cope with a crisis.

Like Helen Klaben, Walter Hudson was also born in Brooklyn, New York, in the early 1940s. But Walter did not get around quite so much as Helen Klaben. At age 12, Walter broke his leg, became bedridden, and started gaining so much weight that, by age 15, he was unable to leave his own bedroom. While Helen was starving in the Alaskan wilderness, Walter was already on the way to becoming one of the heaviest people in the world. Despite his immobility, though, he was happy and well liked, and his family kept him well fed. On a typical morning, Walter would consume two boxes of sausages, a pound of bacon, a dozen eggs, and an entire loaf of bread. His lunch consisted of four Big Macs, four double cheeseburgers, and eight large orders of french fries. Then, for a typical dinner, he'd eat two chickens, four baked potatoes, four sweet potatoes and, just to make it all healthy, would throw in four heads of broccoli. He washed each meal down with six quart-sized bottles of soda and then polished off most of a large layer cake for dessert. And he had lots of between-meal snacks within easy reach as he lay in bed all day.

After hitting 1,197 pounds, Walter Hudson realized that his health was at risk and set about attempting to lose weight. He made some progress, dropping several hundred pounds. But, on December 24, 1991, at age 47, he died. Although Walter was born 4 years after Helen Klaben, she outlived him by 3 decades, surviving a half century after her wilderness ordeal and reaching the age of 76 in 2020.

The contrast between the lives of Helen Klaben and Walter Hudson illustrates one of the key themes of this book: Our bodies and brains are designed to cope with incredible levels of natural adversity, but the same adaptive mechanisms that helped our forebears survive in rugged ancestral environments sometimes make us easy prey to artificial temptations in the modern world.

WHAT KILLED WALTER HUDSON AND ELVIS PRESLEY IS MOST LIKELY GOING TO KILL YOU, TOO

The official cause of Walter Hudson's death was a heart attack.

As King of Rock 'n' Roll, Elvis Presley moved around more than Walter Hudson. But Elvis shared Walter's proclivity for eating massive amounts of fats and carbohydrates. The once svelte rock icon managed to make it all the way up to 350 pounds by age 42. Then, like Walter Hudson, he died of a heart attack.

Knowing nothing else about you, our best statistical bet is that that's the most likely way you'll die as well. Heart disease was the Number 1 killer in the United States in 2018 and 2017. In 2020, the Centers for Disease Control and Prevention estimated that COVID-19 killed 371,000 people. But while COVID made the headlines, heart disease killed more than 650,000 people during the same period. And it was the same heartrending story back in 1990, 1980, 1970, and even way back in 1930.

For people under age 65, heart disease is not the Number 1 danger to their lives. But it is still the Number 2 killer of people in their 40s, which is when it took out Elvis and Walter Hudson. Whether you die of heart disease—and the age at which it takes you out—is partly related to genes you inherited from your parents and grandparents. But it's also partly related to the choices you make about exercise, diet, and drug use.

Over the past decade, cancer, chronic respiratory disease, and strokes are executioners Number 2, 4, and 5, respectively. The odds you will succumb to those three diseases are strongly related to another behavioral choice: whether you smoke.

Unintentional injuries are the Number 3 killer, which can be further divided into poisoning, motor vehicle accidents, and falls. Poisoning in this case doesn't mean accidental ingestion of rat poison or household bleach; it refers mostly to deaths from drug overdoses—with opiates and prescription sedatives being prime executioners in that subcategory. Whether you take an overdose of drugs is, like overeating or underexercising, a behavior over which you have quite a bit of choice. And your choices also have a direct influence over whether you die from a fall or in an automobile accident. Almost a third of automobile accidents involve a drunk driver, so choices about getting high are a significant factor here as well.

WHY DON'T WE PANIC AT THE SIGHT OF CHEESESTEAKS?

Which of the following two clusters makes you feel more fear: Is it (a) sharks, crocodiles, snakes, and black-widow spiders, or are you instead petrified at the very sight of (b) donuts, cheeseburgers, cigarettes, and upholstered furniture? To put it another way, would you be more nervous going for a walkabout in the isolated outback in Northern Australia, where you might encounter the first set of threats, or for breakfast at a rural diner in the American Midwest, where there is a danger of encountering the second set?

Isaac M. Marks was a member of the Royal College of Psychiatrists who worked at the Bethlem Royal Hospital—whose nickname "Bedlam" became synonymous with madness and chaotic confusion. Dr. Marks specialized in the treatment of anxiety, phobia, and obsessive-compulsive disorders, and in 1969, he published his now classic book, *Fears and Phobias.* In that book, Marks noted that people rarely develop phobias to things that are actually likely to kill them in the modern world, such as motor cars, cigarettes, or guns. Instead, people show up at the clinic with intense fears of things that are no longer threats, such as snakes, spiders, dogs, or having to go outside their homes.

Marks was not the first to observe this puzzling discrepancy. The pioneering psychologist G. Stanley Hall had observed as far back as 1897 that

> the intensity of many fears, especially in youth, is out of all proportion to the exciting cause . . . their relative intensity fits past conditions far better than it does present ones . . . serpents

are no longer among our most fatal foes and most of the animal fears do not fit the present conditions of civilized life.

Exactly how irrational is it for someone to be more fearful of sharks, crocodiles, snakes, and black widow spiders compared with donuts, cheeseburgers, cigarettes, and upholstered furniture? In the United States, sharks kill about one person per annum; alligators, also about one; snakes, six; and spiders top our short scary list at seven fatal attacks each year. Add in those killed by ants, bees, wasps, hornets, dogs, pigs, deer, cows, and horses, and the annual total comes to 182 Americans killed by nonhuman organisms. Heart disease, on the other hand (which is more likely to get you if you eat an unhealthy diet, smoke, and laze around on your sofa instead of exercising), knocks out 1,694 people a day. Yes—that's *a day*. The total in 2018 was 655,381, and, as we just noted, it was about the same in 2020.

The Grim Reaper's heart disease division only takes 2 hours and 40 minutes to reach the same quota as the animal death branch brings down in a whole year. And because we had cigarettes on the second list, it's only fair to mention that chronic lung disease and strokes bring down an additional 307,296 people every year. Adding up the numbers, unhealthy diets, smoking, and lack of exercise contribute to 5,295 times more deaths than do attacks by other animals. And in case you're wondering, the ratios don't look that different in Australia, where, despite all the poisonous snakes, crocodiles, spiders, and sharks, only a couple of dozen people are killed each year by nonhuman animals (and even in the land Down Under, most of the nonhuman perpetrators are farm animals). Heart disease, on the other hand, takes out 19,376 Aussies per annum.

What Isaac Marks and G. Stanley Hall before him were arguing was that our fear systems were not evolved to deal with life in modern cities and suburbs. Instead, they were designed to deal with the most common threats in the jungles and savannahs where our ancestors evolved.

Let's take a quick look at the actual dangers that our forebears did face.

WHAT KILLED OUR ANCESTORS?

We first consider our recent ancestors because the Grim Reaper has radically changed his angle of attack in the past century or two. An article in *The New England Journal of Medicine* compared the causes of death in 1900 and 2010. Back in 1900, the top cause of death was pneumonia or influenza, which killed slightly more people than heart disease did in 2010 (and that's not even correcting for the population growth, so pneumonia or influenza in 1900 was still at least four times more dangerous than heart disease is today). Tuberculosis killed more people back in 1900 than cancer did in 2010, and if you throw in the combination of gastrointestinal infections and diphtheria, the 1900 death tally for communicable diseases equals the total of *all* the top 10 causes in 2010. In 2010, only one infectious disease category made it into the top 10—pneumonia or influenza—but the total mortality for that category was 12 times less than it had been in 1900. And in 2010, no other infectious disease even made the list.

The year 2020 was something of a statistical outlier, however. As of June 2021, 574,000 Americans have died from a coronavirus pandemic that began in March 2020. Big number, but during that same time period, 812,500 people died from heart disease. The COVID-19 pandemic is, at the time of this writing, stubbornly persisting into a second year but is likely to dwindle at some point in the next year or so. Heart disease, however, is fully expected to continue at its same old deadly pace. To give another perspective, the 1918 influenza pandemic killed 675,000 Americans, back when the total U.S. population was only 103 million. So, COVID-19's death toll would have had to reach 2,169,000 to match the virulence of the 1918 flu.

The year 1900 was only three or four generations ago, not exactly the ancient past. What if we were to look at the causes of death back when our ancestors were still hunter–gatherers? Our predecessors were hunting and gathering for at least 90% of our species' history, and agriculture came along a mere 10,000 years ago. Based on estimates from archaeological and genetic data, we *Homo sapiens* have been around, in more or less our current form, for at least 200,000 years. And although the agricultural revolution arrived for some of our ancestors 10,000 years ago, most of our them did not start farming until the past 5,000 years or so (making 98% a better estimate for the amount of time our species spent as hunter–gatherers).

Obviously, there wasn't a government agency gathering data on the causes of mortality 11,000 years ago. But anthropologists, archaeologists, and demographers have come up with clever ways to estimate death patterns in the good old days. One method is to look at evidence from ancient burial sites and archaeological digs, which contain bones that can be analyzed to determine how old their owners were at the time of death. Another method is to look at records from hunter–gatherers who were still around during the past century or two in remote regions of Australia, Africa, and South America.

Evolutionary anthropologists Kim Hill, Magdalena Hurtado, and Robert Walker conducted one of the hallmark studies of comparative mortality rates. The research team collected detailed data on 722 deaths among the Hiwi of Venezuela, who had continued to live as hunter–gatherers until the late 20th century. The Hiwi were likely to die violent deaths from homicides (caused by competitions over women, reprisals by jealous husbands, and revenge for past killings) and from accidents associated with the hunter–gatherer lifestyle. In a similar study, Barry Hewlett and colleagues collected details about deaths among Aka pygmies of Central Africa. Compared with the Hiwi, Hewlett et al. found a lower rate of homicide but a similarly high rate of deaths from accidents (which included people falling from trees as they tried to get honey or palm nuts; being trampled by elephants; and in one case, being gored by a captured antelope). Although we don't die in the same kinds of accidents, this is nevertheless a mortality category we share in common with our ancestors; the important variation is that we die not from encounters with wild animals or falling out of trees but from automobile accidents.

The biggest difference between modern mortality statistics and the death tolls for hunter–gatherers, however, is that most hunter–gatherers do not survive until puberty because infectious diseases kill the majority of infants and children. On the positive side of the ledger, though, hunter–gatherers who survive into adulthood almost never die of heart disease and cancer. The lack of heart disease is probably because obesity is almost nonexistent in hunter–gatherers, who have different diets and spend a lot of their time moving around (no lounging on the sofa munching on donuts and cheeseburgers among the Hiwi or the Aka). Kim Hill speculated that the lack of cancer among hunter–gatherers is attributable to their much lower exposure to chemical toxins.

People often think that hunter–gatherers don't die of cancer or heart disease because they don't live long enough. But that's wrong; many of them live well into old age. Michael Gurven and Hillard Kaplan brought together data from a number of studies of hunter–gatherers living in diverse environments and found that a good percentage of those who managed to survive into their teens went on to live for several decades, often into their 60s and even 70s. If they persist long enough to become elders, though, Hiwi and Aka die of infectious diseases, not heart disease or cancer. It's also worth noting that the infectious diseases that kill hunter–gatherers are not influenza epidemics—those became more common after the agricultural revolution, when human beings started living in very large groups concentrated in dense population centers. Instead, hunter–gatherers die of diarrhea and cholera or of diseases they contract from other animals or from the soil.

Animal attacks didn't stop being a danger to our species until very recently, incidentally, when we moved into large urban areas. Even today, although it may be irrational to be afraid of snakes in London, New York, or Sydney, as many as 32,000 people in Africa and 57,000 people in Southeast Asia are estimated to die of snakebite every year. And although large predatory mammals have been largely hunted to extinction, people in Africa and Asia are still taken out by lions and tigers. In his gripping account of a man-eating Siberian tiger, John Vaillant made a convincing case that when large feline predators were more numerous, many thousands of human beings likely ended up as dinner for a big cat.

So, if we consider the history of our species, it's not at all surprising that we are more afraid of venomous and predatory animals than we are of motor vehicles. Cars have only been around for a few ticks on the human evolutionary clock, not long enough to have exerted a significant influence on our genes. Most of the other things that do kill us today, including the rich foods and lack of exercise that contribute to death by heart disease, are not "unnatural," but our relationship to food and exercise has changed radically since the ancestral past.

Our predecessors, like modern hunter–gatherers, did not need to worry about getting enough exercise; their lifestyles forced them to stay on their feet most of the day. And they did not need to worry at all about eating too many sugary and fatty foods. Instead, because starvation was often a possibility, turning down calorie-rich foods was not a wise decision for them. And although throwing meat onto the barbecue increases its carcinogen potential, Harvard anthropologist Richard Wrangham explained that cooking food was a cultural invention that dramatically boosted our ancestors' survival rates (besides killing germs, cooking food breaks down indigestible fibers so that we get many more calories out of cooked as compared with raw food).

But, alas, because of all our modern technological advances in growing, preserving, transporting, cooking, and processing food into irresistibly appetizing dishes, humans in the modern world are moving away from the lean physique of our ancestors toward the beefed-up Las Vegas version of Elvis Presley. As we mentioned in Chapter 1, the World Health Organization estimated that more people around the globe now die of diseases related to obesity than of starvation. Indeed, obesity-related diseases have begun to increase even for young children, so much so that Michelle Obama decided to make this problem her first priority to address when she became U.S. First Lady.

OUR POWERFUL APPETITES OPEN THE DOOR FOR MODERN PARASITES

If you actually needed as many calories as you could find, ripe fruit full of tasty sugars or well-marbled meat densely packed with caloric fat are about as good as you could ask for. So, we inherited nervous systems that respond with pleasurable sensations to sweet flavors or creamy fats. There's a general rule at work here: Many of the behaviors that bring us pleasure today are behaviors that would have increased our ancestors' odds of survival and reproduction: drinking a cool glass of water when we are parched with thirst, sitting by a warm fire after we've been out in the snow, having sex, or eating foods rich in sugars and fats.

There are economic consequences of all this: If it makes us feel good, we're willing to pay for it. The massive food and beverage industry thrives because we need to eat and drink. But the companies providing those foods and beverages are businesses, and they compete to provide products that satisfy their customers' cravings in ways that maximize not the long-term well-being of the public but profit margins during the next financial quarter. From the perspective of public health, it would be wonderful if the supermarket sold only unprocessed fruits and vegetables, nuts, and unsweetened yogurt. Those are the foods that researchers have found to be associated with being trim and healthy. Indeed, if you go to the local chain supermarket, you can probably find swiss chard, garlic, berries, walnuts, avocados, black beans, and unsweetened yogurt. But if you stand in the checkout line at that same market, there's a good chance you'll see that many people's carts contain none of those healthy things but are instead filled to the brim with frozen pizzas, boxes of macaroni and cheese, potato chips, sugar-coated breakfast cereals, jumbo-sized candy bars, giant "economy-sized" bags of cookies, gallon tubs of chocolate fudge ice cream, and 2-liter bottles of artificially colored sugary beverages. Those unhealthy foods are not only less expensive and less likely to go bad than fresh berries and vegetables, but they have been designed to actually taste better than healthy natural foods. Just try offering a young child the choice between a meal of walnuts and berries versus pizza and ice cream.

We willingly allow the purveyors of processed foods to parasitize our ancient appetites for sugars and fats. But all those profits incentivize them to go a few steps further—to bring those tasty, processed foods to you and your children rather than wait for you to drive over to the local supermarket. They're now pushing their most processed and least healthy goods in vending machines everywhere, even in our children's schools. One study found that 83% of junior high schools and high schools had vending machines that sold primarily what the researchers described as "foods of minimal nutritional values (soft drinks, chips and sweets)."

The food industry has become aware of recent concerns about the epidemic of obesity and also that many people now read the labels, scanning for information about the sugar content. In many cases, sugars would be number one on the list, but their clever solution is not to remove the sugar but to break it down into several subcategories so they can list some other ingredient first and to cunningly sneak out the word "sugar," as in a processed breakfast food label that might read: "Ingredients: Oats, corn syrup, raisins, glucose, natural cane syrup, dextrose, may contain traces of actual nuts."

The food industry is at least giving us something that actually has nutritive value, hence triggering a biologically legitimate blast of gratification in the brain's pleasure centers. But modern technology can now bypass all the natural obstacles and give us a "free" dose of pleasure without our having to perform any actions that would have led to survival in the ancestral world. This is done in the form of drugs, such as opioids or cannabis (our brains have receptors for these substances because their natural analogs in our body previously served an adaptive signaling function). Unfortunately, our endocrine systems respond to drugs that make us high by producing other substances that return us to chemical balance, and over time, our systems respond to psychotropic drugs by producing more of the opposing chemicals. So, with repeated regular use, we need more of the pleasure-inducing drug to get us high. One consequence of this natural drug resistance is that people often unintentionally overdose in an attempt to reach a dose strong enough to reinstate the original pleasant feeling. As we noted earlier in this chapter, overdoses from opiates and sedatives are one of the major contributors to the high number of accidental deaths, and those numbers have been dramatically increasing in recent years.

IS THERE ANY WAY TO ESCAPE THE TRAP OF IMMEDIATE GRATIFICATION?

John Platt was a biophysicist and associate director of the Mental Health Research Institute at the University of Michigan. In 1973, he published a brilliant paper on *social traps*, situations in which individuals or groups do things that are initially attractive but "later prove to be unpleasant or lethal and that they see no easy way to back out of or to avoid." He talked about addictions to alcohol, opiates, or cigarettes as examples of such traps. Platt argued that people get drawn into social traps not because they are evil or lazy or stupid but because they are responding to a powerful principle of reinforcement: All animals, our species included, are inclined to repeat anything that brings us immediate rewards and to avoid anything that brings us immediate punishment. Years of research on learning had demonstrated that if a reward or a punishment is delayed, even for a few minutes, it has much less influence on behavior. The nicotine in a cigarette gives you an immediate lift, and although emphysema or lung cancer is a rather severe punishment, those negative consequences don't come until you've smoked for several decades, too late to undo the unhealthy behaviors that caused them. Likewise, eating a bag of potato chips or a pint of cookie dough ice cream results in an immediate jolt of pleasure, but the negative consequence of obesity won't show up for a long while.

Platt also talked about *countertraps*, which are the flip side—in which the immediate effect of a behavior is unpleasant, and the long-term consequence only comes after a long delay. Jogging is a good example of a countertrap: The immediate consequence is to feel unpleasantly out of breath, whereas the rewarding "runner's high" only comes after months of pushing through the initial unpleasantness. On any given day, your natural production of painkilling endorphins doesn't kick in until you've been exercising for 20 or 30 minutes, so there's always a psychological hurdle to overcome at the start of your jogging session.

Because Platt understood social traps to be the result of simple principles of reinforcement and punishment, he was able to offer several suggestions about how to break out of those traps. First, you can convert long-term punishments to immediate ones. Responding to immediate threats is something we are designed to do. For example, if you are finding it hard to stop smoking cigarettes, as most people do, you can keep a gruesome picture of a lung cancer operation that you tape to each new pack of cigarettes and remind yourself to think about the long-term consequences each time you go for the short-term pleasure of a smoke.

Platt also suggested adding new counter-reinforcers to compete with immediate rewards. Placing a rubber band on your wrist and snapping it every time you think about a cigarette makes you pay an immediate price. Another version of that is to destroy three cigarettes for every one you smoke (that brings the cost of each cigarette up to $2, given the going price of $10 for a pack of 20). Similarly, you could put a dollar in a jar every time you eat an unhealthy snack, and, at the end of the week, give all the money to a cause you don't care about.

The flip side of that is to reward yourself for healthy alternatives—to allow yourself to do something fun after you've gone for 2 hours without a cigarette or an unhealthy snack, for example. It helps to keep a record of your progress and to award yourself points every time you reach a goal. Then, when you reach a certain number of points, you give yourself a payoff—maybe call your romantic partner if you reach your daily goal, and go do some fun activity together if you reach your weekly goal—maybe hike down to a local park, where you can have a snack of tasty berries and nuts purchased with the money you saved not buying french fries and double fudge ice cream earlier in the week.

Platt also suggested that, rather than rely completely on your own willpower, you solicit some outside help. Years of research in social psychology has revealed that public commitments provide powerful inducements to follow through. Our ancestors were designed to crave not only calories but also the respect of their friends. So, you don't want to keep your self-improvement program a secret. To the contrary, you want to recruit a friend or relative to administer the points, the rewards, or both. Even better, you can pair up with a partner who is also trying to stick to a health-inducing diet or exercise regimen so that you can reciprocate and also build a team commitment. You might want to post your goals on social media and then do a regular update about your progress.

One study took advantage of the public commitment principle by recruiting participants for a weight-loss program in teams of three friends or relatives. Compared with those who undertook the weight loss program alone, the teams did much better: Of those in groups, 95% completed the weight loss program (compared with 76% in the control group), and 66% of group participants maintained their weight losses 6 months later (compared to only 24% of the solo control subjects).

Two other critically important principles emerged out of half a century of research on the basic rules of learning and reward. One is the idea of *shaping*—or rewarding successive approximations. If your goal is to lose 30 pounds or to run a marathon, you won't be able to accomplish either of those the first day. So, you start with a goal of reducing by 1 pound and running for 5 minutes; then when you reach that goal, you raise the bar, inch by inch, till you've gradually reached the target.

The other essential discovery about reward-based learning is called *stimulus control*. We quickly learn to associate rewards with cues in the environment that signal their arrival (the mere aroma of baking cookies triggers pleasurable expectations of a mouthful of warm chocolate chips). When those cues are present, our brains are set to receive the reward and will do what it takes to get the expected satisfaction. If you want to control impulses toward unhealthy behaviors, you need to recognize what the triggers are and then avoid them. If you want to stop eating sugary snacks, for example, it's almost impossible if you regularly leave them sitting on your kitchen counter. If you want to reduce your alcohol consumption, it's best not to keep a six-pack of your favorite beer and a bottle of your favorite wine chilling in the fridge.

In a clever study, Brian Wansink and Junyong Kim gave people a bowl of popcorn to eat as they watched a movie. Some got their popcorn in a giant oversized jumbo container; others, in a bowl half that size. The researchers also varied whether the popcorn was fresh and tasty or stale (14 days old). People with the jumbo bin in front of them tended to clean it out, eating substantially more, even if the popcorn was stale! So, if you want to eat healthy, fill your fridge and cupboard with healthy foods and leave the unhealthy temptations in the supermarket.

Incidentally, despite knowing all about the benefits of healthy eating, one of us recently stocked up on a giant supply of chocolate-covered treats when the coronavirus food-hoarding panic hit, purchasing more than a pound each of chocolate-covered almonds, chocolate-covered raisins, chocolate-covered coffee beans, chocolate-covered cranberries, and chocolate-covered cherries. It was easy to find a justification: All the treats were dark chocolate with fruit and nuts inside, and who knew whether there would be a run on chocolate? But after putting these "healthy" treats in five jumbo mason jars on the kitchen counter, the temptation to grab a few of each, on every visit to the kitchen, was irresistible.

Psychologists have derived one very useful bit of wisdom from all this: It's a lot easier to preemptively control your environment than to resist temptation on a moment-to-moment basis. Our ancestors had to search long and hard to find calories; we don't. So, to keep ourselves from ending up like Walter Hudson or Elvis Presley, we need to hide the extra food, preferably by leaving the foods we are trying to avoid on the shelf at the store and instead putting lots of healthy fresh fruits, vegetables, and nuts within easy reach.

Besides resisting the immediate rewards of tasty treats, you also need to overcome the immediate obstacles to healthy behavior, those countertraps. You can rearrange your circumstances to help you overcome the obstacles to exercise, though. For instance, instead of driving to work, consider biking. If you can't manage that, you could park a mile away from your office, which will not only force you to get some exercise on the way in but also require a bit more exercise when you return to the car at the end of the day, a time when you may be less motivated.

SUICIDE: WHY YOU DON'T WANT TO DIE

We have discussed how the choices you make have a profound influence on whether you are taken out by each of the top five causes of death. There is another category of top 10 killers that is *completely* determined by people's choices: suicide.

Suicidal thoughts are surprisingly common. According to the National Institute of Mental Health, major depressive disorder is one of the most common mental problems in the United States, and one in 25 American adults has contemplated suicide in the past year alone. Severe depression is higher in women than in men; in young adults under 25 as compared with older adults; and in Whites as compared with Hispanics, Blacks, and Asians. Abraham Lincoln, often regarded as the greatest U.S. president, was so depressed as a young man that his friends tried to hide any sharp objects in his house. Winston Churchill, often regarded as one of the greatest world leaders of all times, was also subject to extreme bouts of depression. And Virginia Woolf, Sylvia Plath, Marilyn Monroe, and Robin Williams did more than think about it; they actually took their own lives.

From a subjective perspective, it's not that hard to figure out why so many people want to check out. Life is hard. Freud even argued that we all have a death instinct that is continually doing battle with our life instincts. From a modern evolutionary perspective, though, suicide is a great puzzle. If evolution is all about differential reproduction, terminating your own life puts an immediate end to any chance of increasing the number of genes you transmit into future generations. So, the very idea of a death instinct is absurd because any such instinct would quickly be selected out of the gene pool. People without the genetic instinct toward self-destruction would reproduce more than those with it.

Evolutionary psychologist David Buss came to Arizona State University for a conference on the psychology of zombies and gave a very interesting talk on the question of whether it's better to be undead than dead. If you die, of course you will miss out on any future reproductive opportunities, but, as Buss pointed out, that's only the start of it. Any children you already have will face additional obstacles if you can't help them out, and any children they have will miss out on the grandparental resources you might have provided. Besides all that, your children's competitors—for mates and jobs, for example—will gain a complementary set of advantages from the support provided by their surviving parents.

Denys deCatanzaro suggested that some instances of suicide are less of an evolutionary puzzle than they might appear at first glance. He and his colleagues found that people who believe they are unlikely to reproduce and who perceive themselves to be a burden to their families are more likely to think about suicide. The high levels of depression and suicide in modern society may be yet another example of a mismatch between our psychological mechanisms and the modern world. Our ancestors were virtually always surrounded by family members, and there was no such a thing as unemployment. In the modern world, a large percentage of the population moves far away from their kin groups and often faces a good deal of uncertainty about employment prospects. Indeed, researchers have found that residential mobility and unemployment are two big risk factors for suicide. Both of these are, of course, related to social isolation and the perception that one is a burden on one's family.

One perennially interesting factoid about suicide is that women are much more likely to attempt suicide, whereas men are more likely to actually die after a suicide attempt. Over the years, there have been a number of squishy psychological explanations of this difference, such as the suggestion that suicidal women don't really intend to end their lives and are simply "crying out for help." But there is a simple explanation in terms of modern technology: Men are more likely to own guns, and guns are the main tool used in fatal suicide attempts. There is a reasonable chance that someone who uses drugs will survive a suicide attempt, for example, but a very low chance of surviving a gunshot wound to the head.

Guns are in fact twice as likely to be used in a suicide as in a homicide. Worse yet, guns are not only used in suicide attempts by their owners, they are also likely to be used in suicides by their teenaged children. Hence, one effective way to prevent suicide is not to own a gun. Some people feel safer if they own a gun, and some people may actually be safer if they are living in a very dangerous part of the world. However, guns are in actuality hardly ever used in self-defense against bad guys as they are in the movies. Firearms are instead much more likely to be used against romantic partners, friends, and family members, and even more likely to be used against oneself.

FEAR OF FALLING AND THE LACK THEREOF

So, our ancestors didn't die of heart attacks, and they didn't die in car accidents, and we modern urbanites don't die from poisonous snake bites or attacks by lions or tigers or bears. But there is one means of death that was common then, and is still common now: death by an accidental fall. According to the World Health Organization, death by falling is the second highest cause of death by injury in the world (second only to motor vehicle accidents). Even there, though, what appears to be a similarity may mask some important differences.

For one thing, our ancestors did a lot more tree climbing, as we discussed in the case of Aka pygmies in search of honey. But most of the fatal falls that happen now take out not youthful tree climbers or mountain climbers but elderly people who are having trouble with balance and whose bones are more brittle.

Although there's less call to climb trees in search of honey or high-hanging fruit, a number of people in the modern world actually go out of the way to climb up into risky locations. Indeed, millions of Americans are obsessed with rock climbing, bouldering, and mountain climbing. According to one estimate, there were 1,863 deaths in climbing accidents in the United States and Canada between 1981 and 2013. Most climbers do everything they can to protect themselves from injuries, investing in high-quality systems of harnesses, woven ropes, carabiners, cams, and helmets designed to reduce the risks as much as possible. But one might wonder what in the world is going on with the phenomenon called "free solo climbing." Free soloists inch themselves straight up steep cliff faces without any protective gear whatsoever. They are "free" not only of annoying and clunky carabiners, cams, and harnesses but of ropes. The Wikipedia page that listed well-known free climbers had 24 links to other pages about the most famous of the lot. Of those 24, 13 were dead—one from speeding on the autobahn, one from falling drunk down a flight of stairs—and surprise, surprise, 11 of those 13 died in a free fall right off the face of a mountain.

Why would anyone purposefully engage in such risky behavior? A clever study conducted in a skateboard park in Brisbane, Australia, provides an important clue. The researchers, Richard Ronay and Bill von Hippel of the University of Queensland, showed up in the skateboard park with a camera and asked young men (who make up most of the trick skateboarding population) if they would, for $20, allow the researchers to film them while they practiced two skateboard tricks. The skateboarders were asked to choose one trick they found easy and one they found difficult—a trick they were working on but that they failed on 50% of the time.

Skaters were asked to practice their tricks 10 times in front of a male experimenter, and then, after a short break, half of them performed the same tricks again in front of the same man. For the other half, though, the researchers introduced an experimental manipulation: An attractive female research assistant showed up to witness the second set of tricks. The researchers recorded the number of tricks that were aborted (jumping off the board to avoid a dangerous fall) as well as those that succeeded and those that failed. When the skateboarders were performing for the attractive female, they were only half as likely to abort the tricks; that is, they were more likely to "go for it." As a consequence, they succeeded more frequently in the difficult tricks. But by going for it under uncertain circumstances, they also fell more.

The skateboarders provided a saliva sample after they had completed both tricks, and the researchers analyzed the saliva for testosterone levels. Young men whose testosterone levels had soared higher in the presence of the attractive female were also more likely to take risks.

Those findings not only provide part of the answer to the question of why some people (mostly young men, by the way) are willing to take on the risks involved in free climbing (and in many other risky behaviors), they also elucidate a more general point that arises from thinking about behavior in evolutionary terms. Every behavioral choice made by any animal, including human beings, involves trade-offs. If you don't leave your hut, you lower the risk of getting bitten by a snake or eaten by a crocodile, but you also won't find any food to eat, and you won't attract any mates. So, our ancestors took risks all the time. Sometimes the risks were small and the payoffs reliable, as in going down to the nearby waterhole, where there was a slight chance of encountering a dangerous animal but a 100% chance they would quench their thirst. And sometimes the risks were bigger, but so were the payoffs, as in climbing up a tall tree to knock down a bee's nest (at the reasonably high risk of being stung by a swarm of bees and the slight possibility of falling to one's death). Those who took those risks occasionally won high payoffs, not only in resources, such as honey, but also in social recognition from their fellow villagers, who got to share in the booty. And as a consequence, taking risks also often increased their mate value. After Philippe Petit managed to sneak onto the roof of one of New York's Twin Towers and walk a tightrope across to the other one, where one slipup would have sent him falling 1,368 feet to his death on the city streets below, he became an instant celebrity and was offered a multimillion-dollar movie deal and potentially lucrative product endorsement opportunities.

If there is a single bit of advice we'd draw from the research on risky behaviors, it is this: Don't climb without a rope (unless there's a camera crew, or someone attractive happens to be watching).

CIVILIZED DISCONTENTS AND ANCESTRAL SOLUTIONS

Modern society has helped us solve numerous ancestral problems. High-calorie foods have helped us fend off starvation. Cars help us travel great distances quickly. Opiates can help us undergo lifesaving surgeries. But because inventions like ice cream, cars, and drugs are relatively modern, our brains haven't had a chance to adapt to the new dangers these products present. Solving the overindulgence problem often comes down to creating a personal environment in which the rewards and punishments more closely match those in our ancestral environment.

The trade-offs between safety and mating in young skate-boarders illuminate another important point: Each of the fundamental motives on the pyramid is intimately connected to others.

Appreciating that point can help us not only understand why we make the choices we do but also suggest ways to avoid bad choices. We talked about avoiding obesity-related health problems by structuring your environment in ways that directly alter your eating or exercise habits. But you can also fulfill your drive to be healthier by connecting it to your drive to have friends, to find mates, or to care for your kin. We mentioned Platt's suggestion that you recruit your social network to help you by making a public commitment to your goals and ask a friend or partner to help reward your healthy choices. And if you have a child, you could put a picture of them on the fridge with a cartoon bubble that says: "Stay healthy so you can watch me graduate from college and get married, Dad!"

Earlier in this chapter, we talked about the dangers posed by other animal species. In the next chapter, we talk about the special dangers posed by the most dangerous animal on the planet: other members of our own species.

BOTTOM LINES: SUGGESTIONS FOR SURVIVAL

In this chapter, we talked about the major causes of mortality and noted that some of the things that kill us today arise from a mismatch between our ancestral desires and the modern world. Here are a few useful bits of advice that stem from the relevant psychological research.

- *Actively rig your reinforcements.* Give yourself immediate rewards for healthy behaviors (a star on an exercise record every time you jog, for example; then, when you reach a certain number of stars, buy yourself a comfy new pair of running shoes) and also *make punishments for unhealthy behaviors immediate* (crumble three cigarettes every time you smoke one, for example).

- *Make your healthy goals public.* If possible, recruit a friend or relative who has a similar goal (to start jogging, for example).
- *Reward progressive approximations.* Set small goals you can easily reach and be sure to notch them up as they become easier.
- *Control your environment.* Put up obstacles in the way of temptations. Don't fill your refrigerator with foods you want to avoid, and if you are prone to suicidal feelings, don't keep a gun in the house.
- *Avoid unnecessary risks of accidents.* Don't climb without a rope.

CHAPTER 3

AVOIDING BULLIES, BARBARIANS, AND MICROPLUNDERERS

Kim Hill and Hillard Kaplan met in 1980 while they were both graduate students in anthropology. After finishing their doctoral dissertations, they were keen for some adventurous fieldwork and heard about a group of Native Americans called the Yora, who lived in a remote region of Peru. Many of the Yora had never made contact with outsiders, so as budding young anthropologists interested in studying human beings under more "natural" ancestral conditions, Hill and Kaplan decided that making contact with the Yora would provide a great opportunity.

There were a couple of wrinkles, though. A month before Hill and Kaplan arrived, a group of Yora had attacked and killed a team of workers from the Royal Dutch Shell oil corporation. For outsiders daring to venture into the unmapped regions of the globe, this was not an isolated event. From another anthropologist, Hill had heard of a group of five missionaries in Ecuador who had made contact with one native group only to be slaughtered 2 days later. Many previous explorers had perished in the jungles of South America, where local natives would sometimes greet intrusions by strangers with showers of poisoned arrows. The explorer Percy Harrison Fawcett had successfully made peace with several hostile tribes on his first foray into the remote jungles of Brazil, but on a later expedition, he was not so lucky. According to a recent book delving into Fawcett's disappearance, the evidence suggests he was killed by a native group when he attempted to go deeper into the jungle. Sydney Possuelo, an authority on isolated tribes in Brazil who has spent more than half a century working with Indigenous groups in that country, says that locals advised him that "in an encounter with the isolated tribes there are two possibilities: Either they get along with you, or they kill you."

Despite the dangers, though, Hill and Kaplan loaded their camping equipment into a boat and ascended to the remote headwaters of the Manu River. When they reached the Yora village, they were met by a group of armed tribesmen. The tribesmen were naked, except for one horrifying detail: Several of them were wearing hard hats with the Shell oil symbol. Given that these head adornments were obviously trophies taken from the recently murdered oil workers, the wisest thing to do would have been to turn around, hop back into their boat, and get the hell out of there. Instead, Hill and Kaplan decided to stick around but to do all they could to seem harmless. This including wearing very few clothes so the locals could see they weren't concealing any weapons, letting the Yora ransack their bags and backpacks to see they had no firearms, giving away a lot of presents, smiling and laughing a lot, and singing happily, all in an attempt to advertise that they were nonthreatening.

Hill and Kaplan pitched their tent right near the river in case they would need to make a quick escape. One night, they heard loud arguing in the village, which they thought might be a debate about whether to kill the two anthropologists and take their belongings. As Hill later described it, "It was pretty tense," adding that he and Kaplan "had a plan that if attacked we would jump in the river in the dark and float underwater downstream to escape (something I learned from our guide who had escaped an attack that way as a boy when his whole village was exterminated)."

Although majoring in anthropology comes with a known risk of dangerous interactions with strangers, Samantha Power went to college with the intention of becoming a sports journalist—a generally safer occupation. After graduating from Yale University with a degree in journalism, however, she did an internship in Washington, DC. There she learned about the war in Bosnia and decided to try her hand at becoming a war correspondent instead. It was a good career move and led to her writing a book that won a Pulitzer Prize, which in turn led to her to being appointed U.N. ambassador.

Whereas Power might have been bonked on the head by a stray volleyball working as a sports journalist, being a war correspondent involved some more serious risks. Besides the dangers of being killed by stray bombs or bullets as she and her fellow journalists purposefully sought out the frontlines of military conflict, Power noted that female correspondents faced another kind of danger. One evening, she was taken at gunpoint by armed Serb soldiers reeking of alcohol, the leader of whom asked her, "Are you a virgin?" On another occasion, she arrived to interview the Bosnian prime minister, who greeted her at the door of his hotel room barely dressed and then spent 15 minutes trying to embrace her until she gave up and ran out without the promised interview. Power noted that all the female correspondents she knew in Bosnia had been surprised by sexual come-ons during attempted interviews, and they were all painfully aware that many of their intended interviewees were part of a military force that had raped an estimated 20,000 Bosnian women during the brutal conflict there.

THE BAD GUYS IN THE GOOD OLD DAYS

If you've ever taken a course in history, it can seem like one damned violent thing after another. Recorded history tells a story of century after century of territorial invasion, rape, and murder. Genghis

Khan's early life in the remote and barely populated backwoods of Outer Mongolia was one such example. Genghis Khan's father had kidnapped and impregnated Khan's mother, and as a boy, Genghis Khan himself was captured and enslaved by a rival group. Later in life, Khan's own wife was kidnapped, and he recruited a local warlord to help him wage an attack on the village where she was being held. From there, he graduated to becoming a warlord himself and went on to become a master of warfare by cavalry, eventually leading his mounted soldiers (the Mongolians) on a systematic rampage throughout all of Asia, even extending his path of conquest and destruction all the way into Eastern Europe.

The Mongol horde's typical modus operandi was to surround a city with thousands of armed horsemen, and if their intended victims did not immediately surrender, to kill all the men, pillage the city, and rape the women. Sometimes, rather than killing the men right away, they would force the prisoners to march in front of their horses to the next city, using them as cannon fodder. When they reached the next city, the Mongol cavalrymen would force the captives into the moats surrounding the city until it was filled with their bodies, and the Mongols' horses could ride across on their corpses.

The early history of Europe is also a gruesomely violent tale. In 40 A.D., the Celts in Britain were invaded by a force of 40,000 Roman soldiers. Resistance was futile, even suicidal. Four centuries later, the Romans themselves were forced to abandon Britain after enduring continuing attacks from Anglo-Saxon and Pict invaders. Later still, the Anglo-Saxon marauders were themselves attacked by invading warriors from Normandy and Scandinavia. Although the history books often depict historic confrontations like that of Hastings in 1066 in antiseptic political terms, what those celebrated battles actually involved were thousands of men hacking each other up with swords, spears, and arrows.

A look at the small-scale societies studied by anthropologists also tells an often brutal tale. A few years ago, Dave filmed Napoleon Chagnon for a documentary series on evolution and behavior. Chagnon was perhaps the world's most famous (and to some infamous) anthropologist. His fame owed to his best-selling ethnography *Yąnomamö: The Fierce People*. When he was researching his book back in 1960, Chagnon went to live among the Yąnomamö, who were one of the few remaining groups in the world still living a lifestyle similar to that of our ancestors—somewhere between hunter–gatherers and early horticulturalists. The Yąnomamö dwelled in the lush jungles bordering Brazil's Orinoco River. In what might have otherwise been a delightful sylvan paradise, the Yąnomamö lived in a near constant state of violent terror. One of the villages Chagnon studied was raided 25 times during his first 15 months of fieldwork. The chronic state of warfare had infiltrated every aspect of Yąnomamö culture, including their myths, their ceremonies, their politics, and their marriage patterns.

Chagnon's classic book opens with a description of an incident in which the members of one village were invited to a feast at a nearby village. While the guests were lounging around in hammocks and enjoying the food, their hosts suddenly attacked them with clubs and bows and arrows. More than a dozen men were killed in that incident, and several young girls and women were taken captive, never to be seen by their families again.

Other classic ethnographies of preindustrial societies from every corner of the globe, such as Leopold Pospisil's 1963 description of the Kapauku Papuans of New Guinea or Adamson Hoebel's 1960 description of the Cheyenne of the North American Great Plains, are rife with descriptions of intergroup warfare and everyday violence.

But aren't there also nonviolent hunter–gatherers? In one classic ethnography, Elizabeth Marshall Thomas dubbed the Kalahari !Kung San "the harmless people." Indeed, when considered alongside the

Yąnomamö, the !Kung San were comparatively harmless. Nevertheless, Thomas's book contains the story of at least one homicide in the small group she studied. Richard Lee, who also studied the !Kung San, estimated their homicide rate at 293 per million. In contrast to the Yąnomamö, that is quite low, but it hardly qualifies as harmless. The rate of homicide among the "harmless people" is roughly equivalent to that in New Orleans, one of the most violent cities in the United States, a nation that itself boasts the highest homicide rate in the modern industrialized world.

VIOLENT INCLINATIONS IN THE MODERN WORLD

These days, we live in a food-rich environment, and people in the modern world don't need to go to war to win status or acquire romantic partners. So, have those violent impulses become vestigial—like gills that we no longer use?

A few years back, Doug asked several hundred students in his psychology class whether they had ever fantasized about committing murder. As it turned out, fully 76% of the men in the class had considered homicide at least once in their lives. More surprisingly, 61% of the women had also considered killing another human being.

Was this just a statistically unusual group? No. The results replicated across two different and fairly large samples (totaling 760 students in all).

When Josh Duntley and David Buss later asked the same question of students at the University of Texas at Austin, they found even higher numbers.

How could so many good people have thought of doing such a bad thing? We also asked people what had triggered their thoughts about killing another person.

The most common trigger was that the other person was threatening them. Homicidal fantasies were also commonly triggered by public humiliation, threats to someone else they cared about, or an actual attack by another person. So, it looks as though we're all cognitively equipped with a readiness to do violence, but most people's violent impulses do not stem from a yearning desire to join the ranks of the raping and plundering bad guys. Instead, they arise from a desire to defend ourselves and those we hold dear. We want to be good guys; indeed, we want to be heroes. Other research, done in several different countries, such as Spain and Poland, indicates that self-defense or defense of loved ones are widely regarded as completely justifiable motivations for violence.

If you pick up the newspaper, it might seem as though things haven't much changed since the days of Mongols and Vikings pillaging, raping, and murdering. The daily news is permeated with stories about acts of violence, police and rioters shooting at one another, unhinged people with machine guns murdering scores of schoolchildren, and tribal warlords pillaging and raping. And the modern era of globalization has opened up niches for a whole new breed of professional violent criminal. After Eastern European hitmen assassinated a woman in London, BBC journalist Misha Glenny conducted an extensive investigation into the worldwide networks of modern organized crime. His findings, documented in the book *McMafia*, were nothing short of horrifying. One of his conclusions was that "in the last two decades, [organized crime] has experienced an unprecedented expansion, now accounting for roughly 15% of the world's GDP [gross domestic product]." Besides former Soviet agents involved in international weapons sales and cyber-terrorism and wealthy drug dealers in Latin America and South Africa paying off police officers and politicians to look the other way, there are the stories of thousands of women from Eastern Europe being lured into Britain or Germany on the promise of high-paying office jobs, only to be beaten, raped, and forced into lives of prostitution.

So, there were bullies raping, pillaging, and murdering in ancestral times, and there are bullies raping, pillaging, and murdering today. But the important question is this: Are the odds of being victimized by the bad guys better or worse if we compare then versus now?

Let's first focus on the modern murder rate, something for which we have reasonably reliable numbers. Unlike other crimes, which often go unreported, most murders do make the public record. At first glance, the modern data look pretty depressing. According to a United Nations tally, worldwide, 464,000 people were murdered in 2017 alone. That does not count an additional 89,000 people killed in war that year or another 26,000 killed in terrorist attacks. That adds up to 579,000 people slaughtered by other people—and all that bloodletting in just 1 year. And just as in the days of yore, it is men who continue to do most of the murdering, committing 90% of the homicides, and close to 100% of the killings in war and terrorist attacks. Women do commit homicide, but it is often in self-defense against a violent man.

Certainly, 579,000 people killed is a gruesome number. It is roughly equivalent to the total combined populations of Pittsburgh, Pennsylvania, and Newark, New Jersey. But is your personal chance of being murdered higher or lower now than it would have been if you lived in the good old days? Given the world population of more than 7 billion, that number translates into a homicide rate of 7.6 per 100,000. When Steven Pinker averaged the data from 27 nonstate societies (hunter–gatherers and horticulturalists), the average number of people killed every year in war alone was 524 per 100,000. That means your chances of being killed in a war in the old days were about 90 times higher than your chances of being killed today. The war deaths from those nonstate societies don't even count the many deaths from day-to-day homicides back then. The Semai, dubbed by their ethnographer "a nonviolent people of Malaya," were one of the least violent groups ever studied. The odds of being murdered among the Semai were even lower than the odds of murder if you lived among the "gentle people" of the !Kung San tribe, and many times lower than the odds of being offed if you lived among the Ya̧nomamö. Nevertheless, homicide rates among the "nonviolent" Semai, although remarkably low for a pre-state group, were higher than those found in almost any American city today (double those of Chicago, for example).

Murder is, of course, not an equal opportunity affair, even in the modern world. If you are a male, if you are a young adult, and if you are African American or a Hispanic in the United States, your odds of dying at another male's hand are much higher than those same odds if you are a White middle-aged and middle-class woman, for example. But even if you're a teenage boy living in inner city Chicago, the odds of dying via homicide are still a lot lower than they would have been living under the typical conditions our ancestors faced.

Steven Pinker argued that several factors have contributed to the dramatic drop in violence since hunter–gatherer times. One was what he called the *pacification process*, which happened when hunter–gatherers traded their traditions of chronic raiding and feuding for the more settled agricultural lifestyle. The second was what Pinker called the *civilization process*, which followed the development of large kingdoms in which responsibility for punishing offenses was taken completely out of the hands of individuals and local feudal lords, and placed under the authority of a centralized state. This factor alone, Pinker estimated, resulted in at least a 10-fold reduction in violent crime (of course, this comes at the cost of a high incarceration rate, which can essentially eliminate your chance of reproducing).

Does that mean you're safe from the bad guys and can feel comfortable letting your guard down? To return to an issue we raised earlier, many modern urban and suburban dwellers encounter unfamiliar men from diverse groups throughout the course of their lives. The odds that those men are terrorists are not zero, but they are much lower than they were for our ancestors, who lived during a time when intergroup marauding was common and during which there was no centralized law enforcement authority to do anything about it. It turns out that, these days, men are much more likely to be killed by a member of their own group than by a stranger. Usually, the perpetrator of a modern-day, male-to-male homicide is someone the victim knows well enough to have insulted in some way. And even young males living in rough neighborhoods are, on average, safer than they were in most places, and at most times, throughout history.

Nevertheless, it remains true that, whether you are venturing into the remote unexplored jungles of South America, as Hill and Kaplan did, braving a modern war zone, as Samantha Power did, or just going for a stroll around a neighborhood in your own home-town, the odds that a stranger is a potential threat to your physical safety are many times higher if that stranger is a male. They are especially high if he is a young adult male and if he is with a group of other young adult males. As anthropologist Richard Wrangham has observed, there is no society in which groups of females go out looking for fights. Indeed, groups of males go out looking for trouble not only in most human societies but even among chimpanzees, whose young male bands wander the borders of their territory and kill any outsider male they encounter. So, there's a reason that people more readily condition fear to strange men than to strange women (as we describe shortly), and there's a reason your mother told you not to wander into strange neighborhoods by yourself.

Speaking of wandering into dangerous neighborhoods, Kim Hill and Hillard Kaplan survived their encounter with the Yaro, and their program of singing, smiling, and looking harmless turned the tense initial encounter into a more friendly and pleasant one. But Hill, now a prominent, and much older and wiser, anthropologist, told us that he thinks it was foolhardy to approach a group that had recently killed outsiders. But if he had it to do over again, he advises that there is a much better way to look harmless: bring along a wife and child. As he puts it, "All humans know that any man who comes to a strange group with wife and children is not intending to kill somebody. . . . Only 'single' males commit violence in groups on each other." Professor Hill doesn't say how you'd get your wife and child to agree to come along, or how to quell your own anxieties about the potential risks to them, but that's another problem.

THE PSYCHOLOGICAL LEGACY OF OUR VIOLENT PAST

Despite the fact that people living in the modern developed world are relatively safer than our ancestors, those millennia of marauding males have left a deep imprint on the collective human psyche. Our research team at Arizona State University has conducted a number of studies into the evolutionary psychology of stereotyping and prejudice. Findings from our labs combine with those from many other researchers to suggest that modern human minds are, in several ways, especially well tuned to information about any strange man who might pose a potential threat of violence.

In one very simple study, we asked people to clear their minds and "think of an angry person." Try this yourself for a few seconds. Get a picture of an angry person in your mind.

Was the person you imagined a woman or a man?

Although we did not specify the sex of the angry person, 71% of the women in our study and 83% of the men spontaneously imagined a man. Furthermore, the most common man that people imagined was not someone whose anger they had personally experienced, which would reflect their own learning experiences. It was instead a perfect stranger, thus more of a ghostly reflection of our ancestors' experiences.

Follow-up studies revealed that people were remarkably quick and accurate in detecting the emotion of anger on a stranger's face—and even quicker and more accurate when that anger was glaring at them from a man's face as compared with a woman's. Besides this remarkable astuteness at detecting *actual* anger on a man's face, other research by our team has found that people are biased to see anger on a man's face *even when it isn't there*. And that is particularly true if people are judging a man from a different racial group, or if they've been primed to feel threatened—either by seeing another angry person, watching a scary movie, or even just sitting alone in a completely dark room.

In another line of research, Harvard psychologists Elizabeth Phelps, Mahzarin Banaji, and their team recorded people's brain activity as they viewed photographs of other people. Earlier investigations had established that if someone learns to associate an electric shock with an image of a threatening animal, such as a snake or a spider, the fear response is more difficult to extinguish (or unlearn) than if the shocks had been paired with pictures of harmless animals (such as butterflies). The researchers found an analogous effect for members of other races: Whites had a hard time extinguishing a fear response to a Black face, and Blacks conversely had a hard time extinguishing fear to a White face. And this outgroup fear-conditioning effect holds particularly for men's faces rather than women's.

But other research by the same team found an interesting exception: When a White participant viewed a Black man, the area of their brain associated with fear automatically starting firing *only* if the man was an unfamiliar stranger. It didn't happen for celebrity pictures of Denzel Washington or Eddie Murphy, for example, whose familiarity led them to be encoded as fellow ingroup members.

Ancestrally, strange men posed a different type of danger to women than they did to other men. Yąnomamö warriors, Mongol cavalrymen, and other marauding males, before and since, were likely to kill the other men in a vanquished group but to rape or abduct the women. As Samantha Power's experiences and observations in Bosnia attest, these threats continue into the modern world. Christine Garver-Apgar and her colleagues found that when women are ovulating and hence more likely to become pregnant, they are more likely to perceive that a strange man has sexually coercive intentions.

It turns out that there is research showing that putting two groups of people onto teams with different colored shirts is enough to get them to ignore race while shifting their focus to who is on which team. Our ancestors probably never traveled far enough to encounter people from other racial groups, although Neanderthals and *Homo sapiens* may have come into contact. But encounters with people who belonged to different tribal groups, who were slightly different from their group, would have been more common, and the main question they had in evaluating strangers, and the same question we confront today, is: "Are they one of us?"

NEW BAD GUYS IN THE 21ST CENTURY: *HOMO PREDATORIUS* AND *HOMO PARASITARIIS*

According to the *Merriam-Webster* dictionary, the word predator refers primarily to an organism that obtains its food by killing and eating other animals. The classic examples of predators are lions and tigers, and, at least during salmon migration season, bears. A secondary definition, however, is used to refer to human beings who injure or exploit others for personal gain, as in predatory lenders, ransomware extortion agents, or sexual predators.

From a biological perspective the term "predator" would more appropriately refer only to cannibals, or to professional hit men, who kill their victims. Organisms that exploit others without killing them are more correctly labeled "parasites." As E.O. Wilson observed, the term "parasite" refers to a predator that eats its prey in units of less than one. When we're being victimized, the distinction is quite an important one because we usually survive encounters with parasites, human or otherwise.

There are also further distinctions between different types of biological parasites, and those distinctions are useful in thinking not only about nonhuman organisms but also about human actions that exploit fundamental motives in ways that do not ultimately serve the goals for which those motives were designed. Biologists talk about a continuum of interspecies exploitation ranging from (a) *mutualism*, in which both species take something from the other but also receive benefits (for example, the relationship between the clownfish that cleans sea anemones in exchange for shelter within the plant's poisonous barbs); through (b) *commensalism*, in which one species gets a benefit from the relationship, and the other is unharmed (for example, the relationship between remoras that ride along with sharks and eat the scraps left over by their host's messy eating habits); (c) *microparasitism*, in which the parasite only takes a tiny toll from the host (as in the case of mosquitos); and (d) *extreme parasitism*, in which the parasitic species extracts a high price from its victims (barnacles that completely consume the gonads of crabs, for example). At its most extreme, parasitism shades into the zone of predation, except that it is done slowly (some parasitic wasp species paralyze caterpillars and lay their eggs inside their hosts' bodies, and when the eggs hatch, the young wasps consume the still-living caterpillar from the inside).

The homicide statistics we reviewed suggested that few of us are likely to end up dead at the hands of true human predators. But all of us regularly have our resources plundered to varying degrees by other humans, who frequently attempt to exploit our fundamental motives in small, and sometimes larger, ways.

Bad guys can now pillage your belongings without ever getting their hands dirty and without ever placing themselves in danger of retaliatory counterattacks of the sort that Yąnomamö warriors or the young Genghis Khan regularly visited on their oppressors. Indeed, modern technology, globalization, and the centralization of power and wealth have made possible a whole host of procedures by which your pocket can be picked in any number of ways, many of which are almost impossible for law enforcement authorities to protect us against, and some of which are perfectly legal.

SIX-GUNS VERSUS FOUNTAIN PENS

Woody Guthrie was a pioneer of the American protest song, and many of his songs drew attention to economic injustices during the Great Depression. In "Pretty Boy Floyd," Guthrie told of the plight of starving farmers who lost their land to the banks during a devastating drought that turned many Midwestern states into a giant dust bowl. In the song, Guthrie suggested that although someone would be labeled as an outlaw if he wielded a six-gun while robbing his victims, a poor family was more likely to be robbed by a wealthy banker wielding a less obvious weapon: a fountain pen.

Robbing someone with a fountain pen didn't end with the Great Depression. The bankers, land developers, and financiers who took away the farmers' lands in the 1930s simply got better at it in the intervening decades. Elie Wiesel survived the concentration camps at Auschwitz and Buchenwald, and went on to write several now classic novels about his experiences, which won him a Nobel Prize and considerable wealth. He lost his $12 million life savings, though, when a trusted friend introduced him to Bernard Madoff, to whom he entrusted his personal wealth as well as another $15 million from the Elie Wiesel Foundation for Humanity. Madoff had been the chairman of the Nasdaq stock exchange, and he used his financial prestige to set up a massive Ponzi scheme, managing to bilk investors for $18 billion. Most of us don't deal with numbers that large in our personal checking accounts, so to get some perspective on how much money that is, consider that a million dollar bills in a stack would reach 358 feet into the air, about as high as a 25-story building. Now imagine 18,000 such piles (stacked next to one another, the piles would stretch for nine football fields). If you spend that money at $1,000 per minute and never took a time out to eat, sleep, or go to the restroom, it would take you more than 34 years until you were done with your shopping spree.

Madoff was not the first major criminal in the financial world, though. The practice of using new investments not to generate real assets but to redistribute illusory "profits" to previous investors and attract still more unwary investors traces at least as far back as Charles Ponzi, after whom this Ponzi scheme is named. Wall Street has a rich history of shady characters capitalizing on investors' desire for easy money with junk bonds, penny stocks, and various other schemes. Pulitzer Prize–winning journalist and author James Stewart dubbed the Wall Street financial wheelers and dealers a "den of thieves." Ponzi's financial descendants don't only steal money from other rich investors on Wall Street. Their explicitly criminal frauds as well as their quasilegal scams and cover-ups have taken a direct toll on your grandfather's retirement fund and many indirect tolls on the financial security of the rest of the American population, even those with no investments.

THE MICROPLUNDERERS

Numerous financial scams, rather than involving the theft of fortunes from Elie Wiesel's charitable foundation or grandma's life savings, fall into the category of microparasitism. Together, those scams add up to the equivalent of swarms of economic mosquitos taking tiny little sips of our blood every time we let down our protective psychological netting by not reading the fine print. A surprising amount of mosquito-style pickpocketing is perfectly legal.

University of Missouri professor Devin Fergus studies the factors that contribute to maintaining economic inequality in the United States, which he has nicknamed "The Land of the Fee." If you look carefully at the bills you pay for everyday expenses—the costs of housing, meals, transportation, and education—you will find an awe-inspiring number of hidden fees, and if you put them into a calculator, you'll likely find they add up to thousands of dollars per year. If you are one of the 44 million Americans who has taken out a student loan to pay for college tuition (and "fees"), the fine print you neglected to read will reveal not only the interest you'll pay but also a host of other little hidden costs: origination fees, deferment and extension costs, early repayment penalties, and massive penalties for late payments. Fergus noted that some students end up paying three or four times the amount of the original loan. There are also hidden fees, sometimes rather large ones, when you borrow money to buy a car or finance a mortgage (title fees, even if you are refinancing a house you already own; more origination fees; a few extra "points"—which tack on several percent of the value of the whole loan so that you can secure the particular interest rate you'll pay for the next 30 years).

When *Consumer Reports* conducted a survey of 2,057 Americans, they found that 85% had encountered a hidden or unexpected fee during the past 2 years. When Dave wanted to sign his kids up for a karate class, he had to ante up not only the fee for the class, which was reasonable, but also a monthly membership fee to the health club LifeTime Fitness, which is where the class was being held. LifeTime Fitness started charging Dave an extra $3 for their monthly magazine, and he needed to fill out a form in writing to stop that mosquito-sized fee. If he took the kids away for the summer and wanted to pause the membership for a couple months, no problem, but there was a "processing fee" that amounted to several hundred dollars for the privilege of not paying the "regular monthly fee" while he wasn't there to use the services.

Telecommunications companies seem to be the biggest offenders: Of the people participating in the *Consumer Reports* survey, 69% reported a hidden fee from their telecommunication provider. One woman objected to a $25 mandatory fee for sports coverage because she never watched sports (that fee is the product of a coercive deal between money-hungry sports teams and the networks that want to cover their games). When the woman tried to cancel her service, she was hit with a $150 "cancellation fee" for a service she never requested in the first place.

And then there's the travel industry. If you go on vacation, you might need to worry about getting your wallet stolen in a crowded public square, but you can be virtually assured that your pocket will be picked in numerous fully legal ways by the airlines that transport you to your destination, the hotels you'll stay in, and the car rental agencies that will assist you in hauling your luggage from the airport to the hotel. To keep their online ticket prices low, airlines now charge you a fee for that luggage. It's not a lot, but if you're traveling a long distance with a family who won't squeeze everything into carry-on luggage, it can add up to more than $100 going and another $100 coming back. Then, before they let you load your luggage into that rental vehicle, and when you are exhausted from your flight, the rental agency will pressure you into buying insurance even though you likely already paid a fee for that coverage as part of your regular auto insurance. If you nevertheless pay the rental company's "highly recommended!!" full coverage, it can cost $30 per day, which would calculate out to $10,950 per year, a rather handsome insurance premium. And if you don't agree to pay an extra $15 per day fee to cover possible road tolls, you may find a hefty charge for any tollbooths you happen to drive through. The tollbooths themselves are now hidden in many cities, so you can't pay cash if you wanted to and may not even realize you were just hit with a fee as you drove through a strange city.

The travel industry may be crawling with microparasitic fees, but the medical industry puts those amateur pickpockets to shame. If you have health insurance, you might not notice most of the fees because they're "free," but only if you ignore the fact that they add up to massive premiums for all of us. The insurance companies often look the other way at overcharging because the amount the government lets them take as profits is a percentage of what they pay out, so their take goes up when your bills go up. Dave recently took his daughter in for a minor leg injury, and the clinic offered to give her a leg brace to take home with her just in case she felt she needed it. Dave asked how much it would cost and was told not to worry because the insurance would cover it. But he inquired about what the insurance company would pay and found out the charge would be $400. He checked on his phone and found the identical leg brace selling for $12. Sounds like highway robbery, but it's actually just business as usual.

Then for women and girls, there's the "pink tax." The New York City Department of Consumer Affairs compared the price of 794 consumer products that were virtually identical but marketed in male and female versions, such as pink T-shirts, bikes, and scooters for girls versus blue versions of the same product for boys, or identical medical supplies for senior women versus men. The female versions cost, on average, 7% more. That might not seem like much when you are considering the purchase of a single bottle of shampoo, but the State of California conducted a similar study and concluded that what they called the "gender tax" compounded to an extra $1,351 per year.

SELF-PROTECTION 101: NOTHING TO FEAR, BUT . . .

Unlike violent crime, which you can take steps to avoid, institution-alized pickpocketing is almost impossible to escape completely. The free market capitalist economy makes it easy for large corporations to pick your pocket and then use a portion of those proceeds to make big contributions to any elected representatives willing to undermine consumer protection. But that open market also lets those corpora-tions compete with one another to offer you a slightly better deal and also to do what they can to avoid having consumers complain too publicly. After Doug was hit with a surprise $300 charge from AT&T for accidentally leaving his phone on for a single evening in Canada, he did a little research and realized that T-Mobile regards Canada as part of North America and adds no surcharges at all if his trip from Phoenix to Seattle happens to extend a few miles further into Vancouver, British Columbia. Because Doug spends a month or two every summer in Vancouver, he was also being hit with a 3% surcharge every time he used his credit card. But a little research revealed that another credit card was willing to forgo all foreign transaction fees in the interest of moving your business over to their ledger. Result: Business moved to new phone carrier and new credit card. So, capitalism taketh away, but it also giveth—if you're willing to do a little comparison shopping.

The forces of the open market also make it such that purveyors of goods and services want to keep their pickpocketing under the radar, and it hurts their sales if their hidden charges become publicly visible. When Doug called AT&T and threatened to complain online, he was refunded $150 of the $300 fee (not enough to keep him as a customer but enough to reduce the motivation to write an online complaint and instead buy dinner for two in a nice restaurant—using the credit card without the international surcharge, of course). *Consumer Reports* found that only three of 10 people fought those annoying hidden charges. But of those who did, fully two out of three got the charges removed from the bill or refunded. The idea that most consumers do not have the time or energy to comparison shop or to seek refunds seems baked into the economic model underlying many of these predatory business practices.

Our proclivity to seek safety in numbers in the face of interpersonal violence does not usually extend to banding together against parasitic institutional practices, which fly under the radar of our group defensive systems. And yet there is something to be said for joining a larger herd to defend oneself against systemic parasitism. Duke Energy in South Carolina was proposing to sneak through a 238% increase in their fixed monthly fee (the minimum they would charge customers even if those customers went away for a month and did not turn on any of the lights or machines in their houses). But when a group of consumers learned of this plan and organized a campaign of public outcry, soliciting the help of Consumer Reports, Inc. (publishers of *Consumer Reports* magazine), the South Carolina Public Service Commission saw the crowd gathering to defend itself and decided to overturn the proposed rate hike. In the modern era, it is easy to organize a crowd defense online, encouraging people to share messages with their friends, and writing emails to complain to elected officials. But all that would work better to the extent that the crowd was organized and mounted a systematic defense, as did the American workers who formed unions back in the days when Woody Guthrie was writing about how the rich crooks could rob you with a fountain pen.

SELF-PROTECTION MASTER LEVEL: FEAR THYSELF

In the Bronx Zoo, there was a classic sign at one exhibit that advertised "World's Most Dangerous Predator."

Above the sign was a mirror.

There is an interesting commonality between warring Yąnomamö and modern organized criminals. From the outside, Yąnomamö men and organized criminals are bad guys: They kill, they steal from one another, and they kidnap women. But from the inside, they don't think of themselves as dangerous bad guys. Yąnomamö and other warlike foragers often explain to anthropologists that they would be happy to live in peace. They only raid one another's villages because they believe they need to protect themselves from their warlike neighbors. Indeed, most of the raids can be simply justified as retaliations for previous raids, the ancient prototype of the feud between the Hatfields and the McCoys.

When Misha Glenny interviewed hoodlums from former Soviet countries, they also, like the Yąnomamö, believed that engaging in violent crime was not something they enjoyed but something necessitated by their circumstances. They weren't bad guys, they told him, just good people making the best go of a bad lot.

It's easy to get trapped into a cyclic pattern of hostile interactions with another person or group even if, for most of us, that conflict typically involves only words rather than machine guns. But before you jump to the conclusion that your only option is to fight fire with fire and prepare to counterattack when someone slights you in any way, you might also consider looking in the mirror and asking whether your reactions are contributing to the problem. Indeed, a number of studies conducted by psychologists have found that, just as people reciprocate hostile and uncooperative behaviors, they also reciprocate cooperative and peaceful gestures, and if you escalate your kindness and deescalate your unpleasantness, you may be surprised to find that you will lose an enemy and maybe even make a new friend.

THE AVENGERS

In this chapter, we've taken the perspective of potential victims, innocent people trying to defend themselves and the other good people they love against threats of violence. From that perspective, the most common emotion is fear. But if we take the perspective of perpetrators—and remember that the clear majority of the population has considered perpetrating homicide—then the most common emotion seems to be self-righteous anger. What could be wrong with self-righteous anger? Don't we need more courageous Wonder Woman–like heroes in this world? More Avengers? Well, only if we trust that all that self-righteous anger would be directed at real bad guys—at the sadistic and evil Dr. Nos and Auric Goldfingers.

But who gets to decide when vengeful violence is justifiable and when it's not? As authors of a social psychology textbook, we are painfully aware of a couple of problems. For one thing, decades of sobering research demonstrate that people are masters of self-serving attributions. For example, 83% of automobile drivers judge themselves as being in the top 30% when it comes to driving safety (of course, two thirds of them are wrong because only 30% of drivers can fit into the top 30%). And among a group of drivers hospitalized after a serious automobile accident, most of whom were judged responsible for the accident, most still judged themselves to be good drivers. Students who score poorly on a test are convinced the test was unfair and the professor failed to get the right ideas across. Those who get *A* grades on an exam think it's a great test that accurately sorts the superior intellects from the duller masses. The prevalence of self-serving biases raises the danger that everyday people feeling self-righteous anger might not always be trusted to decide whether the target of their vengeful feelings actually deserves a death sentence.

On September 14, 2001, Frank Roque drove up to a gas station owned by Balbir Singh Sodhi and shot Singh five times. Roque believed (incorrectly) that Singh's turban identified him as a Muslim. He proclaimed the shooting a justifiable act of retaliation for the September 11th attacks. In Roque's mind, he was Rambo heroically going after the bad guys. Frank Roque is an extreme case, but his is hardly the only case of a violent murderer who thought he was doing good. Every terrorist thinks the same thing. Such cases demonstrate the dangers of combining self-righteous anger with another very human proclivity: the tendency to dehumanize the members of other groups.

When the Spanish conquistadors, accompanied by Jesuit priests, devout Catholics all, conquered the New World, they freely killed Incas and Aztecs with whom they came into conflict. There was a heated controversy in the Catholic church when some of the clergy suggested that the Indians were also humans and should be treated as such. Many church leaders resisted classifying Native Americans as humans because that would have made it sinful to kill them and thus posed an obstacle to empire building.

The tendency to dehumanize members of other groups is still with us today, as was demonstrated in a thought-provoking series of studies by Nour Kteily and his colleagues. In one of Kteily's experiments, Israelis were asked to rate Palestinians on a scale marked with five silhouette figures. On the left, at the bottom of the scale, the researchers' continuum depicted a chimplike primate walking on its hands and feet; on the right, the scale depicted a fully human figure walking upright. In between were three intermediate figures. You may have seen a figure like this on a T-shirt or in a cartoon meant to depict a lighthearted scale of "evolutionary progress." On this humanity scale, Israelis rated Palestinians far below the "fully evolved" upright modern human.

More troubling yet, Israelis were asked how many Palestinian civilians they would be willing to kill to save the life of one Israeli soldier wounded by a Palestinian militant. The answer: 575.

The researchers also asked Palestinians to rate Israelis on the same humanity scale. The average Palestinian rated Israelis as well below the "fully evolved" modern human, closer to a quadruped ancestor. And Palestinians similarly believed that, to save one Palestinian life, it was acceptable to kill many Israelis.

Other research suggests that one part of the problem is that people do not think the members of enemy groups experience emotion in the same way "we" do. Melissa McDonald and her colleagues were able to reduce Israelis' dehumanization of Palestinians by having them read an anger-inducing news story and then informing the Israelis that the Palestinian participants had felt the same emotional response they did.

For purely selfish reasons, acting on your angry self-righteous feelings is not in your self-interest in the modern world. Although the radical voices on the internet might rail against the injustices of a strong centralized government, the historical evidence indicates that ceding the responsibility for righteous vengeance to a central authority resulted in a dramatic drop in violence in comparison with the old system of tribal feuding and individual retribution. Frank Roque was arrested, tried, and is presently spending the rest of his life in prison. Many of his fellow inmates are also there because they thought their violent outburst of homicidal anger was justified even when it involved killing a total stranger in reaction to a perceived slight on the highway. Simply reminding yourself that the people in the other group, just like us, also feel love and fear, and that they also cherish their dogs and children, won't necessarily save the world, but it could save you from ending up in the cell next to Frank Roque.

BOTTOM LINES: SUGGESTIONS FOR AVOIDING BULLIES AND MICROPLUNDERERS

Avoiding the danger of serious violence shares a feature with the danger of eating unhealthy foods: Our immediate automatic reactions can get us in trouble. With regard to microplunderers in the modern world, on the other hand, it is the opposite problem: Our natural radar is not tuned to catch them. We are designed to devote serious attention to growling dogs, not to mosquitos, but small blood losses can add up over time. Thinking about those similarities and differences suggests a few bits of useful advice:

- *To avoid real violence, beware the young male syndrome.* Don't insult young males, especially desperate ones. If some angry young fellow cuts you off in traffic, before honking and giving him the finger, ask yourself how you'd respond if an angry dog was barking at you. Just smile, count to 10 (or better yet, 100), and move into a different lane.
- *Don't look like a threat.* Kim Hill suggested traveling with his family if he were going to contact a potentially hostile group. Becca Neel, Samantha Neufeld, and Steve Neuberg conducted research on how people counteract other people's stereotypes. They found that young males who regularly encounter strangers from other groups who might view them as threatening use tactics such as whistling classical music and wearing a broad smile (rather than a studded black leather jacket).
- *Control your own inner bad guy.* Avoid dehumanizing the members of other groups. A central lesson we encounter throughout this book is this: Underneath their superficial dissimilarities in appearance and customs across human societies, "they" are all human just like "us."
- *Consider the possibility that an unpleasant interaction is, at least partly, your fault.* Even if that's not the case, you can change the direction of a conflict spiral by doing or saying something nice—because people reciprocate positivity as well as negativity.
- *Join with others to fight the microplunderers.* You don't need to start a massive social organization, but you can use the digital crowd to your advantage. Ask for your money back, and if the response isn't favorable, take 5 minutes to write a comment online.
- *Unsubscribe from political and news sources that regularly exploit (and amplify) your fears for profit.*

CHAPTER 4

GETTING ALONG

When Daniel Kahneman was a young boy, according to one biographer, "he had no friends."

Danny was born in 1934 and spent his early childhood in France. Because he and his family were Jews, they were forced to flee Paris when the Nazis invaded in 1942. For several years, the family lived in a chicken coop behind a farmhouse in the south of France. Some of the locals were cooperating with the Nazis, so Danny needed to avoid getting close to other kids who might discover that he was Jewish.

It was not until age 14, after he moved to Israel, that Danny made his first real friend—a boy named Shamir. But even Shamir described Danny as something of an outsider who kept his distance from most of the other kids. Shamir observed of Danny's outsider status, "It was because of his personality, not because he was a refugee."

As an adult, though, Kahneman developed a friendship—with Amos Tversky—that would become legendary. In fact, it led to a Nobel Prize. Despite the fact that Tversky and Kahneman's friendship had earth-shaking scientific consequences, though, it was actually based on a rather mundane rule for forming a strong friendship, which we describe later in the chapter.

But, before examining that modern-world friendship, let's consider what friendship was like for our ancestors.

ROLLING WITH THE HOMIES IN THE OLD-STYLE HOOD

After living among the Maisin people of Papua, New Guinea, cultural psychologist Anne Tietjen described the social relationships of "Iris," a typical Maisin girl. Iris lives in a village of 250 people; the village is perched between the sea on the one side and the tropical rain forest on the other. Iris's father built their tiny thatched hut, which stands on tall stilts, out of Sago palm stalks. Her house is about 10 feet away from her grandparents' home, and her paternal uncles, aunts, and cousins also live in nearby huts. Iris plays with her cousins every day. Iris also helps her family prepare food, which they share with those cousins and their other relatives who live in the village. Although Iris is only 8 years old, her mother and sisters have already taught her most of the tasks she will need to accomplish when she reaches adulthood, including how to cook, how to take care of infants, and how to tend a garden.

Iris's social situation is, in many ways, not unlike that experienced by most people living in non-Western societies and similar to that of the majority of our ancestors. Her friends are mostly biological relatives or in-laws connected to those biological relatives by marriage and family ties. Her friendships are likely to last her entire lifetime and to involve frequent gift-giving and mutual assistance.

Close relationships with our relatives and in-laws were critical to our ancestor's survival. Anthropologist Kim Hill and his colleagues, whose work we mentioned in Chapter 1, tracked the number of calories brought in by every member of a small Aché village. Many of those calories came from gathering fruits and vegetables, some of which the villagers tended in their gardens and others that they picked from the nearby rain forest. Another source of calories came from hunting, mostly small mammals, although, occasionally, a member of the group caught a larger animal, such as a wild pig. Each individual member of the Aché faces a lot of uncertainty about how many calories they will bring in on any given day, and even the best hunters can go long stretches without much luck. By sharing their food, however, the group members provide a risk pool for one another. If a member of the Aché catches a wild pig one day, they cannot store the meat (they have no refrigerators and no technology for drying or storing food). So, they share it with their relatives and neighbors.

Working with Wesley Allen-Arave and Michael Gurven, Hill tracked those food exchanges in minute detail. Over a 2-month period, the researchers painstakingly weighed and counted the food items, and calculated the caloric value, for the exchanges made between 23 households in one Aché village. A typical household kept only about 25% of the foods they acquired on any given day and shared the remaining 75% with their neighbors. Those food exchanges were not random. People gave most to their kin but also shared with nonrelatives. Relatives and friends who had given them more in the past were most likely to receive some of the family's bounty. And if someone got injured or fell sick, other group members shared extra with them, especially so if the injured person had been generous in the past.

Sharing food in such groups is a life-or-death matter because, as Larry Sugiyama found in working with the Shiwiar, a similar group of South American foragers, 65% of them experienced an injury or illness that laid them up for a month or more. And because of luck alone, even the best hunters and gatherers encountered periods when they were unable to generate enough calories to feed themselves or their families. So, by sharing their takes with their relatives and friends who shared with them in the past, the group members serve as safety nets against the very real danger of starvation.

Besides sharing meals, friends can also help one another acquire the ingredients in the first place. Hunter–gatherers often do the hunting part in groups; some individuals circle around to flush animals out of the bush, for example, and others wait to catch those animals as they try to run away. Some anthropologists and historians have argued that group hunting may have been one of the primary drivers of human evolution, which explains how a relatively weak and helpless naked ape could compete with large predators and bring down prey many times their own size, such as mammoths.

In addition to sharing meals and helping one another acquire the raw material for those meals, friends in ancestral groups served many other functions. For one thing, friends helped protect one another from the other dangerous humans out there. Among the fierce Yąnomamö, whom we discussed in Chapter 3, people turn to their friends whenever someone else is out to hurt them. And as we also mention in that same chapter on self-protection, there is safety in simply hanging out in numbers—because predatory male groups are less likely to attack other groups than they are to attack lone individuals. The adaptive benefits of friendship predate the arrival of human beings on the planet. Joan Silk found that friendships among female baboons translate into an evolutionary payoff: The offspring of females with more friends are more likely to survive.

Another benefit of friends in traditional human societies is that they teach one another essential skills, such as how to repair a hut or how to make a canoe. In the case of Iris, the Maisin girl from Papua, New Guinea, her older siblings and cousins taught her how to prepare food and how to care for children. Human beings depend on all that acquired knowledge to survive. Indeed, anthropologist Hillard Kaplan estimated that it takes 2 decades for a man to acquire sufficient knowledge and skill to bring in enough calories to feed himself. And as Rob Boyd, another prominent anthropologist, pointed out, in many of the environments in which humans have managed to survive, such as the frozen areas around the Arctic Circle, a newcomer would die soon without the knowledge the locals acquired over generations.

When British explorers equipped with the latest technology for making fires, keeping warm, and catching their food (guns and fishing poles) first tried to explore the frozen reaches of Northern Canada and Alaska, most of them died. One man who managed to beat the odds was John Rae, the first European to find the long-sought Northwest Passage. Although he was born in Scotland and had studied medicine, Rae befriended members of the Cree tribe, from whom he learned how to make and maintain snowshoes, hunt caribou, and cure the meat. Rae also befriended Inuit Eskimos, from whom he learned how to sled, create homemade goggles to protect himself against snow blindness, and build an igloo (which provided more protection from the cold than the fanciest European tent).

We mentioned that traditional people mostly formed friendships with others to whom they were related by blood or marriage. However, there were some notable exceptions to that general rule. When they married, our ancestors often moved into another village with their new spouse. Even if they stayed in the same village, their relatives often brought in spouses from other villages. And there were occasional visitors from other villages, who included not only distant second cousins but also unrelated individuals interested in trading. Turkana cattle herders in East Africa form friendships (called *lopai*) with herders who live outside their yearly orbit of migration and can turn to them in tough times.

Recent evidence suggests that our ancestors began trading goods, such as the obsidian used to make sharp axe blades, more than a hundred thousand years before the advent of agriculture, during the historical period when they were still hunting and gathering. Thus, trade has been around almost since the beginning of *Homo sapiens* itself. Although human beings may have always found it easiest to befriend their relatives and other people with whom they interacted on a daily basis, getting along with strangers was also a skill that helped our ancestors survive and reproduce.

KAHNEMAN'S NOBEL PRIZE–WINNING FRIENDSHIP

As a teenager in Israel, Danny Kahneman took a vocational test that identified him as a likely fit for the field of psychology. That made great sense to a kid interested in what makes people tick, and after studying psychology at Hebrew University, Kahneman went to the University of California, Berkeley, for his doctorate. In 1961, he returned to Hebrew University to become a psychology professor.

In 1969, in what Kahneman later described as a fateful decision, he invited a younger professor named Amos Tversky to give a guest lecture to the students in his seminar. Tversky's visit to the class led to a lively debate, and later that week, he and Kahneman met for lunch to discuss doing a study together. The study was designed to examine how sophisticated researchers think about statistics. According to Kahneman, that first study revealed that "even statisticians are not very good intuitive statisticians." Working on that study also led Kahneman to a realization:

> While writing the article that reported these findings, Amos and I discovered that we enjoyed working together. Amos was always very funny, and in his presence I became funny as well, so we spent hours of solid work in continuous amusement. . . . We were sufficiently similar to understand each other easily, and sufficiently different to surprise each other. We developed a routine in which we spent much of our working days together, often on long walks. For the next fourteen years our collaboration was the focus of our lives, and the work we did together during those years was the best either of us ever did.

Those long walks and entertaining conversations led to a series of highly influential scientific papers. A look on *Google Scholar* reveals that Daniel Kahneman's work has been cited by other scientists a stunning 428,699 times. Although Kahneman has done a great deal of important work with other authors, his most highly cited research papers have a short list of authors: either Tversky and Kahneman or Kahneman and Tversky. All of those scientific citations attest to something much more important: Kahneman's friendship with Amos Tversky, and the ideas they tossed around during their long walks together, led to a revolutionary change in the way other psychologists and economists now think about how people make decisions.

Three decades later, in 2002, Kahneman was awarded a Nobel Prize in economics. His acceptance speech opened with a picture of his friend Amos. His first words were: "The work on which the award was given . . . was done jointly with Amos Tversky during a long period of unusually close collaboration. He should have been here." Tversky had died in 1996, and the Nobel Prize is not given posthumously, but Kahneman said, "I feel it is a joint prize. We were twinned for more than a decade."

FRIENDSHIPS IN THE MODERN WORLD

The alliance between Daniel Kahneman and Amos Tversky illustrated many of the characteristics of modern friendships. Kahneman grew up in Paris speaking French; Tversky grew up speaking Hebrew in Haifa. Paris is 803 miles away from Haifa, and to get there on foot, you'd need to scale several mountain ranges. Having a friend who was born a continent away would never have happened in the ancestral past, when friends came either from your own small village or from another village within a day's walk of where you grew up. Our ancestors' friendship choices were quite limited—to whoever belonged to their small group and lived near them. People living in the modern world, by contrast, can freely choose their friends from a large population of possibilities, as Kahneman and Tversky did. So, mobility in the modern world has opened up opportunities, but it comes at the cost of separating you from close family members who could be counted on to share their daily repasts with you.

All that mobility has another profound consequence for friendships in the modern world. Because so many people move around from place to place or from job to job, modern friendships are much less permanent than those of our ancestors. For both of us (Doug and Dave), most of our friends from childhood were replaced by a different set of friends in high school, then those were replaced by another set in college, and yet another set in adulthood.

There's another big difference as well: Unlike the ancestral world, where friendships were almost solely determined by membership in a common tribal group, modern friendships are more likely to be based on common individual characteristics. Both of us have had good friends from different religious and ethnic groups whose ancestors hailed from completely different continents than ours. Rather than tribal similarities, our friends instead share with us some special intellectual interests and social attitudes.

To some extent, modern technology can help us stay connected with our old friends and family members. Not only is it easy to hop on a plane and move to another continent, it is also now remarkably easy to pick up a cell phone and chat with those folks back home or with the ones who hopped a plane to move a thousand miles in the opposite direction. But if one of our ancestors had moved to another village after marriage, and it was a few miles away, keeping in daily touch with their friends and family members was simply not an option.

There is the question of whether virtual contact is quite the same as actual contact, though. With the advent of the telephone came the ability to exchange words but the loss of most of the non-verbal cues, such as the winks, nods, and eye contact we use to distinguish sarcasm and humor from sincerity. Email made things still worse, removing even our friends' tone of voice from the dialogue and breaking whole conversations into bits and pieces that might unfold over a few days. Text messages then reduced email messages to a few lines of characters, although with the addition of emoticons to stand in for real emotional cues, and sped things up (now if your friend on another continent doesn't respond in 4 minutes, perhaps because they were in the midst of an amorous dinner, you can send a follow-up text saying, "Are you alive??? ☹☹☹!!!").

Currently, a great deal of research is being conducted on the pros and cons of virtual contact compared to real contact. Some of the evidence suggests that virtual contacts can be positive, especially for people who are normally a bit shy, for example. But other research suggests that young people who spend relatively less time in actual contact with their friends are more depressed and anxious than those who spend a smaller proportion of time interacting on various social media.

Robert Putnam is a political scientist who examined historical trends in social participation over the past century. He argued that modern technology has been undermining real social contacts for the past 50 years. During that time, Americans have become less and less likely to join social groups, with declining participation in bowling teams; scout troops; parent–teacher associations; trade unions; and professional organizations, such as the American Medical Association and the American Bar Association. Modern Americans are also less likely than their parents' and grandparents' generations to entertain friends at home, drop in on the neighbors, or meet up with friends at a tavern. Two of the main culprits were 20th century technologies: cars and televisions in combination with an increasing desire for money (another modern cultural artifact that did not exist for most of our ancestors). Modern people who spend more time commuting to work and who spend more time in front of a television set (perhaps watching reruns of *Friends*), are less likely to have any time left over for real interactions with their real friends and neighbors.

During the time we were writing this, modern friendships encountered a whole new challenge: social distancing designed to lower the risk of transmitting the COVID-19 virus. For more than a year, most of the usual contacts with friends at work, at the gym, at the pub had to be put on hold. If you happened to bump into a friend or neighbor at the store, there's a good chance the two of you were speaking through a face mask, which would hide any of the usual smiles and other expressions that facilitate normal conversation. In the place of actual contacts, however, there was an increase in virtual meetings in which people could see one another's faces and actually chat in a manner that was at least more natural than faceless phone calls or text messages. To what extent this is a harbinger of friendships in the future is hard to tell and will depend to some extent on developments in medical science and public policy.

SOME FEATURES OF FRIENDSHIP THAT TRAVELED OVER THE CENTURIES

Despite all the technological advances and setbacks, there are still traces of the ancestral past in modern friendships. One such holdover is a strong tendency to befriend other people who are similar to us. A half century of research by sociologists and social psychologists has found that modern friends resemble one another not only in ethnicity, religion, and political attitudes but even food and beverage preferences. We are, of course, simply more likely to be exposed to people from our own groups, but it seems to go beyond mere exposure. People who move to a new place actively seek out people who are similar to them, and Mark Schaller's research suggests that if you discover that I share your attitudes, you infer that we may be kin.

Lisa DeBruine and her colleagues have done a series of studies in which participants are asked to make judgments about other people depicted in photographs. The photographs are actually morphed images that digitally combine two other people's likeness. Sometimes, one of the photos that makes up the morph is the participants' own face. Participants are unaware of this, but they like the person who looks like them more than other people whose images are made up of two strangers. More critically, we even trust the person who looks more like us.

Another study by Jeremy Bailenson found that people were more likely to vote for an unfamiliar candidate if that person's face was morphed with theirs. And several studies by Brett Pelham have found that we even prefer people whose names have similar letters to ours, so that Dave Kenrick likes someone named Dan Kennedy more than someone named Seamus O'Toole.

Despite being raised on different continents, Kahneman and Tversky were certainly similar in many ways. Kahneman's parents were born in Lithuania, and so was Tversky's mother. Both Danny and Amos shared a trait of unusually high intelligence. They had both been undergraduates at Hebrew University (although at different times), and they both then went on to earn their PhDs in the United States. And perhaps most important, they both shared a passionate interest in human psychology. Indeed, after finishing their doctorates, they both returned to Hebrew University in Israel to become psychology professors.

Although the preference for similarity inclines us to seek out our own tribal members as friends, that preference for physical and ethnic similarity can be overridden by psychological similarities. One study compared people's willingness to work on a team with someone from the same race who had different political attitudes versus someone from a different race who shared their political attitudes. There was a strong preference for the person who shared the person's attitudes rather than their race. And another study, conducted by Doug and FangFang Chen, found that sharing similar attitudes counts for even more if people initially expect to disagree. When Democrats found out that a Republican agreed with them on topics such as birth control and abortion, it led to more of a boost in liking than if they found out that another Democrat shared their opinions on controversial topics (which they already expected). These findings can explain friendships such as the one that developed between Mikhail Gorbachev, the leader of the Soviet Union, and Margaret Thatcher, the Conservative Prime Minister of one of the world's most prominent capitalistic and democratic countries.

Another relic of the ancestral past is the profound importance of proximity in friendship choice. We come to like others who are physically close to us. In a classic social psychological study, Leon Festinger and his colleagues observed the formation of friendships among college students moving into a college dorm at the Massachusetts Institute of Technology (MIT). People were almost twice as likely to strike up a friendship with someone who lived one door down compared with another person who lived two doors away. If two people lived four doors away from one another, on the other hand, their odds were 10 to 1 against their becoming friends. Other research done with police academy cadets found that friendships were most likely to form between people who were seated near one another in class. For one thing, it is simply more likely that we will interact with someone sitting right next to us or living in the next apartment. What is impressive, though, is how even a few feet can alter who becomes friends. Kahneman and Tversky may have grown up far away from one another, but as adults, they ended up as professors in the same department at the same university. Thus, they were certain to come into contact when they walked down the hallway, or went to the main office to get a cup of coffee, or pick up their mail (there was no electronic communication in those days, and the office mailroom was a social hot spot). Although they both eventually migrated to the United States, the two of them were neighbors in the psychology department at Hebrew University for more than a decade.

When anthropologist Dan Hruschka examined friendships in a sample of 60 societies from around the world, he found one other commonality that applied to hunter–gatherer groups, agricultural societies, and modern urban cultures: Friends provide mutual aid for one another. Friends in modern urban societies are not as likely to share food with one another on a daily basis, but they do exchange material goods (tools, books, cups of sugar, manual labor for moving a couch), information (how to fix a leaky faucet, write a term paper, or change a tire), and social support (lending an ear or a shoulder to cry on when we face life's stressors). In the case of Kahneman and Tversky, who were young professors, their alliance and the influential papers they published as a result not only helped them survive in a "publish or perish" environment but led each of them to receive offers at other internationally prominent universities with world-class psychology departments (Tversky landed a professorial slot at Stanford University, and Kahneman moved to the University of British Columbia and then to Berkeley and Princeton University).

Like our ancestors, modern people still regard friendship as essential. In one study of Arizona State University (ASU) undergrads, our research team asked people what they would be doing if they were trying to (a) find meaning in purpose in life, (b) become self-actualized (or reach their own personal potential), or (c) maximize their sense of well-being with their lives. Then participants rated the extent to which those behaviors would be linked to fundamental goals, such as self-protection, status-seeking, and kin care. People said that *affiliation* (defined as making and keeping friends) was the most important goal linked to their subjective sense of well-being. And when people thought about finding meaning in life, making and keeping friends came in second only to caring for family members. When people thought about self-actualization, affiliation also ranked at the top (for men, status was a little more important, but for women, making and keeping friends was just as important as gaining status).

A broader sample of Americans in a 2005 Gallup Poll said that they value friends as much as they value money and their jobs. And people are well advised to place such paramount value on friendships. After reviewing decades of literature on friendship, the psychological anthropologist Robin Dunbar concluded that "friendship is the single most important factor influencing our health, well-being, and happiness." Dunbar estimated that only giving up smoking has a bigger effect on mortality than friendship.

FRIENDSHIP STYLES: HIS, HERS, AND THEIRS

We mentioned that Daniel Kahneman and Amos Tversky published many highly cited scientific papers together. But Tversky wasn't Kahneman's only academic ally by any means. Despite Kahneman's reticence as a child, he made a lot of friends as an adult professor. The eminent economist Richard Thaler (who also won a Nobel Prize for his work on behavioral economics) mentions Danny frequently and warmly in describing Thaler's own work (much of which was done with Kahneman). Kahneman also conducted research with numerous prominent psychologists including Norbert Schwarz, Paul Slovic, Anne Treisman, Dan Ariely, and Ed Diener (a founder of the field of positive psychology). Indeed, the friendless boy Danny Kahneman grew up not only to make a lot of friends but to become the hub of an immense social network of close collaborators.

In one sense, the number and nature of Kahneman's adult friendships is a typical guy thing. Having a lot of friends whose time together is spent working on common projects is more typical of men than of women. Women are more likely to have a smaller number of deeper friendships that focus on socially supporting one another. These sex differences make sense in light of the ancestral past. Our hunter–gatherer grandfathers often went out in relatively large groups to hunt and sometimes to make war with other bands of males. Our ancestral grandmothers were likely to stay back in the village sharing child care, gathering fruits and vegetables, and preparing food with their daughters or one or two close friends.

Shelley Taylor is a prominent social psychologist at the University of California, Los Angeles, who has studied the links between relationships and health. She has made a strong case that early research on stress overemphasized fight-or-flight responses, which are linked to the hormones adrenaline, noradrenaline, and testosterone. Testosterone is found in much higher concentrations in men than in women (being produced in the adrenal glands by both sexes but also in the testes, which are only found in men). Taylor also observed that boys from the earliest age often interact with their friends in competitive contests, and this play aggression is important in developing later fighting skills and establishing dominance hierarchies. Play fighting, also found in monkeys and other apes, often results in one "alpha male" rising to the top of the dominance ladder. Female primates, on the other hand, are more likely to respond by "tending and befriending": gathering their offspring and huddling into a group. Taylor linked tending and befriending to a different set of hormones, most notably oxytocin, which appears to be related to prosocial and caring behaviors.

One team of researchers, led by former ASU doctoral student Jaimie Krems, found that sex differences in friendship patterns played themselves out in different patterns of friendship jealousy. Women, who have a smaller number of more intensely close relationships, were more likely to become jealous if their best friend started hanging out with another individual woman. However, men were more likely to feel jealous if a member of their team started hanging out with another team of guys. That male friendships are less intimate and more focused on group competition has another consequence: Women are more attractive as friends, both to other women and to men. Women are much less likely to nominate a man as a close friend than men are to nominate a woman.

In an interesting study, Brian Gillespie and his colleagues asked gay, lesbian, heterosexual, and bisexual men and women whom they planned to hang out with on their birthday. Heterosexual women and lesbians named twice as many other women as men friends, whereas heterosexual men showed a (slightly less pronounced) bias to name more guys than women. Gay men and bisexual women, on the other hand, were pretty egalitarian in their choices, and bisexual men actually showed a slight reversal, nominating slightly more women than men friends.

HOW TO WIN FRIENDS

To summarize what we've covered so far in this chapter: Researchers have found some fairly universal patterns in friendships. People tend to make friends most easily with people who are similar to them; who are physically close to them; and who are likely to provide useful goods, services, or information, or otherwise help them get ahead in life. All those decades of research into friendship formation—in other primates, in hunter–gatherers, in modern college students, in police cadets, and in people moving into new apartments—contain some useful lessons. Here, we focus on just five of them.

Make Yourself Useful

Vangie Keefe is married to Doug's close friend from graduate school, Rich Keefe, and she is the mother of Richie Keefe, who has been a lifelong friend of Dave. She is also perhaps the most beloved person either of us has ever met. Wherever Vangie goes, she is helping someone, including not only her large network of friends and coworkers but the many members of her extended Filipino American family. Although she spends most of her time in Seattle, whenever one of her old friends from Phoenix falls seriously ill, Vangie takes a leave from her day job (as a nurse) and comes down to help out. When Doug was passing through Seattle with Dave's younger brother, Liam, Vangie not only insisted that the two of them stay in her small apartment there (while she and Rich moved out and stayed at her mom's house), but she came by every day to make sure we were doing well and then took Liam on a tour of some of the fun sights nearby. And when Doug fell ill with what turned out to be a potentially fatal variant of asthma, Vangie called him up and advised him how to check his blood oxygen levels, and then when the results came in, she insisted that he get to the nearest hospital, which probably saved his life. What is most amazing about Vangie is that despite helping other people from morning till night, she is always smiling and truly seems delighted to see the next person who walks through her door. There are a lot of people walking through her door, too, because besides all the extensive medical knowledge she is so willing to share, she's also an excellent cook and frequently hosts large dinner parties. If she comes over to your house for dinner, though, her first question is, "What can I do to help?"

Danny Kahneman's friendship with Amos Tversky, which resulted in so many astounding professional benefits for both of them, was based on mutual usefulness. One key to making that friendship work was that, as Kahneman noted, they truly had fun in one another's company. Much of their work generating new ideas for groundbreaking experiments was done during their long and pleasant walks together.

The prominent evolutionary psychologists John Tooby and Leda Cosmides noted that, from the perspective of your selfish genes, being helpful to others is actually a good investment. To the extent that you can be counted on to help out your friends, especially with a skill that other people don't have (such as Vangie Keefe's knowledge of medicine or Amos Tversky's knowledge of statistical reasoning), you make yourself irreplaceable. When you are later down and out and need some help, those friends you helped earlier will be more eager to help you because from a purely selfish standpoint, they won't want to lose such a valuable asset. As a consequence, it seems as though we are wired to feel good when we do something nice for another person.

The oft-heard admonishment not to combine work and play is generally bad advice. When you and a friend are working together to accomplish something, that is just as much fun as trying to avoid work. And sometimes you can, in fact, work and play at the same time. Doug has spent many afterwork hours hanging out drinking coffee or hiking around with his friend, Rich Keefe (Vangie's husband) and Ed Sadalla. But during the course of all their casual hours hanging out, a lot of useful things have been accomplished. Not only are Keefe and Sadalla endless fonts of information about medicine, diet, and the best new nonfiction book, but among Doug's most cited academic articles are several papers written with these two old buddies.

Helping someone prepare a meal or bringing over a gift of food is one of the most time-honored ways of making yourself useful. As we noted at the beginning of this chapter in our discussion of people living under more traditional circumstances, like Iris from New Guinea, that's how our ancestors spent a lot of their waking hours. So, even if you invite friends over for dinner, you should give them something to do if they ask—even if it's to pour themselves a glass of wine and bring that bottle outside to see if anyone else wants some.

Focus on Real Commonalities

Besides having been raised in different countries, Kahneman and Tversky differed in a number of other ways. Kahneman was reserved, serious, and conflict averse; Tversky was outgoing, argumentative, and a bit of a comic. But in the most important ways, they were remarkably similar. Kahneman had been regarded as an ominously bright intellectual in high school, and this in the context of a culture in which intelligence was highly valued. Tversky was so smart that the distinguished University of Michigan professor Richard Nisbett made up the following one-item IQ test: The sooner you realized that Amos Tversky was smarter than you, the smarter you are. And besides being notably intelligent, even in the class of world-class college professors, both Kahneman and Tversky were obsessed with understanding the flaws in people's ability to think logically.

Kahneman and Tversky's highly productive friendship—based on a deep commonality of interests—was hardly unique. Indeed, history is made of such alliances. Michelle Obama's rise from lower middle-class kid in South Side Chicago to Princeton student, to Harvard Law School graduate, to dean at the University of Chicago, to First Lady of the United States dining with the Queen of England, is hardly a story of a rugged individual going it alone. Instead, it is a story of mutually supportive lifelong friendships. In high school, Michelle made friends with Santita Jackson, who rode the same school bus. They were drawn to each other because they were both studious and inquisitive. It turned out, though, that Santita happened to have a wealthy and influential father, the Reverend Jesse Jackson, who had worked alongside Martin Luther King, Jr., and had even run for president. Michelle's close friendship with Santita Jackson as well as her other connections to a web of close friends in Chicago no doubt played a role in her husband's entry into local and, later, national politics.

Frederick Douglass's biography is a prototypical heroic epic of an individual pulling himself up from the bottom to the top rung of society's status hierarchy. He began life as a slave and ended it as an internationally influential author and speaker whose eloquently expressed ideas shaped modern views of race relations and had a profound impact on Abraham Lincoln's Emancipation Proclamation. But part of Douglass's personal success owed to his ability to form strong working friendships, such as his alliance with American abolitionist William Lloyd Garrison, who sponsored Douglass's early career as a public speaker, and his friendship with British abolitionist Julia Griffiths, who raised funds for Douglass's cause in England and later moved to Upstate New York to help him edit his abolitionist newspaper *North Star*. Douglass's friendships also demonstrate how shared values and attitudes can override differences in racial and ethnic background.

If you move into a new neighborhood or take a new job, it makes sense to figure out the ways in which your new neighbors or coworkers are similar to you in their hobbies, the sports they enjoy, their attitudes, their food preferences, or their political attitudes. To the extent to which you emphasize those common links, you're more likely to fit in and make new friends. If you find instead that your political or religious beliefs differ from those of someone you've just met, emphasizing those differences is the best way to get them to dislike you. Some classic research in social psychology by Milton Rosenbaum found that the repulsion power of attitudinal disagreement was even stronger than the attraction power of agreement. This is not to say you ought to pretend to agree with someone whose beliefs you actually find abhorrent, only that you are ill advised to begin with a conversion about the dangers of religious dogmatism if you notice your new office mate is wearing a crucifix around her neck, and you are an atheist. Better to emphasize your shared passion for tennis or cooking shows.

You can also build similarities over time. Over the past 2 decades, Doug has formed what has become the closest alliance of his adult professional life with his colleague Steve Neuberg. Neuberg comes from a different cultural background than Doug. Rather than being a shantytown Irish Catholic from a family of criminals who nearly dropped out of a community college, as Doug did, Steve grew up in a wealthy Jewish family, went to an Ivy League university, and was even president of his fraternity. They also began their careers with very different research interests. Steve and Doug would often debate the relative merits of the social cognitive perspective versus the evolutionary perspective on social behavior. Social cognition researchers had traditionally focused on the immediate conscious influences on behavior (how my impression of you would be influenced by what I had just been thinking about before I met you, for example); evolutionary psychologists have traditionally been more interested in how our reactions to others are influenced by innate mechanisms that would have been adaptive for our ancestors (automatically noticing an angry face or an attractive person making a flirtation gesture, for example).

But Steve and Doug had offices with doors across the hall from one another for a decade, and after debating the relative merits of our viewpoints every day for a few years, we decided to begin doing some studies integrating our two different perspectives. The result has been almost 70 papers published together (many in our field's most prominent journals); several grants exploring how basic thought processes and economic decision making are influenced by evolved motives (as in the pyramid around which this book is organized); a social psychology textbook now in its seventh edition; and a large number of former

109

students who are themselves now working as professors in universities around the world and have produced several hundred of their own published papers in prominent journals, many following up on work they began in Steve and Doug's joint lab.

Beware of Fast but False Friends

Although our ancestors interacted mostly with people they knew well, those of us living in the modern urban world come in contact with strangers every day. Just walking across the campus at ASU to get lunch on the main street in nearby Tempe, we are likely to pass thousands of strangers, including not only dense crowds of college students, professors, and university administrators but also gardeners, business owners, restaurant workers, traveling salespeople, homeless people, and throngs of out-of-town visitors in town to see a football game or visit their relatives. Some of those people might even talk to us, asking for directions, offering us a coupon for a nearby restaurant, asking us to contribute to a cause, or trying to panhandle money. Every day, we also receive dozens of digital communications from people we don't know; some from folks in the psychology business; others from strangers asking for advice; and others trying to sell us something, get us involved in their cause, or get us to contribute to their organization.

Most of the strangers you encounter on a daily basis are harmless, but a few want to exploit you in some way, even if it's only to get you to part with a few of your hard-earned dollars. Our colleague Bob Cialdini has done years of research into the social influence process, particularly delving into the way compliance professionals exploit everyday rules of thumb that normally help us make sound and efficient decisions about who to trust. One of those everyday rules of thumb is to trust people who are related to us in some way, who have those features we associate with members of our own tribe.

Hence, salespeople will often quickly begin calling you by your first name and will find some tribal connection: "No kidding! You're from Milwaukee. My wife's family is from Milwaukee! What a small world!" Some of the requests for donations we get in our email hijack those friendship cues: "Hey, Doug, did you see Amy's message last night?" Sounds exactly like a message from a real friend, but it is actually a request from a political organization full of people Doug has never met but who, of course, know his name from his email address.

A related trick is to share something in a way that only a friend normally does. Before trying to sell you on buying one of their automobiles, car salespeople will frequently offer you a Coke, a coffee, or a bottle of water. In one study by Dennis Regan, freshmen at Stanford participated in a psychology experiment along with another student (who was actually a confederate of the experimenter). The "other student" left the room for a few minutes then returned, saying he had asked the experimenter if it was okay to buy himself a Coke and adding, "I bought one for you, too." Later on, during a pause in the experiment, the Coke-sharing confederate passed a note to the real subject, saying that he was selling raffle tickets to build a new gym at his old high school and that he'd win $50 if he sold the highest number of tickets. He mentioned it would really help out if the subject wanted to buy any. Compared with a control condition in which the confederate didn't give the subject a Coke, having previously given that small gift resulted in nearly twice as many tickets sold.

Although most of us are completely unaware of it, we tend to like other people whose nonverbal behaviors are similar to ours— who scratch their head when we scratch our head, shake their foot when we shake ours. This research has become well known in the field of marketing, with the following result: Salespeople and online marketers are now being trained to imitate the nonverbal behaviors of their customers (for example, mimic a customer's hand and foot movements) and to speak at the same pace as the customer, while also saying, "you know" at the end of their sentences if the customer does . . . you know. And other research evidence suggests that such apparently superficial mimicking increases tips, sells more electronic equipment, and leads to better outcomes in business negotiations.

Of course, buying a few extra raffle tickets from another student is no great cost, but you should think twice before taking out a $40,000 car loan because the salesperson gives you a Coke, calls you by your first name, says he has a cousin from your hometown, and scratches his head every time you do.

One good way to avoid being conned by false friends is to use reliable cues to group membership. The most reliable cue is a long history of actual interactions with real friends.

Keep the Old

Strangers can be charming but dangerous, especially when they fake the cues of friendship. Facebook "friends" you haven't actually met might also be suspect. Hell, half of them might be paid purveyors of misinformation trying to get you to show up at a prearranged political gang fight!

So, who can you trust to be a real friend? Well, old friends make especially good friends because you have a good record of their reliability and trustworthiness, and if you've done well by them, you are also valuable to them. And kin make good friends, too, because they share a deep biological connection with you, and those shared genes lead them to be relatively more likely to have your interests at heart.

Give Your Friends the Credit and Gratitude They Deserve

Of course, friendships have their ups and downs, and they require tending. Even Kahneman and Tversky's friendship ran into some bumps. Besides having led to a lot of shared laughter and pleasant times, their work together had generated a long series of increasingly influential papers, job offers at major universities, invitations to consult with world leaders, and awards. Ironically, it was that very success that began to tear them apart. Kahneman began to feel envious because Tversky was getting the lion's share of the credit. As one example, Tversky had received a lucrative MacArthur genius award for the work he'd done with Kahneman, but the award had not even mentioned Kahneman. And although they'd always enjoyed debating about ideas, Kahneman began to take Tversky's criticisms as personal put-downs.

The tendency for some people to compete with their friends for recognition was examined in a study Doug conducted with Josh Ackerman (a former ASU student who is now a psychology professor at the University of Michigan, where Tversky had gotten his PhD) and Mark Schaller (another former ASU student, who is now a psychology professor at the University of British Columbia, where Kahneman went after leaving Israel). In that study, students were asked to recruit either a close friend or a family member to participate along with them. The task they would work on (with their friend, their relative, or, in the control condition, a stranger) involved difficult questions from a test that they were told was used by major corporations to predict professional success. In reality, the questions were difficult items from the Graduate Record Examination (something like the SAT or ACT, only used to select college students for admission into doctoral programs). If you were a participant, you and your friend would have been given different questions, but in the end, rather than getting feedback about your individual performance, you would learn only your team score. Regardless of your actual performance, you would be told that your pair had performed exceptionally well: above 93% of all the other participants, in fact. You would then be asked who you thought should get the most credit for the stellar performance.

When students were paired with strangers, they tended to give themselves more of the credit. If they were paired with a relative, however, they tended to give more credit to their family member. Those results were the same whether the participants themselves were men or women. What was most interesting, however, is what happened when people were paired with friends. In that case, women treated their friends as kin, giving them more credit than they took for themselves. Men, however, gave more credit to themselves rather than their friends. This result is consistent with other findings suggesting that men's relationships are more competitive (even as children, boys compete with one another much more than girls, who tend to play cooperatively).

So, one punchline of those findings is this: You should go out of your way to acknowledge your friends' contributions to any team efforts and to explicitly give them credit.

We have discussed the profound importance of making yourself useful to others. On the other side of that equation, if someone does anything to help you in any way, be sure to clearly express your thanks. Indeed, there's research suggesting that clearly communicating gratitude for a favor is highly rewarding for both parties, making both the person being thanked and the person doing the thanking feel that the relationship is more intimate and more communal. Expressing gratitude also has the benefit of generating more rewards in the future; it feels better to give to someone who appreciates the gift. In one clever field study, the researchers had servers at an upscale East Coast restaurant record their tip size when they wrote, "Thank you" on the bill. They compared those tips with a control condition in which the servers wrote nothing. Merely jotting down the words "Thank you" boosted tips 11% (in an upscale restaurant, that can add up to a lot of money before your pen runs out of ink).

University of California, San Diego, psychologist Mike McCullough has done a number of studies on the effects of gratitude, and he pointed out that gratitude is a two-edged sword (or a two-scooped ice cream cone). It not only reinforces the gift giver for providing the benefit but also motivates the gift receiver to want to do something nice in return.

When it comes to providing mutual benefits, it's good to keep in mind that close friendships tend to work on a communal rather than an exchange model—with benefits flowing to the friend who currently needs help—and no need for careful accounting or immediate repayment. Hence, good friends don't count what their friends do or don't do for them. At the same time, good friends don't take and take without ever giving back. Even the closest friends will notice if things are too one-sided for too long. So, if you haven't done something nice for a friend in a while, consider bringing them a small gift (a cup of coffee, a chocolate bar, or even a short note complimenting them about something you know they might be proud of). And if they ask you for some help with something that is really important to them, it's best when you can just say yes.

We close the chapter by suggesting one particular gift you can give a friend. It's one that seems free but that is becoming increasingly rare in the modern technologically dominated world: Attention. In a series of studies, Yohsuke Ohtsubo and colleagues found that if you pay more attention to another person, they are more likely to assume you understand them, accept them, and care more about their well-being. So, the next time you are talking to a friend, turn off the ringer on your cell phone and don't watch the basketball game playing on the wide-screen TV behind their heads. Make eye contact and pay attention to what they're saying. And if you are in a virtual meeting, be sure to turn on the video, turn off the mute, and look directly at the screen rather than gazing off to the side to read your email.

BOTTOM LINES: SUGGESTIONS FOR GETTING ALONG

Although ancestral friendship networks were made up of kin and in-laws, there were also often beneficial alliances with nonrelatives. Those of us living in the modern world are still inclined to befriend others who are nearby, who share resources with us, and who are similar to us in various ways. A few potentially useful pointers follow from considering modern friendships in light of the ancestral past:

- *Make yourself useful.* It's okay to mix work and play.
- *Base your friendships on real commonalities.* Find similarities with those around you, and build on those similarities over time.
- *Beware of false friends.* Our simple and automatic tendency to trust friends can be used against us by those who aren't.
- *Keep the old.* When it comes to old friends, you have a good record of their reliability and trustworthiness, and if you've done well by them, you are also valuable to them. And don't forget that kin make good friends, too.
- *Give your friends the credit, gratitude, and attention, they deserve.*

CHAPTER 5

GETTING AHEAD

Bob Cialdini was a star of his high school baseball team in Milwaukee, Wisconsin, and he had a dream: "I wanted to be Willie Mays, or Mickey Mantle." When a scout for the Chicago White Sox offered Bob a contract to play professional ball with one of the White Sox's minor league teams, that dream seemed like it might come true.

As Bob tells the story a half century later, he was eager to accept the deal. But just as he was about to sign the contract, the scout asked: "Are you good in school, son?" Cialdini replied that, yes, he was.

"Are you good enough to go to college?" Again, yes.

"Are you good enough to complete a college education?"

When he answered yes to that as well, the scout said, "Go to school, kid. You're not really good enough to make it to the majors."

Bob found that feedback painful to hear at the time but now realizes it was a great act of kindness. By the time he'd have realized he was never going to make the major leagues, he figures, he would have found himself living in Cozad, Nebraska, perhaps with a wife and dependent child, and the college option long past. At that point, he reckons his best option might have been landing a job as assistant manager at the local Pizza Hut.

But Cialdini did in fact go to college, and although he had to work part-time as a garbage collector to pay his expenses, he excelled at his classes. A fortuitous upturn in his prospects came when he volunteered in a comparative psychology lab to conduct research on a study of alarm pheromones in earthworms. Those lowly earthworms resulted in Cialdini's first big academic success: coauthorship on a paper published in the prestigious journal *Science*.

That publication would have been a ticket to a graduate program studying animal behavior. But, before he set off on that course, chance intervened again. He had developed a mad crush on a young woman who happened to be taking a social psychology class and decided to sit in on the class to be near her. Although the romance did not progress, Cialdini found himself in love with the class. He asked the professor about graduate schools in social psychology but was informed that most application deadlines had already passed. Cialdini didn't give up, though, and searched around for a program that might still be accepting applications.

Cialdini discovered that the deadline had not passed at the University of North Carolina, which had a strong social psychology program. He got accepted, and when he arrived, he teamed up with an emerging young professor named Chet Insko, who taught Bob how to conduct research and publish scientific papers. Cialdini was a natural at designing and conducting laboratory experiments, and was also a good writer, so by the time he took his first job as a professor in a new program at Arizona State University, he was already a rising star.

Doug (one of this book's authors) was a student in Cialdini's first graduate seminar. Cialdini at the time did not appear the prototype of a rising academic superstar. Wearing scruffy bell-bottoms, gaudy dashiki shirts, and sporting a Vinnie Barbarino haircut, he drove around in an orange Plymouth Duster that looked like something straight out of Appalachia. In the low-rent apartment complex where he lived, there were two murders (one of which was a mob hit, with Cialdini first on the scene to try to pull the victim out of his exploded car).

But appearances notwithstanding, Cialdini was about to make another sharp turn in his career—one that would eventually result in his becoming a world-renowned leader inside and outside the academic world. Cialdini had decided to venture outside the familiar comforts of the university laboratory to try to discover the social influence techniques used by professional influence agents, the salespeople, cult recruiters, and politicians who so skillfully get people to say "yes" to giving up their precious money, time, and votes.

Hiding the fact that he was a college professor, Cialdini went undercover, taking various part-time sales jobs. His experiences led him to write a book called *Influence: Science and Practice,* first published in 1985. The book was wildly successful. It has sold more than 5 million copies worldwide and has been translated into over 30 languages. In articles in *The New York Times* and in popular books, such as *Nudge* by Nobel Prize–winning economist Richard Thaler, you will see Cialdini hailed as the "guru of social influence." Cialdini's success in studying the psychology of influence led to attainments in other domains as well; he has been consulted by politicians (at 10 Downing Street and in the Barack Obama administration) and by business leaders at Fortune 500 companies (which inspired a sartorial change from scruffy jeans to fancy Italian suits). By any measure, it is safe to say Bob Cialdini has succeeded at getting ahead in the modern world.

Is there anything in common between getting ahead in the modern world and getting ahead as a hunter–gatherer on the African savannah? We now turn to that question.

GETTING AHEAD IN THE YEARS BEHIND

The !Kung San Bushmen of the Kalahari, still living a hunter–gatherer lifestyle in the 20th century, had few status distinctions. Bushmen who were verbally articulate or who were good hunters did earn special respect within their groups. But the best hunters did not accumulate resources; they instead shared the wealth with others. Anyone who bragged about his successes was criticized, so saying, "It was nothing" gained more respect than announcing, "I am the greatest."

Anthropologist Chris von Rueden has studied social status among Amazon foragers. He joined forces with psychologist Mark Van Vugt, who studies leadership in modern societies, to investigate the similarities and differences between getting ahead in those two very different worlds. In small-scale societies, humility is mandatory, and anyone who tries to stand above his fellows is ostracized. If an uppity individual tries to bully other group members, he may even be executed. Besides humility, those who command respect within small-scale societies tend to have specific knowledge (how to build a sturdy hut, fish, prepare food, or make a good canoe), and general wisdom (seeing connections between current problems and similar problems in the past, for example). Leaders in small-scale societies also tend to have good verbal skills, which allow them to demonstrate their knowledge and wisdom, and to persuade others. They also tend to have large networks of kin and friends whom they have helped in the past and who trust them to make decisions for the group good.

Being a leader in a small-scale society carries some important benefits: Other people share more of their resources with you, and if you are a man, you are more successful in attracting mates. We discuss the link between status and finding mates in the next chapter. But, for now, we simply note that women were more likely to marry men based on the man's status, and men were consequently more likely to compete for status in traditional societies. Being a leader also carried costs. Yǎnomamö headmen got drawn into petty, and sometimes dangerous, conflicts between other group members. And they were expected to take more risks. The leaders patrolled the group's perimeter at night, for example, which increased their odds of being killed if they bumped into an enemy group without comrades to help them fight.

For around 200,000 years, our ancestors lived in bands, like those of the !Kung, composed largely of extended family groupings, including cousins and in-laws. Because people moved around a lot, there wasn't much in the way of accumulated capital, so status distinctions, although potentially important, were relatively small. But during the most recent 5% of human history, things changed. Beginning around 10,000 years ago, agriculture and the domestication of large animals allowed some individuals to accumulate much more wealth than others.

The development of agriculture led to the formation of larger tribal groups and chiefdoms that included people who were not all so closely related. Chiefs emerged to manage the conflicts arising within and between these larger groups. Over time, there was also an increasing division of labor, with some members of society becoming soldiers and some taking on political and religious roles. A consequence of these developments was a steeper social hierarchy. Not only did the hierarchy reach higher at the top, it also got lower at the bottom, with many societies, including the Egyptians, Greeks, Romans, and early American colonists, enslaving the members of other groups.

Over time, the agricultural revolution also facilitated the growth of large cities, which, in turn, led to the emergence of a broad middle class comprising mostly merchants and artisans. This development was magnified following the late 1700s, when the industrial revolution made it possible for some members of the merchant class to accumulate extremely high levels of wealth, as in the case of the Rockefellers, Guggenheims, and Carnegies.

GETTING BEHIND IN THE YEARS AHEAD

There were not many rungs on the hunter–gatherer status hierarchy, but there are many in the modern world. Consider just the gradations in income between the richest and poorest people in American and European society today. In 2019, Walmart employed 2.3 million workers who earned an average annual salary of $21,952. Walmart's CEO that year earned $23,620,352 (1,076 times as much as his typical employee). Walmart is not particularly anomalous; across the 350 largest U.S. companies, the average CEO earns about $21 million a year, almost as much as Walmart's CEO, and fully 320 times more than the average employee in those same companies.

Besides the number of rungs on the social ladder in the modern world, there is another unique problem at the bottom of the ladder: unemployment. In the hunter–gatherer world, everyone had a job to do, although the number of hours worked per day was less than it is in the modern world. In 2019, four out of 100 Americans were out of work, as were almost seven out of 100 Europeans. After the COVID-19 virus hit in 2020, the European unemployment rate increased a bit, from 6.6 to 7.2, whereas the American rate shot up to 15%. That means that for every six adult Americans with a job, there was one person with an income of $0. Among African Americans in Michigan in the spring and summer of 2020, it was much worse: Fully one in three were unemployed.

If a modern American does have a job, they work an average of 44 hours per week and spend another 4.5 hours commuting to and from work. A typical hunter–gatherer toiled for about 5 hours a day.

The skyward expansion of rungs on the modern social ladder means that even if you are doing well, there are almost always people way above you to provide unpleasant sources of social comparison. These invidious contrasts get magnified by the media, which deliver stories about the rich and famous into everyone's living room on a daily basis. Whether we care or not, we are fed a never-ending diet of stories about pop stars like Rihanna and Jay-Z making billions of dollars from their exclusive clothing lines, and others, like Jeff Bezos and Richard Branson, who are so filthy rich, they are funding their own personal space programs.

But all the news is not bad for us everyday people. Besides being many more rungs, there are also many more ladders. In a hunter–gatherer group, there was not much division of labor, except between the sexes (with women doing more of the gathering and domestic care, and men, more hunting). But in the modern world, you can excel (or at least get by) in many different ways. The U.S. Bureau of Labor Statistics lists 867 different occupations, ranging from accountants, auditors, and architects through gambling dealers and morticians, to veterinary assistants and zoologists. There are 72 different occupations in the "educational instruction" category alone, including postsecondary conservation science teachers, kinder-garten special education teachers, and library technicians. Within every one of these occupational groups, there is a status hierarchy. Among academic psychologists, you gain status from publishing articles in journals, such as *Psychological Review* or *Behavioral and Brain Sciences*, but those achievements would make no impression whatsoever on a group of accountants or special forces officers.

The sex difference in competition for status in foraging societies continued after the agricultural revolution. Although there were exceptions, such as Cleopatra in Egypt and the Empress Wu Zetian in China, most of the world's leaders were men up until modern times. In the modern world, leaders continue to have masculine characteristics, such as deeper voices and taller stature. However, there are more opportunities for women to increase their status today. In 2020, 23% of U.S. congressional representatives and 26% of U.S. senators were women. In Sweden, fully 47% of parliament members were women. Analyses of election results show that, when a woman runs against a man in a U.S. election, she stands as good a chance of winning as he does. Although people still stereotypically associate leadership with masculine traits, those stereotypes don't translate into preferences. Indeed, people generally find women more trustworthy and understand that high levels of masculinity can be associated with exploitative bullying tactics. Being a bully might be valued in a wartime leader, but it is regarded as a handicap if people are thinking about who they want as their boss or who will help different groups within their country get along.

Being well-connected to a large network of relatives and friends continues to be a factor in gaining status in modern societies (think of the Kennedy clan or the Bush family), and, as in the old days, people still prefer leaders whom they perceive as generous and fair (in the run-up to the 2020 U.S. presidential election, there was as much discussion of Joe Biden's willingness to share his personal cell phone number with working class people he met on the train as of his previous experience working as a senator and vice president).

Your definition of getting ahead or getting respect may not include accumulating a pile of money that's obscenely larger than everyone else's, and it's fine if your goals do not include climbing up the social hierarchy. But we are similar to our ancestors in that most of us continue to desire, and to benefit from, winning respect and admiration from the other members of our groups.

So, what are some pathways for you to achieve the fundamental human need for status and respect? We organize the remainder of this chapter into three categories: figuring out how to choose the right career, doing your personal best in that career, and being a good team player.

CHOOSING THE RIGHT CAREER: FOLLOW YOUR DREAM?

It can be a daunting task to decide which of the 867 occupational categories is right for you or to advise a teenage relative about how to make the choice. Bob Cialdini had to choose between a highly tempting opportunity to earn a salary playing professional baseball, his youthful dream, and a long-focus opportunity to earn a college degree for which he would need to work part time as a garbage collector. In the long run, his decision turned out to be a wise one. When we asked him if he had any advice that generalized beyond the specifics of deciding about being a minor league baseball player, he replied, "Everybody's going to tell you 'go for your dream!' . . . (but) it's not enough just to have an aspiration." Cialdini advised, "Follow your dream, but first investigate the extent to which you're good at what that dream requires you to be."

Lots of kids who are good at sports dream of living the rich and famous lifestyles of professional athletes, such as Serena Williams or Lionel Messi. But what is the probability a talented and ambitious young athlete will be able to convert those aspirations into reality?

Every year 1,108,441 kids play high school football, but only 67,887 go on to play college football. How many get drafted into the NFL (National Football League)? Just 255. Those are not good odds (4,346 to 1, to be exact). The odds are even worse for basketball (11,371 to 1), and although they seem slightly better for baseball (584 to 1), remember that a lot of baseball contracts are to play in those minor league teams like the Great Falls Voyagers or the Omaha Storm Chasers (from Cozad, Nebraska, with its notorious Pizza Hut). If that doesn't give you pause, consider this: Most professional football players who may make millions while they are playing the sport are bankrupt within a few years of leaving the game—at the ripe old age of 35!

Or maybe you dream instead of making it as a professional musician, nurturing hopes that your band will be the next Green Day or that you'll personally be the next Rihanna, Luis Fonsi, or Shakira. Compared with earning money as a professional athlete, there are a lot more local opportunities for musicians, such as playing the neighborhood bar. But those local gigs are unlikely to make you enough money to live on, much less support a family. And among those few who can manage to call themselves professional musicians, fewer than 1% make it into the mainstream, and only two in 1,000 make it big. So, if you're dreaming of a career making music, you'll also need to dream up a good day job as well.

Finding Out Which Day Jobs Are in Demand

The first question to ask about a particular career path is whether it will lead you into an economic oasis or leave you financially forsaken in the desert of destitution. Most kids who aspire to be professional athletes or rock stars are going to end up penniless in the desert. But a little research can help you find your way to one of those income oases.

In 2018, *U.S. News & World Report* published a list of the best jobs. Number 3 was a physician's assistant. On that job, you'd make an average salary of $101,000 and could expect to see 37% more such positions opening up over the next decade. Number 2 was a dentist, earning an average salary of $153,000, with an expected 17% more openings in the next few years. On top of the heap was software developer, with an annual salary around $100,000 and an expected increase in demand of 30% in the future.

Matching Your Personality to Your Chosen Occupation

Before you sign up for a program in software development or dentistry, though, you ought to ask yourself another question: Will I personally be happy in this job?

How in the world can you tell in advance whether your personality will fit with a particular job? Turns out there are decades of hard scientific data exploring which personality traits will lead you to be happy in which types of jobs. John L. Holland was a personality psychologist who worked in the sociology department at Johns Hopkins University. He collected data on thousands of college students in different majors as well as adult women and men in different occupations, and found a clear linkage between an individual's personality and the career they chose. A lot depends on whether your personality is a good fit with those of the other people in your chosen occupational environment.

Using the statistical data on job preferences, Holland was able to collapse the many types of jobs in a much smaller number of categories:

- *Realistic* jobs include those in information technology like that top software developer job. They also include jobs in law enforcement and the military as well as those hard-to-get jobs as professional athletes. In general, realistic types are people who are good at completing practical tasks that require mechanical dexterity and physical courage. According to Robert Hogan, a prominent personality psychologist who also runs a successful business, people in realistic occupations tend to be introverted rather than extraverted, and also to be action oriented, tough, and conforming.
- *Investigative* jobs are those in science fields. You'd enjoy an investigative job if you are someone who likes to identify and

127

solve problems, and to design new systems to solve those problems. Investigative types are cerebral, analytical, and introverted. They also like to challenge authority (science is about new ideas, after all, not accepting the status quo). Think of Rosalind Franklin, who was instrumental in discovering the structure of DNA.

- *Artistic* jobs are those involving art, music, literature, philosophy, architecture, and landscaping. Artistic types like to design and create products and they get a kick out of entertaining people. Like Andy Warhol, Frida Kahlo, and those whiz kids in the "creative" department at an advertising agency, they are imaginative, colorful, and nonconforming.

- *Social* jobs are those in teaching, medicine, social work, and human resources. They involve helping and teaching other people. If you are an altruistic, helpful, and sympathetic person, such as Jaimie Escalante or Florence Nightingale, you'd do well in a social career.

- *Enterprising* careers involve jobs in sales, politics, or management. Enterprising types are good at persuading and manipulating other people. Other people tend to perceive enterprising types as aggressive, bold, and outgoing. Vincent van Gogh took a job as an art salesman in his uncle's business. Although he should have been happy bringing home a paycheck, he was miserable because he was basically an introvert trying to do a job requiring a high degree of extroversion.

- *Conventional* jobs include most jobs in an office: secretaries and administrative assistants as well as accountants, tax lawyers, and finance analysts. Conventional types like the rules, which are consistent with their conforming, procedural, orderly, and detail-oriented personalities. But they tend to be unimaginative and would be miserable in a job as an artist.

In general, you would be maximally satisfied with, most productive in, and least likely to quit a job that matches your personal traits, and you would be next most satisfied with a job in an adjacent position on the preceding list. An artistic type, for example, might also feel at home in an investigative or social career. But if you take a job in a much different category; if you are an investigative type in a job that requires you to be enterprising, for example, you're likely to be dissatisfied.

Showing Up

Once you've made a career choice, you need to figure out how to succeed in that career.

A number of highly accomplished people have argued that the main ingredient to success is simply giving it your best try. Thomas Edison, who invented the light bulb and the phonograph, said that genius is "one per cent percent inspiration, ninety-nine per cent perspiration." Angela Duckworth, a psychologist who has conducted extensive research on "grit" (perseverance toward long-term goals), said, "As much as talent counts, effort counts twice." And Ben Hogan, who won nine major golf championships, said, "Golf is a game of luck. The more I practice, the luckier I get."

A couple of years back, Dave's 10-year-old daughter, Greta, told him she wanted to try out for her school's volleyball team. Although Greta had never even played the game, her two closest friends, who were experienced volleyball players, were trying out for the team. Besides Doug's sister Janice, Greta is the only sports-oriented member of our immediate family, and her athletic inclinations certainly did not come from genes or experiences contributed by her father or grandfather. But Dave dutifully bought her a ball.

Unfortunately, it immediately became clear not only that volleyball isn't something that comes naturally but that she was going

to need some work. Dave himself could barely hit the ball properly and did not know the first thing about how to train her to play
volleyball. If those weren't enough handicaps, it was August in
Phoenix, with midday temperatures running 115 degrees. But Greta
wanted to make the team, so they went out in the evening and practiced. And they got up early the next morning and practiced again.
They did this for several days, and Dave realized something amazing
about her progress over that short time. There wasn't any! On the
day of the tryouts, though, Dave suggested:

> When you try out today, I want you to run as hard as you can
> for every ball that they hit to you, even if you know there's no
> chance you could possibly hit it back. The coach will really like
> that, and it will make her think that once you learn how to play,
> you'll have a lot of heart.

Greta did try her heart out in the first day of tryouts but
did predictably badly and came home depressed. She got up and
went back the next day, though, and again tried her best despite
the likelihood she'd be eliminated. In the end, though, she actually made the team. Turns out most of the other kids who weren't
stars had self-selected out, so all the kids who stuck it out till the
last day of tryouts made the final cut, no matter how unstarlike
their initial abilities. And then, Greta showed up for practice and
games every day, and her team went on to be undefeated. She
wasn't the team's star by any means, but she made the team again
the following year.

When personal computers first became available, Doug's
friend David Funder, who was then a new professor at Harvard,
had a simple piece of advice about how to survive in the publish-
or-perish world of academia. Funder had learned not to set
himself up with the daunting expectation of completing a long,

perfectly organized, eloquent paper with seamless documentation for every point. This perfectionism hurdle frequently leaves aspiring authors spending month after month trying to read everything that might possibly be relevant and then forgetting what it was they intended to say in the first place. Instead, Funder would simply open up his computer every day and just read what he'd written the day before. When he got to the end, he'd set the small goal of writing just one sentence. One sentence a day isn't a daunting task. But it was enough to get him started, and he would often end up getting on a roll, adding several pages. Three pages a day is almost a thousand in a year—enough to fill two or three books!

GETTING BY VERSUS GETTING IN THE GROOVE

Not everyone wants to move to the head of the class. There is something to be said for just getting by. Research on the determinants of happiness finds that the biggest boost in life satisfaction comes from just getting out of the gutter. People who live in very poor countries—in Africa and former Soviet states—are less happy than those who live in Europe or Canada, for example. Within the relatively wealthy countries, the very poorest people are the least happy.

If you're a guy, there's another reason to avoid the bottom of the totem pole: Women are attracted to men who have some wealth and social status. But above that, the benefits are not so clear. Very wealthy Americans are not substantially happier than those with middle-class incomes. And when our research team looked more deeply at the relationship between a man's income and his attractiveness, most of the boost in attractiveness came at the low end. We found that guys who make a middle-class living are way more attractive than poor guys. But really wealthy guys don't gain that much more. And once you've moved up to the middle, it takes a lot more effort to move further up in the hierarchy because there are fewer and fewer spots with each step up. There are 115,000 corporals in the U.S. Army, 30,000 captains, 14,000 colonels, and 363 generals. And then there are the costs that come with leadership: People expect those at the top to make good decisions and to lead the group in the right direction. Followers get angry when leaders don't perform.

Of course, there are also benefits to moving up besides the incremental gains in happiness and sex appeal. Whether it makes you effusively blissful and irresistible, there is still something to be said for a higher salary, a nice office, and other people to work for you on the mundane tasks. Between the two of us, we've had some lower level jobs: stocking clerk, dishwasher, hotel doorman, and factory line worker, for example, as well as higher prestige jobs with pleasant offices and administrative support. Generally, the higher prestige jobs are a lot easier in almost every way.

Timothy Judge and his colleagues conducted a meta-analysis of the studies examining the link between job satisfaction and job performance, including 312 different research samples and a total of 54,417 subjects. Although there was some inconsistency across different studies, the researchers found an overall solid correlation between how well a person performs their job and how satisfied they are with that job. The researchers considered several processes that could lead to the performance–satisfaction link: Having a good attitude toward your work might cause you to work harder, for example, or working harder might, conversely, cause you to like your job more.

Classical models of organizational psychology conceptualized work as a means to an end. To the extent that you view work in an instrumental way, you will be most happy with the highest paycheck. On the *instrumental* view, the relationship between job performance and job satisfaction would follow to the extent that harder work led to better job performance, which in turn led to bigger paychecks. You'd be equally happy, on that model, if you could get the same big paycheck with a lot less work, but you realize you need to work to get the payoff.

But theories of *intrinsic motivation* suggest that rather than wanting "money for nothing," we are designed to enjoy working as an end in itself. In line with the theory of intrinsic work motivation, Steven Brown and Robert Peterson found that salespeople who expended more effort on the job were more satisfied with their jobs above and beyond the effect of their efforts on any extrinsic payoffs. And the link between hard work and job satisfaction wasn't peculiar to sales jobs: A meta-analysis of 11 other studies revealed a similar relationship across several different occupations. People who work harder come to like their jobs more—independent of any outside rewards.

From an evolutionary perspective, why wouldn't we be designed to conserve calories and laze around as much as possible? Maybe it's because our ancestors who enjoyed working reaped genetic benefits as well. The hard workers were more likely to solve important problems and generate resources to carry them, and their kin, through difficult times. And our ancestors who solved problems and generated resources would also have been more attractive as potential mates. The short-term goal—the felt satisfaction from working—might thus link to deeper ultimate goals: generating resources and status, and acquiring mates. Of course, we need not be consciously in touch with that linkage for it to work (people hard at work don't need to say to themselves, "I'm enjoying work because it will enhance my survival and reproduction" any more than people need to think, "I'm enjoying this sexual experience; it will pass on my genes" or "I'm enjoying these chocolate-covered cherries because they will contribute to my somatic resource account, therefore increasing my survival"). All we need to know is that it feels good to eat, love, and work.

EMBRACING FAILURE

If you're trying to get better at any skill-related activity, you are bound to fail. At that point, you can either make a global attribution—tell yourself that you are a loser—or you can instead ask yourself what you learned from your failure. Thomas Edison again had the perfect philosophy on the matter when he said: "I have not failed. I've just found 10,000 ways that won't work."

Read a biography of almost any successful person, and you'll likely learn about a lot of failures that that person lived through. The great ornithologist John James Audubon lost his fortunes several times over and spent some time not only in poverty but also in a state of clinical depression. He was not a biologist by training, and he was turned down for membership in prestigious scientific societies. Yet he persisted in his (unrealistic) goal of making life-sized paintings of all the birds of North America and eventually won great acclaim (although not great wealth).

Stacey Abrams lost her bid to become governor of Georgia. Her opponent was Brian Kemp, who, as secretary of state, had been in charge of elections and voter registration, and had overseen a massive purging of hundreds of thousands of voter registrations. Those purges were found to have selectively reduced votes by African Americans. Abrams, who is African American, lost by a narrow margin. Rather than throw up her hands in defeat and drop out of politics in the face of such powerful vested interests, however, Abrams founded an organization to fight voter suppression and personally oversaw a massive campaign to register voters in Georgia, which was credited with turning around the results of the 2020 presidential and senatorial elections in that state.

PACING YOURSELF

Using Thomas Edison as your role model can have an unintended danger. Maybe you don't have the temperament to sleep in the office, skip meals, and avoid family responsibilities. Even though genius is 99% perspiration, that doesn't mean you need to be working up a sweat 99% of the time for every minute of every day during every week of every year. Sometimes you are up for a sprint, but other times it's fine just to jog along slowly, and sometimes you might even sit out a round. Even Abraham Lincoln and Teddy Roosevelt took some breaks (Roosevelt completely disappeared for 2 years right in the middle of his career, dropping out of politics to work on his ranch in the Dakotas after his young wife and mother died on the same day).

The Nobel Prize–winning economist, political scientist, and psychologist Herbert Simon was an incredibly prolific and thoughtful researcher and writer. One his most useful contributions was to coin the term *satisfice*, which refers to decision making under conditions in which it is impossible to optimize—to arrive at a perfect solution that takes all possible relevant facts into consideration. When you satisfice, you don't strive for perfection, but you stop at "good enough." Usually, you can come up with a good enough solution in a small fraction of the time it would take to come up with a perfect solution.

Part of pacing yourself is to be patient. Success in most fields is more of a long slow marathon than a sprint. K. Anders Ericsson is a Florida State University psychologist who had done a postdoc with Herb Simon. In an influential paper, Ericsson reviewed evidence that people become experts in their crafts not so much by innate talent as by continued practice over a period of 10 years. Ericsson and his colleagues found that deliberate practice in tasks as diverse as medicine, computer programming, physics, chess, sports, typing, juggling, dance, and violin playing actually led to changes in experts' bodies and brains that enabled them to excel at their specific vocation.

ROBOPARASITES IN THE WORKPLACE

What Do People Do All Day? This is the title of a charming 1968 children's book by Richard Scarry in which Blacksmith Fox and Grocer Cat productively pass their time in Busytown, where "some workers work indoors, and some work outdoors. Some work up in the sky and some work underground." In the real world, people aren't quite so efficient as they seem in Busytown. In fact, one study of 1,989 office workers in the United Kingdom suggests that the answer to the question "What do people do all day?" is: mostly fritter away productive time. The average worker in that study, conducted in 2016, spent 44 minutes (during working hours) checking social media, more than 60 minutes reading news websites, 40 minutes chatting with coworkers about nonwork-related activities, plus another 14 minutes text messaging. Only 2 hours, 53 minutes, were spent actually working on productive job-related tasks. Another study of American workers found that young workers are the worst offenders, wasting 70 minutes a day on mobile devices alone.

Technological time parasites are even more of a problem when it comes to preparing for your professional life. A study by James Roberts and his colleagues found that college students frittered away 143 minutes on text messaging and emails, and 81 minutes on social media, such as Facebook, Twitter, and Instagram. Another study, by Andrew Lepp and colleagues, found that more cell phone use translates into lower grades. Cell phones not only distract students when they should be studying but even interfere with learning in the classroom because students check their messages and emails, and surf the internet, during class time.

Besides cell phones, video games and television shows help us waste hours that could be spent learning or doing something productive. The American Academy of Pediatrics recommends that children and teenagers limit their total screen time to no more than 1 hour or 2 hours a day. If you are a parent, though, you learn quickly that extracting a young person from a video device is a lot like trying to take methamphetamines away from an addict.

If, as Andrew Carnegie argued, the world takes off its hat to those who can move up their productivity rates from 25% to 50%, you could be doing a lot better on your job if put your cell phone in airplane mode while you're at work. Better yet, clock your productive work hours and set aside hours when you absolutely do not answer emails or text messages, or look at anything online that isn't directly related to your job. If you are working on a salary, remind yourself that the contract is that you actually *work* from 9 to 5, and if you working independently, remind yourself that you could easily be twice as productive if you turn off those robodistractions. Outside of work hours, or if you are a student, you will go a lot further if you limit yourself to a strict budget of an hour a day of nonproductive screen time. A lot of actual work is done on computers, of course, and sometimes social networking is a part of your job, but it is important to turn off any notifications that will disrupt you if you are doing research or preparing a presentation or report on your computer. You probably do have mail, and one of the lunatics in Washington probably did just say something outrageous, but you don't want to know about it until the work day is over.

BEING A TEAM PLAYER

Dean Keith Simonton is a psychologist who has studied the determinants of "greatness"—the experiences and traits that distinguish those individuals who rise to prominence in their chosen fields. One of the key experiences leading to great success is exposure to other successful people. When Richard Roberts (who won a Nobel Prize in Physiology/Medicine) was asked to write an article on the 10 rules for winning a Nobel Prize, his Rule Number 5 was: "Work in the laboratory of a previous Nobel Prize winner"; Rule Number 6 was: "Even better than Rule 5, try to work in the laboratory of a future Nobel Prize winner." More than half of those who win a Nobel Prize had a Nobel Prize winner for a mentor. And beyond the one-to-one relationship with a particular mentor, your larger network of associations is also critically important. Roberts noted that nine different winners of the Nobel Prize had worked in the same medical research lab at Cambridge University. And an analysis of 19.9 million scientific papers and 2.1 million patents indicated that scientific papers done by teams have more impact.

Although particular individuals are often singled out for great accomplishments, there are very few stories of individuals who made it without a team. We opened the chapter by talking about Robert Cialdini, who was Doug's mentor in grad school and went on to become an internationally respected scholar, a consultant at Fortune 500 corporations, and an advisor to the British government. If you look on Google Scholar, you will see that almost every single one of Cialdini's widely cited research papers were published along with a team of graduate students and other colleagues who worked with him.

Some beginning researchers think they have to make their mark single-handedly—to stand out as an individual. Graduate students with this individualistic mindset avoid working in teams, keep their brilliant ideas to themselves, and feel it is beneath their dignity to work as an apprentice for their advisor. Some don't feel it is worth their while to be the second or third author on a scientific paper. As a consequence, students like this often end up as the leading author—but on an unpublished paper.

By instead working with a mentor who has already learned enough of the ropes to have had some successes, you learn what they know by doing what they are good at. By starting small, helping out on a team, you also get some experience learning what can go wrong and what works. By working on a larger team, you also gain lots of other benefits. In the scientific world, you are pooling your risks with others. Sometimes your ideas are wrong, but you get to find out sooner when you have a team working together to test them. Some of your teammates' ideas are right, and you get to share in the benefits when they are. You also get to profit from group intelligence. Researchers who have studied team performance find that teams are almost always more likely to solve a problem than are individuals. Teams often outperform the best team member. How can that be? Because problems as well as solutions are usually multifaceted, and different people know different things.

There's also the efficiency of division of labor. We talked earlier about Holland's circumplex of job types (realistic, investigative, artistic, social, enterprising, and conventional). Teams made up of artistic geniuses don't do nearly as well as teams in which there is someone to make sure everything is working properly and someone else making sure there are resources to keep the team going.

Team spirit works on a number of levels. Group members who take a collectivist approach do better than those who are "looking out for Number 1." One classic study had students play an economic game in which they could choose to either cooperate or compete. Cooperative choices by both players resulted in the best group outcomes, but a competitive choice could bring you more personal payoff—if your partner made the cooperative decision. If both players made that selfish choice, though, they both got the lowest payoff. Ironically, students who were majoring in economics walked away with substantially less money than other students. Why? They were operating on the classical economic assumption that the world works best when everyone makes a selfish choice. That assumption applies to market pricing when people are exchanging merchandise with strangers, but it does not apply when you are involved in an interdependent working relationship that lasts any amount of time. What happened in the economic game is that the other players started off cooperatively but then matched the selfish choices made by the economists rather than continue to let themselves be exploited.

In real teams, of course, the long-term consequence of slacking off and letting others do all the work is that you get a bad reputation and no one wants to work with you. If you are cooperative and scratch other people's backs, they will be happy to scratch yours in return.

DRIVING FOR DOMINANCE VERSUS WINNING PRESTIGE

Let's say you've picked a job that is compatible with your personality; you've shown up and worked hard; persisted in the face of the inevitable setbacks, failures, and distractions; and you've been a good team player. Now you have the opportunity to move into a position of authority over others. What kind of a leader should you be?

Robert Hogan grew up in a working-class family, then joined the U.S. Navy, where he supervised a gunnery crew and did a lot of reading. When he finished his military term, he took advantage of the GI Bill and enrolled as a student at the University of California. He came from a working-class background in which conflicts were more likely to be resolved by fistfights than legal suits, though, and on his first day of class, he got into a fistfight with a fraternity boy. But Hogan did exceptionally well in his studies and went on to graduate school, where he studied personality psychology. He published a couple of impressive papers and landed a prestigious job at Johns Hopkins University, where he became friends with John Holland. Inspired by Holland's work on job satisfaction and the occupational circumplex, Hogan began to study the influence of personality traits on job performance. After realizing how bad a job businesses were doing at choosing the right employees, he and his wife, Joyce, an industrial psychologist, started a business using psychological science to better match employees to their jobs and to help large companies pick leaders.

Doug met the Hogans when their business was just starting out with a small handful of employees. Three decades later, Hogan Assessment has expanded from a small business into to a corporation housed in a new $12 million, 35,000-square-foot office building, with tests in 47 languages used in 56 countries and in more than half of Fortune 500 businesses.

Doug got to watch Hogan as he went about his daily business as a department chair and a beginning CEO of a start-up business. As a department chair, Hogan would go around to all the faculty's offices every day and ask how they were doing. When the faculty described a project they were working on, Hogan would often encourage them to think of the project in broader terms and aim to publish the work in a higher prestige outlet. Hogan was in a good position to do this, having been an editor of the most prestigious journal in the field of personality and social psychology and having published influential papers in other prominent journals. In dealing with the employees of his business, he was likewise highly engaged and encouraging, and also especially generous. He regularly treated his employees to meals in high-end restaurants, for example, and went out of his way to express his appreciation for good performance.

Hogan's experiences in business and as a researcher investigating the science of leadership led him to develop some strong opinions about what makes a good leader and what makes a bad leader. In his book *Personality and the Fate of Organizations*, he argued that the characteristics of a good leader are the same in a Chinese factory as in an American internet corporation as on a farm in rural France. Besides being hardworking and resilient under stress, good leaders are socially sensitive; they pay close attention to employee relationships and are good at building teams. They also typically have a vision and are able to transform that vision into reality. At the top of the list of desirable traits, good leaders are trustworthy, they treat their employees fairly, and they follow through on their commitments.

The majority of people who are placed into positions of leadership, Hogan argued, are not good leaders. He observed that bad leadership is not only costly but can also be absolutely disastrous, pointing to examples, such as Foday Sankoh, who promised the people of Sierra Leone great social reforms and a share of the profits from the country's diamond mines but, instead, looted the country and encouraged his soldiers to plunder and murder. Another example of a bad leader is Philip J. Purcell, who was fired as the CEO of Morgan Stanley. He was described by former employees as ruthless, autocratic, remote, and intolerant of dissent. He demanded that his employees pledge loyalty to him over the organization. He did not listen when people talked and was fond of belittling investment bankers who worked for the firm. According to one of his former business associates, "Purcell was hated for his intense arrogance by almost everyone who worked for him."

Bad leaders often score high on a set of personality characteristics that University of British Columbia psychologist Del Paulhus called the "Dark Triad": narcissism, Machiavellianism, and psychopathy. Narcissists are "grandiose self-promoters who continually crave attention," which leads them to frequently take center stage. Machiavellians, on the other hand, differ from narcissists in their especially high scores on manipulativeness. They have a proclivity to get involved in white-collar crime, like those notorious stock swindlers who bilked investors out of hundreds of millions of dollars. Psychopaths are the most malevolent of the group, scoring high on all the dark characteristics: being simultaneously callous, impulsive, manipulative, and self-aggrandizing.

People who score high on Dark Triad measures share a tendency of being outgoing and socially skillful. They are quite willing to advertise their strengths and even claim strengths they don't have, which leads them to make good first impressions and to do well on job interviews. Their high level of self-confidence makes them appear, at first, like potentially good leaders. In the long run, though, they tend to make life miserable for those around them.

COERCION VERSUS EXPERTISE

Evolutionary psychologist Joe Henrich and his colleagues Francisco Gil-White and Joey Cheng distinguished between two paths to status in human groups: prestige versus dominance. Many other animals have dominance hierarchies in which status is conferred by physical intimidation—by bullying one's way to the top. In most other species, including our primate cousins, dominance is acquired mostly by being bigger and more aggressive than the other group members. Sometimes human leaders rise to the top because they have the characteristics that would have made for alpha status in chimpanzee groups: being large and aggressive (think of dictators like Idi Amin or Vladimir Putin). Dominant leaders inspire fear in others, and people go out of their way not to cross paths with them. But human beings also have a different path to status—prestige— which is freely conferred upon individuals who have skills that other group members want to imitate. And the most effective human leaders are not the toughest or most aggressive individuals around but the most knowledgeable (think of Samantha Power, discussed in Chapter 3, whose appointment to the post of United Nations ambassador traced to her authorship of a Pulitzer Prize–winning book on the Bosnian conflict). Prestigious leaders inspire admiration, and people go out of their way to get near a prestigious leader, hoping to learn what they know.

Charleen Case and Jon Maner found that dominance-oriented group leaders sometimes damage the very groups they are charged with leading. For example, dominant leaders went out of their way to reduce communication among their subordinates and to prevent subordinates from developing close alliances. Maner and Nicole Mead found that when dominant leaders' hold on leadership was shaky, they prioritized their own power over the group's good—withholding useful information from the rest of the group and excluding another group member who had potentially useful skills but who would have threatened the dominant leader's position in the group.

Why are dominant leaders sometimes appealing to followers? The inclination to choose tall, muscular, aggressive, and dominant leaders (who also happen to usually be males) may have made sense when our ancestors' small groups were at war with neighboring groups (which, according to Harvard anthropologist Richard Wrangham, may have been most of the time). In the modern professional world, though, leaders are never called on to go into combat. In general, dominant aggressive leaders may fit our ancestral stereotype of warlords, but they do not fit the prototype of effective leaders in a modern organization. The most effective leaders tend to build positive social relationships, promote teamwork, and put their group's welfare ahead of their own. So, if you strive for prestige, you are likely to be a more effective leader than if you compete for dominance.

Returning to our opening example of Bob Cialdini, he has been the prototypical prestige-focused leader. As a young man, he had the early athletic prowess that could have facilitated dominance behaviors (in addition to his skills with a baseball bat, he also was known to have a fistfight or two growing up in his working-class neighborhood). But when he matured, his position as the guru of social influence came without ever threatening anyone or knocking aside competitors. In 5 decades of working with him, Doug never even heard Cialdini raise his voice (except to give a lecture to a room full of 500 rapt audience members). Instead, Cialdini's success has been solely attributable to acquiring scientific and practical knowledge, and building successful teams, which, in turn, have made others want to be around him and share some of his wisdom.

Striving to be a prestigious leader like Cialdini brings another advantage over competing to win social position by dominance, bullying, and Machiavellian scheming. People will like you rather than secretly hope to see you fall.

BOTTOM LINES: SUGGESTIONS FOR GETTING AHEAD

In the ancestral world, there were not that many rungs on the social ladder, there were not 867 job categories, and no one was unemployed. We now encounter more freedom to follow our own unique talents, but we carry some baggage from the ancestral world into the modern workplace. Understanding what we're hauling around from the past yields a few potentially useful bits of wisdom for making a go of it in today's world:

- *Find out which jobs are in demand.* The existence of so many occupational categories and a constantly shifting economy make it possible to match your personality and talents to the right occupation.
- *Show up and work hard.* People who do more than just "get by" enjoy their work more and put in better job performances with less stress.

- *Embrace failure.* Our ancestors were inventive, but not all their inventions worked. Learn from your mistakes.
- *Avoid time-sucking roboparasites.* Ask yourself whether and when your digital devices are helping or hindering your ability to accomplish what you hope to accomplish.
- *Be a team player.* Others value you more when your efforts don't just help yourself.
- *Go for prestige rather than dominance.* Some people bully their way into positions of power, but that strategy generates resentment, and we prefer to follow leaders who use their expertise to further the group's joint efforts.

CHAPTER 6

FINDING TRUE LOVE

In June 1982, Sharon Clark was 40 years old and managing a flea market in a small town in Indiana. One day, a tall, dark, and charming man named Giovanni Vigliotto drove up in a long white Cadillac. He wanted to rent a booth to sell $50,000 worth of merchandise (that translates into about $135,000 in 2021 dollars, quite a bit for a flea market). As Sharon described Giovanni, "He was dressed like a rich cowboy, with two big gold bracelets and a chain with gold toothpicks." Although Sharon was not initially attracted to this flashy stranger, he grew on her when he presented her with eight dozen roses and told her the heartrending story of how his parents and sisters had been murdered by the Nazis, who had invaded Sicily. Giovanni was able to charm Sharon further by speaking in seven different languages and describing his extensive world travels. After they dated briefly, he suggested that they should pair up and open a chain of antique shops in Texas. Sharon found his passionate ambitions exciting, so she sold her house and loaded her belongings into a van they had rented.

They first drove to Florida to see Sharon's mom, and Giovanni, always exuberant, suggested that her mother join up with them in Texas. They loaded her mom's jewelry and belongings into the van, and then, because Giovanni had business in Dayton, Ohio, the couple drove there next. Giovanni, who often made mysterious phone calls, said he needed to go ahead by himself to Detroit, but he gave Sharon $80 in cash and a jeep they had purchased, with instructions about where to meet him. When she got to Detroit, though, she found a note from Giovanni instructing her to meet him in Ontario, Canada.

Giovanni never showed up in Ontario. Instead, it finally dawned on Sharon that she had been conned. Giovanni had taken off for parts unknown, hauling $44,000 worth of her belongings, $11,000 worth of her money, and her mother's jewelry.

Unable to get any help from the authorities, who don't have the resources to intervene in every nasty marital spat, Sharon thought she would try to track Giovanni down herself. Because he was obviously a man who traveled widely, though, her chances of actually finding him were virtually nonexistent. She did have one potentially useful clue: Giovanni had left behind a road atlas in which he had circled a number of different towns across the country—those with large flea markets. It angered her to think he might well be selling off her belongings at one of those locations, so she decided to try her hand at being an amateur detective and teamed up with another young flea marketer whom Giovanni had cheated out of money and belongings. They scraped together $1,000 and began driving to all the circled cities on the map.

After having visited flea markets in several states, they had only $3 left and were about to give up. But just then, Sharon spotted Giovanni in a flea market in Panama City, Florida.

Sharon convinced the local police to detain Vigliotto, and it turned out there was already a warrant for his arrest in Arizona. There, Vigliotto had married Patricia Ann Gardiner, and 3 weeks after that ceremony, he had disappeared with $43,000 of Patricia's money.

At his trial in Arizona, another woman, Joan Bacarella of Manalapan, New Jersey, showed up to tell the tale of how Vigliotto had stolen $40,000 of her money after proposing to marry her. And the prosecutor received dozens of calls from other women who reported similar stories. When authorities began investigating, they turned up 82 different marriages in nine different states, Canada, Britain, Italy, and Hong Kong. So, Vigliotto was honest about being a world traveler, at least, but it turns out that his name was probably not Giovanni Vigliotto. That was just one of 120 different aliases he had used over the years. The best guess was that his real name was Frederick Bertram Jiff, and that, rather than having been born in Sicily and victimized by invading German forces, he had been born in Brooklyn, New York. Although he never did come clean about his real name, he admitted to having married 105 different women, without ever having gone to the trouble of divorcing any of the first 104.

Although the story of Giovanni Vigliotto and his 105 wives is hardly typical, it does contain several lessons for what is, from an evolutionary perspective, and from the perspective of merely wanting to live a happy and fulfilling life, one of the most important decisions you will make. Finding the right mate can change your life for the better, but sometimes it's hard to distinguish Mr. or Ms. Right from Mr. or Ms. Vigliotto.

ANCESTRAL ROMANCE

If you could go back in time and tell one of your hunter–gatherer great-great-grandfathers the story of Giovanni Vigliotto and his 105 wives, he'd likely think you were feeding him a fairy tale. Not that he would have disapproved of Vigliotto's *polygyny*—one man with more than one wife—because virtually all human societies throughout history have permitted one man to marry multiple women. It's just that, before the agricultural revolution, the logistics involved in attracting 105 different mates would have been virtually impossible. Anthropologist Frank Marlowe studied mate choice among the Hadza of Tanzania (one of the world's few remaining hunter–gatherer groups), and he estimated that, over the course of their entire lifetime, a typical hunter–gatherer would have met no more than a few dozen possible mates, and would have been unlikely to have the personal and social resources to charm more than one or two of those potential mates into marrying him. And of course, his reputation would have preceded him in that smaller world.

Consider a few of the other hunter–gatherer groups that were still around during the early and middle 20th century. Among the nomadic Kalahari Bushmen studied by Elizabeth Marshall Thomas in the 1950s, women might have been willing to share a husband if he were an especially good hunter, but most men could not afford to support more than one wife. Sometimes two sisters would pair up with the same man, and Thomas had heard tell of one man who managed to attract four wives.

The Yąnomamö, who lived in the Orinoco Basin between Venezuela and Brazil, were more settled than the Bushmen and lived in more permanent villages. They grew a few crops to supplement the calories gained through hunting and gathering. Some successful Yąnomamö men were able to attract more than one wife, but the few available young women had multiple men competing for their attention, and most fellows were lucky to find even one wife. Indeed, there was the ever-present danger that a woman could be kidnapped by men from other villages. Napoleon Chagnon, who began studying the Yąnomamö during the 1960s, did encounter one man who had nevertheless managed to accumulate 11 wives.

A third group, the Kapauku Papuans, were still living in Stone Age conditions when the anthropologist Leopold Pospisil lived with them during the 1950s. They had no metal tools of any kind, but they had made the transition to rudimentary agriculture, raising crops as well as domesticated pigs. These practices permitted some hardworking Kapauku men to accumulate many more resources than others. Husbands would clear the forest before their wives took over the job of tending their gardens. Ambitious men would clear additional patches of ground and were able to attract additional wives, but they would have to pay for each wife. In this group, though, even the wealthiest men might manage to get 10 women to marry them, far shy of Vigliotto's 105.

The advent of advanced agriculture and division of labor led to the concentration of large populations into cities, making it possible for some individuals, such as the Egyptian pharaohs, to accumulate great wealth and power. Under these circumstances, extreme polygyny became much more common. Rajinder Singh, the wealthy maharajah of the Indian state of Patiala during the late 1800s, had 365 wives. But Singh was an outlier both in terms of immense wealth and number of spouses. Even for the wealthiest and most powerful ruling men throughout history, 105 wives would have been a notably high number.

From the small number of societies we just discussed, it should be apparent that romance among our ancestors was hardly limited to one rigid pattern. There were many variations between various hunter–gatherer, early horticultural, and advanced agricultural societies. For example, although virtually all human societies throughout history allowed polygyny, a tiny few even had occasional *polyandry*— one woman with more than one husband. In some societies, there were strict rules about which cousins you could and could not marry; in others, no such constraints.

Alongside all the cross-cultural variations, though, there are many commonalities in how, when, and why women and men in different human societies become attracted to one another. Women in virtually all societies throughout history have tended to marry at a much younger age than have men. This tendency is linked to the fact that men have universally placed a premium on youth, health, and other signs of fertility (such as smooth skin and relatively rounded hips and breasts). Women, on the other hand, have universally been more likely to marry men with abilities to, and success at, generating resources. Among hunter–gatherers, men who are good hunters and who are physically strong had an easier time finding a wife, but it took those men many years to develop those resource-generating skills.

Women in traditional societies placed high value on men who were good providers, as did their parents when they were choosing husbands for their daughters. Women in hunter–gatherer societies often had little say in who they married because their elders frequently made the choice for them while they were still children. However, even in those unliberated societies, women could exercise choice in several ways. For one thing, a woman could run off with, or have an affair with, a man to whom she was more attracted. For another, women often deserted men who mistreated them and, in these cases, either returned to their families or took up with another man who promised to treat them better. Indeed, when anthropologists have asked women in traditional societies about the traits they desire in a man, they place a high premium on a man's being kind, which often translates simply into not beating his wife frequently. Women in hunter–gatherer groups are frequently beaten by their husbands because the husbands suspect them of adultery, which, despite the threat of violence, is nevertheless quite common. The prevalence of adultery owes partly to the fact that polygynous older men often marry the desirable younger women, leaving a number of healthy and virile young men desperate to please any woman who is being mistreated or underappreciated by her current husband or by his more senior wives.

The Tiwi society of North Australia seems to violate some of the general rules we just described. For one thing, Tiwi men marry women much older than themselves, if they marry at all. In one group of Tiwi, 35 men were under the age of 30, and only one of these men was married—to a widow much older than him. Several men in their thirties were also married to much older widows. This particular group was not unusual; it was customary for Tiwi men to marry late and to marry much older women. Older Tiwi women, like women in other societies, have likely gone through menopause. This raises a puzzling question: Why don't young Tiwi men marry younger, more fertile, women?

The answer is that every single one of the fertile young women are already married to the few old men who have managed to live to a ripe old age. And those old codgers jealously guard their younger wives. In the same group, for example, in which nearly all the men under 30 were unmarried, one 65-year-old man had managed to marry 21 different women. One of his wives had not yet reached puberty, so she was still living with her parents.

If you were a Tiwi man in your 20s or 30s, the only way to acquire a young wife was to have one of the elders betroth his new-born daughter to you. Older men were the only ones with young fertile wives, and those older men made the decision about whom their daughters married. But the powerful old men were most likely to bestow their daughters not on young men but on other old men, who could reciprocate in kind. Hence, young men were often trying to seduce the young wives of the older patriarchs—and were sometimes successful. But if a young man were discovered doing that, the punishment was severe: being called out in a public contest by the old man who had been cuckolded and allowing the old man to throw spears at him until one of those missiles drew blood (ideally from an arm or a leg, so the young Romeo didn't suffer a potentially fatal blow to his chest or abdomen, but this required artful dodging by the young man). If the young fellow was too agile in avoiding the older fellow's spears, the other elders would step in and begin throwing spears at the perpetrator from multiple directions.

Eventually, though, the old codgers died and left behind several widows. Because all Tiwi women were required to be married, regardless of their age, and because the older men all had young wives and were uninterested in marrying the postmenopausal women, a young man could get a start in the game by marrying an old widow, whose male relatives would repay him the favor by promising him one of their own daughters in the future.

A Tiwi girl went to live with her husband after she reached puberty, but a Tiwi man did not actually begin having children until he was well into his 40s. Following the rule that all females had to be married, Tiwi girls were betrothed at birth; they thus had no say in whom they married. Older widows (who were also required to be married) could exercise some influence on whom their sons or brothers chose as their new husband.

Despite its unique features, Tiwi society demonstrated two universals, although in exaggerated form. First, men were strongly attracted to youthful women, and, second, high-status men were more successful at acquiring the desirable younger wives. Another similarity to other traditional societies is that Tiwi family members played a central role in determining whom a person married. Although it may seem obvious, it is also worth noting one other universal feature of mate choice in traditional societies: Our ancestors typically married others whom they had known for many years and whom their family members and friends also knew or knew of (if they came from a nearby village).

MATE SELECTION IN OTHER SPECIES

Before examining the features that human beings in modern societies value in a mate, it is worth going one more step back to consider the similarities and differences between all human beings and other mammalian species. In all mammals, dominance in males is virtually always valued by females choosing mates. This is linked to what biologists call *differential parental investment.* In any species in which one sex is obligated to make an initially higher investment in the offspring, that sex will be more selective about choosing mates. It's analogous to the difference between spending $150 for dinner at a gourmet restaurant versus $7 at a local hole-in-the wall. Before choosing an expensive restaurant, you're a lot more likely to read the reviews and compare your options. For female mammals, including *Homo sapiens*, there is no $7 dinner. Carrying offspring inside your body and nursing them afterward is always a big investment. Because males can get by with little investment—just a few minutes and some sperm—but females cannot, females are more likely to read the reviews and choose the males who have demonstrated that the genes carried in that sperm are higher quality than those of their competitors.

As a consequence of this sex difference in obligatory parental investment, males in most vertebrate species tend to be larger and more competitive and to have features like antlers or peacock's feathers. This is linked to what Charles Darwin called *sexual selection,* in which features that help one sex attract the other (such as colorful feathers) or that help the members of one sex dominate their competitors (such as antlers or large size) become more prevalent over generations. Parental investment and sexual selection go hand in hand because higher parental investment in one sex leads that sex to be choosy, which, in turn, leads to more sexually selected traits in the other sex.

Sexual selection on human males has had less extreme results than in species, such as elephant seals, in which the males are several times larger than the females and are inclined to a lifetime of bloody competition. Because human males also invest in the offspring, human females also compete among themselves, at least for desirable long-term mates. This is true of many species of birds, but it is not true for 95% of other mammalian species in which the male invests little besides his sperm.

Humans are also different from other mammals in the relative preference for youth in females. Richard Wrangham and his colleagues found that, even in our close relatives, chimpanzees, the males did not seem to prefer mating with the younger as opposed to older females. Why the difference? Probably because human females, but not chimpanzee females, go through menopause. Female chimpanzees, like females in most mammalian species, continue producing babies until they die, and older females are generally more successful in caring for their young. Human females, who live much longer lives than chimps, shift their energy resources from bearing new babies to helping their families and grandchildren. The combination of investment by grandparents and by fathers is part of a broader picture of extended family care by human families. Anthropologist Kim Hill argued that humans are, like white-fronted bee-eaters and a few other birds, "cooperative breeders."

Two important points need be made about comparing mating in humans and other species. First, if we want to understand mating in human beings, it is helpful to think about ourselves in the context of the wider animal kingdom. Second, besides commonalities, each species is unique, and humans, despite sharing certain characteristics with chimpanzees, peacocks, and elephant seals, are not exactly like any of those species. In particular, because of human family attachments, men and women are, at least in some important ways, very much alike in their mating strategies.

MODERN LOVE

A 2019 paper published in the *Proceedings of the National Academy of Sciences* highlighted a few of the radical ways that modern mate choice has changed—not only since hunter–gatherer times but even in the past few decades. As recently as 1940, the most common way for people to meet their spouses was through their family. At that time, it was also quite common to meet through friends or to meet in primary or secondary school. In other words, people in the

1940s, like our ancient ancestors, married others who were part of their intimate networks and thus known to themselves and to their family and friends.

Since that time, though, there has been a steady drop in the number of romantic partners who meet through family or who knew one another in elementary or high school. Each of those categories only accounts for a little more than 5% of marriages today. Meeting through friends became increasingly important in the 1970s and 1980s but began dropping in importance around the year 2000.

In 2020, the two most likely ways to procure a marriage partner were to meet a stranger online (about 40% of marriages) or to meet a stranger in a bar or restaurant (more than 25% of marriages). Meeting through friends accounted for another 20% of marriages. What this means is that the majority of people are now marrying other people they did not know while they were growing up and whom their family members do not know.

Cari Goetz and her colleagues reviewed a number of ways in which mating in the modern world is mismatched with the world in which our ancestors evolved. Instead of meeting a few dozen potential partners in your whole life, as did members of the Hadza tribe, many people now attend colleges, where, in a single day on campus, they may pass by hundreds or even thousands of healthy young single individuals. In an online dating app, a young person doesn't even need to leave their college dorm room to encounter hordes of possible mates. They can swipe through dozens of potential mates in just a few minutes.

Another contrast with traditional mate choice is that now there is the possibility of very short-term relationships—even one-night stands—in which no members of one's family or of one's partners' family become involved in the decision. Such relationships not only involve anonymity but also open up the door for deceptive self-presentation. Without information from a lifetime of acquaintance or the knowledge provided by family and friends, it can be difficult to determine whether the new partner is who, or what, they claim to be. One British woman got involved with a charming man she met online who claimed to be wealthy diamond merchant. He managed to get access to her checking account and left her with a $200,000 credit card bill. Turns out, he was a convicted fraudster who had done the same to other women as well—a digital age version of Giovanni Vigliotto.

The possibility of short-term relationships might also be facilitated by another important change from the ancestral world: the existence of reliable birth control. Birth control should, in theory, level the playing field for men and women because it can reduce or remove the cost of pregnancy, which would have historically been a cost selectively born by the female. Even though birth control has been around for half a century, however, women, in general, remain more reluctant to get involved in casual sexual relationships. In one series of studies conducted by Doug and his colleagues, college students were asked the minimum level of intelligence they'd require before dating someone, or before having sex with someone, or before marrying someone. Women and men both wanted a partner to be at least "average" in intelligence to qualify for a date and wanted someone substantially above average for a marriage partner. However, the sexes diverged when it came to what they were willing to settle for in a sexual partner. Females demanded more intelligence in a sexual partner than in a date, but college men actually were willing to have sex with someone who was substantially below average in intelligence.

Another change in the modern world is that women now get married at much later ages. Whereas hunter–gatherer women often moved in with their betrothed partners shortly after they reached puberty, at around 14 years of age, modern women marry, on average, at age 28—twice that age. This is particularly striking because puberty comes much earlier in the modern world—at a mere 10 years old for girls in Europe (because of greatly increased access to food, which leads to earlier maturity). Men in the modern world now marry at an average age of 30. In most hunter–gatherer societies, by contrast, guys typically first got married in their late teens (except a few like the Tiwi because the elderly patriarchs had rigged the system to monopolize all the young wives). Although boys still reach puberty a couple of years later than do girls, men in the modern world are, like women, typically marrying fully 15 years after they reach sexual maturity.

Have the multitudinous available options made possible by urban living and internet dating services changed what men and women look for in a partner? One change is that people can now marry those who share their specific interests, hobbies, and personality characteristics and not merely tribal membership. Indeed, in Honolulu, Hawaii, more than 40% of marriages are between people of different racial groups. Even so, we modern humans still use many of the same criteria as our ancestors in evaluating mates. Women and men both place high priority on cooperativeness and kindness in a spouse, as did our hunter–gatherer ancestors. At the same time, some of the ancestral sex differences have persisted. High-status men in the modern United States, like high-status men in traditional societies, have an easier time attracting wives. Physical attractiveness is a desirable characteristic in both sexes, although it is somewhat more important to men judging women.

If you simply survey people about what they'd like in an ideal mate, both sexes will check "yes" to good looks, great personality, intelligence, wealth, kindness, and so on. But in real life, unless you are a movie star who happened to also go to Harvard, you have to make some trade-offs. Doug's former student Norm Li used his background in economics to devise a way to find out which characteristics people prioritize: He gave them a "mating budget." In some cases, participants got the equivalent of a movie star's mating budget and could afford anything they wanted in a spouse. But other participants got a budget more like most of us have in real life: If you invest a lot in good looks, you have less remaining to spend on getting a partner with social status. Under those circumstances, men and women revealed very different priorities: Women regarded good looks as a luxury but some degree of social status as a necessity. The reverse was true for men: Social status was a luxury they could afford to live without, but men regarded some level of attractiveness as a necessity.

Other research that Doug conducted with Jill Sundie (another former economist turned psychologist) found that, although women did place much more emphasis on income when choosing a mate, the biggest boost was in going from poverty to a middle-class income. After that, further increases in a man's income did not buy much in the way of increased attractiveness. So, saying that women desire social status and wealth in a husband doesn't mean that men have to be millionaires. Good thing, or most of our male ancestors would not have reproduced.

Another commonality between traditional societies and modern societies is that relative youth continues to be valued in a woman more than in a man. Other research conducted by our team found that women in North America and Europe, like women in societies all around the world, tend to prefer marrying slightly older men, whereas men's preferences change over the lifespan. Young men are interested in women around their age, but as men age, they come to increasingly prefer brides younger than themselves. Other research has found that relatively younger women not only garner higher bride prices in Asian societies, they also earn higher salaries as prostitutes, and they are also more likely to be clicked on by American men on the dating service OKCupid. This raises the stakes of women's decision making: They have a shorter window in which to pick the correct mate.

Jonathan Gottschall and his colleagues did an intensive analysis of 658 folktales from 48 different societies, comparing the romantic themes in those traditional folktales with those in 240 works of Western literature. The analysis revealed that love stories in Western literature mirrored those in traditional societies in several ways: Male characters in societies all around the world are, compared with female characters, much more likely to be depicted as seeking a physically attractive partner, whereas women are more likely to be depicted as seeking a partner with wealth or social status. Much more important than status, however, women are universally portrayed as seeking a partner who is kind.

What counts as "physically attractive" is different in a woman as compared with a man. For men judging women, cues associated with youth, such as large eyes and relatively smaller facial features, are considered attractive. Women judging a man, on the other hand, view a large jaw and more mature facial features as more handsome than less mature features. Facial symmetry is considered attractive in both sexes.

Doug Jones and Kim Hill showed facial photographs of Americans, Brazilians, and Paraguayan Indians both to Venezuelan natives living in a traditional society and to other Americans, Brazilians, and Paraguayans. They found that people who were preferred in one culture were also ranked as attractive by the members of different cultures. That is, a member of the Aché tribe in Venezuela ranked Americans and Brazilians of European descent the same way Americans and Euro Brazilians did. This suggests that standards of attractiveness are not completely arbitrary and culturally relative, as social scientists once believed.

SEX, ATTRACTION, AND REPRODUCTION

From an evolutionary perspective, everything about an animal has been designed to maximize reproduction: what it eats, how it moves around, whether it is big or small, and whether it chooses to have many offspring or only a few. How an animal chooses its mates—whether based on how red their heads are (as in hummingbirds) or how large and aggressive they are (as in elephant seals)—seems obviously linked to reproductive success. But what about nonproductive sex? Bonobos (pygmy chimpanzees), which are closely related to us, engage in a lot of recreational sex of both the heterosexual and homosexual variety. Females frequently rub their genitals against one another to reduce tensions, and some females develop long-term bonds, which include a sexual element. Males also engage in mutual masturbatory behaviors with other males. In human beings, of course, there is recreational sex of both the heterosexual and homosexual variety, and there are also romantic attractions and long-term bonds between individuals of the same sex.

There are interesting theoretical discussions about whether nonreproductive sex is itself adaptive, in an evolutionary sense, or whether it is a by-product of other adaptive behaviors, perhaps in interaction with environmental factors. Studying Samoan *fa'afafine*—men who show a preference for other men as sexual partners—Paul Vasey and Doug VanderLaan investigated the possibility that homosexual men might compensate for the absence of offspring by investing more resources in nieces and nephews. The evidence on that theory is somewhat mixed, and there are other theories about the possible adaptiveness of homosexual preference. Other researchers have noted that homosexual men's preferences do not show a reversal of heterosexual men's. Michael Bailey and his team found that homosexual men are not attracted to status in the men they desire, as are heterosexual women; instead, they prefer physically attractive guys. In research conducted with Rich Keefe, Angela Bryan, Alicia Barr, and Stephanie Brown, Doug found that homosexual men showed the same preference for youth that heterosexual men show. These findings suggest that sexual preferences and sexual identity are largely independent of one another. Much of what we discuss next is based on research conducted on heterosexual men and women, but it also has implications for people whose preferences lean in other directions. Whatever the outcomes of the intellectual debates about the origins of sexual preference, it is clear that human sexual behaviors, like bonobo sexual behaviors, are not always associated with a drive to produce offspring. This fact reminds us once again of an idea we note in the Introduction: something evolutionary biologists call the *naturalistic fallacy,* the mistaken tendency to associate "natural" with "good." When it comes to going forth and multiplying, natural selection has generally acted to produce animals designed to reproduce their genes at all costs, but that does not imply that doing so is morally good in some way. Indeed, in an overcrowded world, following any evolved "natural" inclinations to produce as many offspring as possible is likely to increase overpopulation, with attendant problems for the environment and, according to political scientists, even an increase in international conflict. So, one could easily argue that nonproductive sex is the more ethical choice in the modern world.

SHOPPING ON THE MATING MARKET: A FEW CONSUMER TIPS

Psychologist Barry Schwartz talked about the "paradox of choice" in the modern world. Walk into a suburban supermarket for a few dinner ingredients, and you will have to select among 20 types of cooking oil, a dozen varieties of canned tomatoes, and a hundred varieties of wine to go with your meal. Freedom of choice sounds great, but it can become cognitively overwhelming and hamper our capacity to make a simple decision. It can be especially stressful if you are making a really important decision about an expensive purchase, such as choosing one automobile from the hundreds of makes, models, special options, and pricing points available, knowing you'll have to live with the choice for years.

If the paradox of choice can slow you down when you're trying to choose an automobile, it can be truly crippling when it comes to choosing a mate.

Our ancestors usually had little choice in mating partners. A girl's parents typically arranged her marriage, and a boy had to wait a few years longer and see if he could impress the parents of one of a few available girls in his village or the next one down the river. But in modern-day Toronto, Amsterdam, or Los Angeles, a girl or boy gets to make their choice from thousands upon thousands of possibilities. In Los Angeles in 2019, approximately 1 million people were in the prime mating window between the ages of 14 (by which the average Angeleno has reached puberty) and 29 (when the average Angeleno first gets married). And of course, modern Los Angeles residents are not limited to just the local pool of choices; some also consider potential mates from San Diego, San Francisco, Seattle, or even São Paulo or Shanghai. They don't even need to board a plane, train, or automobile to check out options in those faraway locations. Just sit at home in Santa Monica and expand the search area on a dating app.

In case you're thinking you'll never find your perfect soul mate unless you carefully search the world (or at least all of greater Los Angeles), it's worth considering a study by Usha Gupta and Pushpa Singh. Those researchers compared love and marital satisfaction in Indian couples whose marriages had been arranged to a similar sample of couples who had chosen their own spouse based on romantic love. Gupta and Singh found that people who had chosen their own spouse were initially more in love but that their love decreased over time. Love between couples in arranged marriages, on the other hand, increased over time so that after a few years together, couples in arranged marriages felt better about the relationship than did those who married for love. So, should you simply go back to letting your parents pick who you date, like in traditional societies? Well, maybe not. Not all the research comparing arranged marriages with love-based marriages has found the same results, and a whole lot depends on how you and your partner treat one another once you get into a relationship (the topic of the next chapter). Most of the readers of this book will likely be involved in choosing their own mate, of course, but perhaps there's a middle ground. Indeed, other research has suggested that European and American parents are likely to encourage their children to choose partners based not on superficial attractiveness but on traits that will make them reliable long-term partners. Not a bad thing to keep in mind when youthful passions are involved.

One bottom line suggestion is this: Shop locally. Pick your mate from the people you get to know personally or from people your relatives and friends know personally. Although few potential mates are professional scammers, many people misrepresent themselves in smaller, and yet significant, ways. Fully 71% of people who had used online dating apps thought it was "very common" for people on such apps to lie about themselves to appear more desirable. Is that his real height? Her real age? A photo that is 10 years old or 10 stone lighter than the current version? And if neither you nor your relatives and friends know the person, it's hard to predict what they will be like in a real relationship, whatever their ability to make a good first impression. Shopping locally not only eases the paradox of choice, but it also helps you avoid the Giovanni Vigliottos and their female equivalents.

DISPOSABLE OR LIFETIME WARRANTY?

Besides choosing a partner, there is another important, but simpler, choice to be made: Are you interested in a long-term or a short-term relationship? Most of us will respond by saying we want a long-term partner (after all, being interested in commitment makes both men and women more desirable), but it's worth being honest with yourself. Look at your past relationships. Did you really just date nine women in a row who just weren't "The One"? Despite claiming you want to settle down, do you find yourself quickly tiring of each new romantic partner and eager to flirt with the next available stranger you meet? Or, on the other side, despite telling yourself you want to be the next free-loving Mick Jagger or Madonna Ciccone, do you find ending a relationship to be a painful, miserable experience? Being honest about which game you are playing will save you and your potential partners a lot of grief.

Of course, there is evidence that people can and do change their strategies, depending on their age, their personal characteristics, and the pool of available mates.

Given that both men and women care for human offspring, some of our decisions about mates are the same regardless of our gender or sociosexual orientation. However, because we are nevertheless still mammals, with all the attendant consequences of differential parental investment and sexual selection, it makes some sense to arrange our initial advice about partner choice into "his" and "hers" columns.

FINDING MR. RIGHT

Eighty-four percent of women say that having a successful marriage is either very important or one of the most important things in their lives. And a majority of women who are currently dating or cohabiting with a man would prefer to be married. So, let's begin by looking at the research evidence on what kind of guy you should be seeking if you want a good husband.

First, it's important to consider personality, and the findings here apply both to men and women seeking marital partners. Evidence suggests that people who score high in what personality researchers call "neuroticism" are more likely to get divorced. You don't need to administer a personality test to a potential date to determine their level of neuroticism; you can simply observe their behavior over time or talk to people who know them well. People high in neuroticism have a hard time hiding their negative feelings; they react to stress with elevated levels of anxiety, depression, hostility, and moodiness. Conversely, people who are emotionally stable in the face of stress are less likely to get divorced.

Besides emotional instability, low levels of conscientiousness are associated with higher divorce rates. Conscientious people are orderly, efficient, hardworking, and thorough compared with lazy, careless, and sloppy. A study by University of Texas psychologist Sam Gosling and his colleagues found a simple one-item test for conscientiousness: Look at how neat the person's room is. People high in conscientiousness had neat, organized college dorm rooms, people low in conscientiousness were content to live in much messier digs. One possibility is that people who are neurotic and low in conscientiousness get divorces more because they are more likely to get angry or can't follow the rules, but it may simply be that their partners find it difficult to deal with moodiness and disorder over the long haul.

Conscientiousness may also be a signal for another desirable feature of a husband—the ability to generate resources. Conscientious guys show up for work regularly and strive to do a good job, so they are consequently more likely to do well in their careers. Another factor that predicts the ability to generate resources is intelligence: People with higher IQs tend to earn more. A closely related factor is education: People with more years of education tend to earn higher salaries, and education itself predicts lower divorce rates. Education, intelligence, and conscientiousness are interconnected: Getting more years of education is linked to being intelligent, but it is also a sign of conscientiousness because success in school is linked to being willing and able to finish assignments and to show up for classes.

It is also important to beware of fake investors. Research by Doug's former student Josh Ackerman (now a professor at the University of Michigan) found that men compared with women are more likely to say, "I love you" early in a relationship, perhaps as a way of signaling long-term commitment (which may or may not be sincere). Playboy types, of course, are the ones who may say it but not really mean it. Those fast guys also like to hear a woman say, "I love you" *before* the couple has started having sex because they take it as a sign that sexual intimacy is likely to increase in the near future. More committed type men (who adopt what psychologists call a "restricted" mating strategy) are similar to women in feeling especially good when their partner says, "I love you" *after* they have started having sex because they take it as a sign of commitment. But, for the same reason, playboy types who were delighted to hear expressions of love before sex would rather not hear those same amorous intimations after sex.

How can you tell whether a guy is the committed type or the playboy hit-and-run type? You could try looking at his style of dress and the car he drives. If he drives a sports car, dresses with impressive urban style, and has musclebound arms covered with tattoos, don't expect him to want to meet your parents. Giovanni Vigliotto's gold jewelry, big white Cadillac, and propensity to flash a lot of cash were not the signs of the kind of guy about to settle down. If, on the other hand, a fellow drives a reliable *Consumer Reports* best buy automobile and dresses in a less flashy fashion, he may be a bit less exciting, but he's more likely to stick around. Assuming you've followed our advice to pick someone familiar to either you or your friends and family, you may already know about or can inquire about his past love life. Otherwise, you can ask. If he says he's had 10 partners in the past year—but only because none of them really understood him—assume you won't either.

FINDING MR. RIGHT NOW

Although most women prefer a long-term relationship, it can often be difficult to predict whether a relationship will last, so consciously considering what you want in a short-term partner could be worthwhile. After all, if you have a one-night stand with an Olympic athlete, your children will at least have athletic genes. On the other hand, if you fall for an average guy who promises you the world and then suddenly disappears, you're still raising the kid on your own, and now your kid can't make the track team.

If you are in the market for short-term partners, there are some things to consider. For one, it's useful to know about what biologists call "true signals of genetic fitness." These are basically traits that can't be faked, borrowed, or stolen. If you're choosing between a good-looking muscular guy (features that generally indicate health and disease avoidance) and a guy who's driving a flashy Ferrari, the Ferrari could have been rented or bought on credit—but not so for the good looks. Beyond those superficialities, someone in the market for a short-term partner might want to consider how applicable a potential partner's traits would be to your child having a happy, successful life. So, if the muscular guy is homeless and friendless, but the guy with the Ferrari is a well-known tech billionaire, perhaps the guy with the Ferrari is a better choice. You may want to pick a guy whose strengths match your area of expertise. If you know a lot about science, you may be better able to tell a genius from a fraud; if you're a regular rock climber, you may be better able to tell an elite athlete from a klutz with nice calves; and if you're a trained artist, you may be better able to pick the next Picasso from a flash in the pan.

You may still want to avoid guys high in neuroticism and low in conscientiousness. Not only will these traits be frustrating if the guy does stick around, passing these traits on to your children may

169

cause your children to be less happy (after all, there is a genetic component to happiness). But of course, just as a guy can fake status with a knockoff Rolex, guys pursuing a relationship may present themselves as nicer than they really are, and your date might be unusually nice if he believes he's about to have sex.

FINDING MR. EVERY-OTHER-WEEKEND

Of course, many relationships are neither anonymous one-night stands nor ever-lasting fairy-tale romances. So, you may want to find a guy who maximizes the trade-off between good genes and potential investment.

Interestingly, the fellow you fancy may change, depending on your ovulation cycle. Kristina Durante and Doug's former students Vlad Griskevicius and Norm Li examined women's reactions to different types of guys when the women were at different phases of their ovulatory cycle. That research revealed that when women are ovulating (and most likely to become pregnant), they are not only more attracted to the bad boy sexy cad types over the "good dad"–type guys, but they are actually likely to believe that the bad boy types will make more devoted partners and better dads.

Some scientists have suggested that women might try to optimize their mating strategy by pursuing a *dual-mating strategy*; that is, marrying a good provider and then sneaking off to mate with a less committed guy with better genes. While this strategy is not unheard of, it is risky. Although everything in life requires trade-offs, people engaging in this dual strategy are risking losses in mate retention (the committed partner is going to become much less committed), kin care (you may end up with nobody to help raise the kid), and even future mate acquisition (fidelity is still considered a highly attractive quality in mates). And, while modern societies no longer allow men to throw spears at their wife's lovers, this strategy still leads to quite a few murders every year. A much safer strategy would be to "split the difference" ahead of time: Find a partner with acceptably good genes who is still willing to help provide for the offspring in one way or another. Indeed, research by University of California, Los Angeles, psychologist Martie Haselton suggests that women with attractive partners don't find other men attractive, even when they are ovulating.

FINDING A GOOD WIFE

When it comes to picking a long-term partner, a lot of what counts as good advice for the goose also counts as good advice for the gander. A man looking for a good long-term partner is well advised to look for personality traits of emotional stability and conscientiousness, which are associated with happier and longer lasting marriages for both sexes. When women are thinking about attracting a man as a long-term mate, they are more likely to show off their kindness and community orientation, likely reflecting an implicit understanding of the ancestral tendency for men to choose those traits as evidence of good mothering abilities. Indeed, rather than deluding yourself into thinking you can tame someone with a shrewish personality, it makes sense to look for a partner who is easy to get along with from the start. People usually show their best sides at first, so if a potential partner makes a bad first impression, assume it will only get worse when the stresses of a shared life, bills, and cranky kids start up. But at the same time, a woman looking for a committed relationship may want you to demonstrate signs of commitment and good genes, so don't be too quick to run away if she lets you pay for dinner or dares you to climb up a steep cliff.

As we suggested for women seeking a husband, a man seeking a wife may also want to find out about his intended partner's previous relationships as well as whether her parents are still married, because both previous divorces and parental divorce are correlated with increased risk of divorce. Now, busting out a scale of all possible risk factors for divorce on your first date may not lead to a second date, and you might get a drink thrown in your face somewhere between your question about family suicides and childhood cancer. But if your date tells you that, although she hasn't actually filed for divorce from her third husband, she's sure that you two are soul mates, perhaps take your time to get to know her before buying a ring or having unprotected sex.

In fact, just like women, if you're a man seeking a wife for the rest of your life, you might do well to delete the apps entirely and look for someone you know. And while it can be quite difficult to turn down a woman dressed like Shakira at the Super Bowl, women who dress more conservatively are more likely to be communicating an interest in domestic as opposed to night life. Kristina Durante, Norm Li, and Martie Haselton found that women wear more revealing outfits, depending on whether they are ovulating, so perhaps you don't need to eliminate every woman who shows her midriff. And women who go to church regularly are also signaling their long-term orientation, whereas those who hang out in bars are signaling the opposite. Similarity is important in long-term relationships, so if you aren't religious, consider secular alternatives, such as volunteering at a charity, which would allow you to meet people showing true signals of caring and also permit you to demonstrate your own willingness to commit and help others.

FINDING A GOOD TIME

If you are a man looking for a short-term partner, though, you might want to be on the lookout for someone who likes a good drinking party. When Christian Rudder, the mathematician who helped start OKCupid, analyzed the data from their millions of users, he reported that the single best question that predicted whether a woman would have sex on the first date was, "Do you like the taste of beer?" Psychologists Jason Weeden, Amber Dukes, and Rob Kurzban also found that marijuana use was associated with a person's having a more "unrestricted" mating orientation.

So, ganja-loving, cerveza-swigging women are statistically more likely to have a one-night stand. But maybe not with you. Women who are unselective about commitment tend to be highly selective when it comes to picking exactly which guy qualifies for their short-term love. So, for every hour you spend out at the bar, you might need to spend 2 hours at the gym or 4 hours practicing with your band.

DON'T PROJECT

Speaking of knowing how to read the signals, guys will also find it useful to be aware of the research on men's inclination to "project" their sexual desires onto attractive women. The phenomenon was demonstrated in an experiment by Jon Maner and a team of researchers from our labs at Arizona State University. If you were a subject in that experiment, you would have viewed a romantic movie clip that ends with the handsome male character passionately kissing the beautiful and sexually alluring ingenue. Afterward, you would have been shown a series of photographs and asked to play amateur psychoanalyst. You'd have been told that some of the people in the photos had been asked to think about strongly emotion-inducing situations but to try to suppress any expressions of those emotions on their faces. Your job would have been to search for subtle emotional cues in the targets' facial expressions.

Men who had seen the romantically arousing film were—compared with men in the control conditions—more likely to guess that the person in the photo was feeling strong sexual desire, but only if that person was a physically attractive woman. The photos had actually been chosen because their facial expressions were emotionally neutral, incidentally, so the men were seeing something that wasn't there. Other research suggests that men are generally predisposed to overperceive sexual interest in women, an inclination that can lead to trouble if a man is on a date with a woman whom he finds attractive but who might not be as enthusiastic about him. Hence, it's important for men in an amorous frame of mind to double-check to make sure that their partners are reciprocating those feelings.

MARKETING YOURSELF

When you are on the mating market, you're not just a shopper. You're also the merchandise. So, at the same time you are trying to find a good deal, you are also marketing yourself.

Marketing sometimes gets a bad rap, having acquired the connotation of dressing up undistinguished products in shiny wrappers decorated with attention-grabbing messages: "New!" "Improved!" "Best!" But our former students and friends who have taken positions in marketing departments point out that good marketing doesn't just move merchandise for the sake of moving merchandise. It also serves an important function by making potential consumers aware of products with features that might be particularly beneficial to them.

The mating market is certainly replete with examples of bad marketing: people overselling themselves, making claims on which they can't really deliver. One of our favorite stories about this phenomenon was told to us by a physician who worked in an emergency room. A man was brought in with a badly broken leg he sustained on the way home from a night out at the dance clubs. The emergency room staff needed to cut off his jeans, but when they did, they discovered something unexpected. He had taped a large sausage to the inside of his upper thigh. One wonders whether he'd considered the consequences if he'd actually managed to find a woman who was attracted enough to accompany such a "well-hung" guy back to his apartment. At least if he had chosen to purchase some cold-pressed olive oil and a can of crushed organic fire-roasted tomatoes on his last trip to the supermarket, he could offer her a satisfying dinner. At the same time, just as you don't want to oversell yourself, it's not a good idea to go around in unwashed hair and a ratty T-shirt, assuming your true soul mate would surely see through to your inner magnificence.

Owing to the powerful evolutionary influence of differential parental investment, mating for all mammals involves males showing off their wares and females being picky customers. As we noted, this is to some extent true for human beings as well, although in species like ours in which the male helps take care of the offspring, the males are also selective, and the females need to do some marketing as well, especially if they are looking for a long-term partner. A female interested in marketing herself to a potential short-term partner, on the other hand, has a somewhat easier time, as illustrated in a classic study by Russell Clark and Elaine Hatfield. If you were one of the college students who served as unknowing participants in that study, you would have been approached by another student of the opposite sex who introduced themselves by saying, "I have been noticing you around campus. I find you very attractive." After this, the other student would have sometimes followed with the question "Would you go out tonight?" The experimental assistants were not fashion models but moderately attractive college students, and about half of the men and the women responded with a "yes."

In another condition, the question was instead "Would you come over to my apartment?" In that case, the results diverged radically by sex. Now, more than 60% of the men said yes, but only 3% of the women responded affirmatively. In still another condition, the question was even more forward: "Would you go to bed with me?" In that case, not a single one of the women said yes, and several told the guy to get lost. But the number of men saying yes—to a total stranger inviting them to have sex—jumped to 70%. Men were more willing to agree to have sex with a stranger than to agree to go on a date. A few guys even asked whether they needed to wait till tonight.

The surprising aspect of those findings is not that women were turned off by a man making an explicit sexual offer but that so many of them responded favorably to the offer of a date. There's another study, by Michael Cunningham, that also contains a lesson for a man wanting to meet a woman he has seen around but does not yet know. Subjects in that field study were patrons at one of several large, middle-class suburban bars in the Chicago area. They were approached by a member of the opposite sex who sometimes opened with what Cunningham called a "cute-flippant" line, such as, "You remind me of someone I used to date." Only about a quarter of the women responded positively to such an approach. But when the guy took the very simple and innocuous approach of saying, "Hi!" more than 70% of the women responded favorably. What's nice about this finding is that it suggests that a man's best strategy for meeting a woman is the one least likely to result in making a fool of himself.

Oh, when men in those same bars were approached by a woman, it didn't really matter much what line she used. Every single man responded favorably to the woman who said, "Hi," but almost 90% responded positively to the cute-flippant line as well. So, it looks as though a woman's best strategy is simply to show up. Indeed, the bigger problem for a woman may be fending off unwanted mating overtures from men. Research by Josh Ackerman found that whereas men's friends are likely to help them meet women to date, women's friends are more often likely to help them fend off men who want to meet them.

Because both sexes invest heavily in long-term relationships and marriages, both women and men have to work to attract long-term partners. Research by our team at Arizona State University found that when women are in a romantic frame of mind, they tend to show off their kindness and agreeableness. This makes sense because kindness and agreeableness are desirable characteristics in a wife and a mother. Men also show off their altruistic side when they're in a romantic frame of mind—for the same reason. And both sexes show off their creative intelligence if they're thinking about long-term mates.

Men also show off in various ways when they're thinking about attracting short-term mates—spending more on conspicuous goods and saying more clever things, for example. Under the influence of short-term mating motivation, men put on their best peacock performances, saying, in effect, "Look at me!" But women thinking about short-term mates don't show off at all. Aware that men are all too easy when it comes to short-term relationships, women seem to be saying instead, "Show me what you've got."

Some other research indicates that both men and women are quite sensitive to sex ratios in deciding whether they'll play a short-term or a long-term relationship and what exactly they'll demand in a mate. When there is a surplus of available men around, it's a buyer's market for women, who consequently demand more commitment and are more selective about the men they're interested in. Men in such a market are more willing to settle down and be faithful, and they are more inclined to go into debt to show off their material wealth.

Our colleague Norm Li suggested a lesson from the work on sex ratios: You'll do better if you choose a place or occupation in which you are in the minority sex. New York City, Philadelphia, Detroit, and Kansas City all have more than 120 single women for every 100 single men, so a guy who moves to one of those cities will have an easier time finding a date. Most big cities have more women than men, but there are exceptions—such as St. Louis—where there are more men than women.

If you're a young woman choosing a college major, you'll meet more men in computer science, mechanical engineering, and finance classes than you will in psychology, education, or nursing classes (and you might simultaneously help those fields toward their goals of attracting a more sexually diverse student body). The converse is true for a man. If you've already chosen your occupation and like where you live, you can still choose leisure activities that optimize the chances of meeting someone of the sex you're most interested in. Dance classes tend to have a surplus of women, and rock gyms have a surplus of men, for example.

If you're a man looking for a long-term mate, it pays to advertise your intellectual and resource-generating skills, and to avoid looking poverty stricken. Dressing nicely is never a bad idea for a guy. If you're seeking a long-term mate, this does not mean dressing flashy; we're talking about J. Crew rather than Motley Crue or William Z in his pink jacket. There's a study by J. Marshall Townsend in which students judged the attractiveness of people who were either physically attractive or average looking, and who were dressed either in fine garb (a dress jacket and clean white dress shirt) or wearing a Burger King server's outfit. For men judging a woman, her attire did not matter as much as her physical attractiveness. A good-looking woman dressed in a Burger King outfit was more desirable as a mate than an average-looking woman dressed in upscale clothes. Bella Hadid doesn't have to dress to the nines to still be a 10. But the reverse was true for women judging men: The average looking guy in the upscale clothes was judged as more desirable than the handsome man in the Burger King outfit. Even a guy who looks like one of the Hemsworth brothers needs to dress for success to succeed in attracting women.

Besides simply dressing for success, obviously a man interested in attracting a woman for a long-term relationship should also play the long game and actually pursue skills that will generate resources over the long haul: stay in college, work hard, be responsible, don't throw money away partying, and invest in stocks and bonds rather than flashy cars.

Maybe the most important thing for a modern man to keep in mind harks back to the research done in traditional societies and the analysis of classic folktales in which women place a paramount value on "being nice." In fact, that is still the case. In one study, women judged the desirability of men who were described (by people who knew them) as displaying either dominant traits (assertive, bold, and talkative, for example) or nondominant characteristics (introverted, quiet, and timid). The men were further described as either highly agreeable (considerate, cooperative, and kind, for example) or disagreeable (rude, selfish, and unsympathetic). The guys described as dominant were rated as attractive, but only if they were also nice. Nice guys who were nondominant were preferred to guys who were dominant but disagreeable, and not by a small margin. Women really dislike disagreeable men. As the researchers who conducted this study pointed out, the findings refute the stereotype that "nice guys finish last."

It is true that socially dominant guys finish first, and this is especially true in competing for short-term mates, but if those dominant fellows are also unpleasant, that disqualifies them in most women's estimation. The winning combination seems to be a guy who expresses self-confidence and boldness but is also nice. It may not matter if you are as filthy rich and talented as Kanye West, but for the rest of us fellows down here in the real world, we are better off modeling our public persona after Tom Hanks.

TWO OTHER OPTIONS: SIMPLY BEING YOURSELF AND SIMPLY BEING ALONE

Two final notes: As evolutionary psychology has gained popularity, casual readers have sometimes assumed that the approach implies a moral imperative to pass on our genes, and this misconception has reinforced the idea that a man's value is related to his ability to have sex and a woman's value is related to her ability to get married. But remember the naturalistic fallacy. The fact is, there are almost 8 billion people in the world, and the population has doubled over the past 50 years. There is no shortage of people passing on their genes. Even if half the world decided to stop having kids, the population wouldn't go down in our time. With 8 billion people out there, there's also plenty of genetic diversity.

So, if you're having trouble finding someone you like, or you have some health problems that make childbearing difficult, or you just don't feel like having kids, that's totally fine. If you still feel a compulsion to help your genes into future generations, you can help raise your nieces, your nephews, or your cousins. Or you can satisfy a parental desire by adopting someone unrelated to you. You can spend your time volunteering or working on medical research. Or you can simply stay home and watch TV. In any case, there's no rational reason to feel bad about not having kids or to feel bad about being alone. Psychologist Bella DePaulo has gathered data showing that, although single people believe that marriage will make them much happier, the actual happiness benefit from marriage is relatively small and tends to diminish over time. And contrary to the assumption that single people are social isolates, single people actually have more friends and closer relationships with their families than do married people.

Even if you do want to date, you don't necessarily have to turn yourself into a robot, honing the "perfect partner algorithm." We are designed to be good at both selecting mates and acquiring mates, and we are adaptable. So don't call off your engagement with someone you've been with for years just because you met them at a bar instead of at church, or because their parents are divorced, or because they have too many muscles (in case you were seconds away from calling off your engagement because your fiancé has nice abs). If you're seriously involved with someone, you probably picked them for a reason. And they probably picked you for a reason as well.

BOTTOM LINES: SUGGESTIONS FOR FINDING ROMANCE

Our ancestors most frequently paired up with partners known to them and to their families. The modern world has a lot more options in the mate selection arena, including short-term relationships with strangers, birth control to limit the reproductive consequences of such encounters, and increasingly later ages of first marriage. In their criteria for desirable mates, men and women have some similarities and some important differences. Understanding how all that works can yield a few potentially useful rules of thumb:

- *Avoid the paradox of choice.* Shop locally.
- *Decide whether you are seeking a short-term or a long-term relationship.* And be sure your intended partners are adopting the same strategy.
- *Some characteristics signal partners who are easier to hang on to for the long-term.* These include emotional stability, conscientiousness, and a restricted mating orientation.
- *Some characteristics are more indicative of, or desirable in, short-term partners.* These include having an extraverted and exciting personality; being especially fit and attractive; and, apparently, liking the taste of beer.
- *Remember that you are both seller and buyer on the mating market.* It's best not to oversell yourself or claim characteristics you don't possess but also not to undersell yourself. Start by saying, "Hi" and being agreeable.

- *Look for a local market with a sex ratio that favors your preferences.* Choosing the right academic major or right city to live in can influence your mate choice options.
- *Enjoy being single.* This applies whether you are shopping around among long-term partners or are consciously off the mating market. Remember that single people have better relationships with friends and relatives.

CHAPTER 7

HOW DO FOOLS STAY IN LOVE?

Marya Skłodowska was regarded as "remarkably gifted" by her teachers, but growing up in Warsaw in the 1860s and 1870s, she knew she would not even be permitted to attend a Polish university. So, she worked as a governess to help send her older sister, Bronisława, to study medicine in Paris. The original plan had been for Bronisława to reciprocate by helping Marya migrate from Poland to France. That plan was disrupted when the handsome eldest son of the family for whom Marya worked fell in love with her, and they made plans to marry. But when his father heard about the plan, he flew into a rage, disgusted that his son would consider marrying a woman beneath his station—someone who was penniless and worked as a governess.

Marya grew pessimistic about her life situation, but Bronisława insisted that she come to Paris after all. So, Marya gave up her work as a governess and left for France, where she soon immersed herself in studying physics, chemistry, and math at the University of Paris. She also began signing her name in the French style: as Marie.

Although Marie was regarded as attractive by her male classmates at the University of Paris, she had, according to her biographer, "ruled love and marriage out of her life's program." This decision stemmed partly from her earlier romantic humiliation and partly from her increasing passion for science, which she saw as incompatible with romance and family life.

But then, her story took another turn, when she met a tall, dark-haired, young scientist named Pierre. Quite a few women were interested in this brilliant and handsome young man, but, like Marie, Pierre was reluctant to get into a relationship. He felt that love and marriage would be a distraction from the pursuit of science. After being drawn together by their mutual fascination with the physics of magnetic fields, though, their shared scientific interests quickly changed into a compelling romantic attraction toward one another.

Pierre proposed marriage, but Marie turned him down because she wanted to return to her beloved homeland. After she returned to Poland, though, Pierre did not give up his suit. He sent her passionate letters, urging her to return to Paris, where she could continue her scientific pursuits and be with him.

In the end, Pierre convinced her to come back to Paris to marry him. As she described her relationship with Pierre to a childhood friend back in Poland,

> fate has made us deeply attached to each other, and we cannot endure the idea of separating. . . . When you receive this letter, write to me: Madame Curie, School of Physics and Chemistry, 42 Rue Lhomond. This is my name from now on.

That name—Madame Curie—would become known worldwide because between romantic bike rides around the French countryside, during which they would stop to eat bread, cheese, and peaches, Marie and Pierre found time to devote to their deeply shared scientific passions. The couple conducted their research in a cold shed without the support of a university, with no team of lab assistants, and with no real research budget. Marie had to split her time between her scientific research and caring for their young daughter Irène, and their personal finances were quite strained. But all their hard work together began to pay off. They made intriguing discoveries about the magnetic properties of uranium, and they discovered a new element, which they named radium. The Curies also coined the term "radioactivity." In 1903, Marie and Pierre were awarded a joint Nobel Prize in Physics.

Winning a joint Nobel Prize made Marie and Pierre Curie a statistically unusual couple, but in some ways, their story is typical for our species. We consider how as we discuss long-term romantic relationships in the long view of evolutionary history.

STAYING TOGETHER FOR THE FIRST FEW MILLION YEARS

Monogamy—to some—is for the birds. And indeed, in 90% of avian species, the males and females pair up to care for their young. But according to a review by comparative anthropologist Kit Opie and his colleagues, bonds between mothers and fathers are found in only 3% of the 6,400 mammal species. Because female mammals carry the young inside their bodies and nurse them afterward, the inputs of fathers are not as necessary. Monkeys, our cousins in the primate order, stand out because more than 25% of them have bonded relationships between fathers and mothers. But among us apes, only humans and gibbons have monogamous bonds, whereas the other 18 species, such as our closest relatives—chimps and gorillas—are father-absent like the rest of the mammalian class.

Our common ancestor with chimps likely did not have parental bonds, yet the best available evidence suggests that those bonds are not some recent cultural invention. Our human ancestors were pairing up throughout history, and the practice may go as far back as *Australopithecus afarensis*. Regardless of when the practice entered the hominid line, all societies ever studied by anthropologists have bonds between fathers and mothers.

Those bonds are not always monogamous. The vast majority of human societies have allowed *polygynous marriages*—one man marrying multiple women—and a small fraction also allowed *poly-androus marriages*—one woman marrying multiple men. But even within polygamous societies, most couples are monogamous—composed of one man and one woman. Of 375 marriages among Aché foragers examined by anthropologists Kim Hill and Magdaleno Hurtado, 15 involved one man and two women (none of the Aché men in their sample had more than two wives). However, the Aché also had a high divorce rate, and people frequently changed partners. There was also polyandry, but it was rare. Only one of the Aché marriages also involved one woman and two men (who were brothers).

Among the warlike Yąnomamö studied by Napoleon Chagnon, intergroup fighting sometimes involved killing another group's women and abducting their wives—and, as we noted in Chapter 6, one man had 11 wives. However, many others had difficulty finding even a first wife, and young Yąnomamö men often kept their wives near them to prevent them running off or being abducted. !Kung San foragers on the Kalahari also allowed polygyny, but only a few men acquired enough resources to have two wives.

When it comes to forming parental relationships, why are humans more like birds than most other mammals? One thing we have in common with birds, but not with most mammals, is that our offspring are born quite helpless. Without inputs from the father, fewer of those helpless and needy offspring would survive. Besides providing resources, fathers also help protect the offspring from being attacked by other males who might want to mate with the mother or by other females in the group who have offspring that might compete with theirs. In other primates, both male suitors and female competitors are known to engage in infanticide and abuse of unprotected offspring.

Because hunter–gatherer women were commonly abducted, and because it was difficult for men to find available female partners, losing a wife could mean the end of a man's reproductive opportunities. For a woman, losing a husband meant losing the resources and protection he provided for her and their offspring. Husbands and wives greatly promoted one another's welfare in many other ways as well. Even among the Tiwi of Northern Australia, when young men first married a postmenopausal widow who was past the age when she could bear offspring, an elderly wife helped her young husband gain respect and status, and she increased his prospects of later acquiring a younger wife (for more details, see Chapter 6).

Despite the many benefits men and women derived from pairing together, marriages among hunter–gatherers were not always idyllically happy affairs. Hunter–gatherer men frequently beat their wives, and if they suspected their wives of being unfaithful, hunter–gatherer men sometimes injured them severely or even killed them. One Yąnomamö man described by Chagnon killed his wife's lover and then cut off both of her ears. Chagnon also described other women comparing the scars on their scalps that their husbands had inflicted with fighting sticks or axes. Men's violence, of course, increased the woman's desire to run off with someone else who promised to treat her better and to call on her brothers to protect her when her husband came stalking. Indeed, the Yąnomamö have a word— *shuwahimau*—to describe running away from a cruel husband to find a new one.

Despite all the spousal violence and frequent divorces, though, some couples remained together for life. Hill and Hurtado met one Aché couple who had been together for 47 years.

STAYING TOGETHER IN THE MODERN WORLD

In contemporary societies, the rates of both marriage and divorce have been decreasing over the past half century. In the United States in 1960, 90% of men older than 25 and 92% of women in the same age bracket had been married at least once. By 2014, the percentage of both men and women who had never married had more than doubled: Up to 23% of adult men were now single as were 17% of women. Two factors contributing to this trend were: (a) people were waiting longer to get married, and (b) a larger percentage of people were living together without bothering to officially tie the knot. But that's not the whole story: Only about a quarter of singles are in cohabiting couples, and the bulk of unmarried adults are living alone.

Along with decreasing marriage rates over those years, though, divorce rates have also declined. This is partly because people are getting married later, and later marriages are more likely to last.

Staying together for modern couples, as for our ancestors, has its trade-offs and its obstacles. Jealousy and spousal violence did not end with the advent of agriculture; Roman and Greek men also frequently beat their wives and occasionally killed them if they suspected infidelity. In the postclassical world, partner violence is still common, although it is lower in developed countries in modern Europe and North America than in the Middle East and in poorer countries around the world. Of women in the United States and Canada, 1% to 3% said they had been physically assaulted by an intimate partner during the past year, whereas the comparable figure in Nicaragua and Peru was closer to 30%. A number of studies have found that women are as likely to physically assault their boyfriends or husbands as to be assaulted by them, but women are, compared with men, less likely to severely injure or kill their partners when they assault them. Indeed, 84% of spousal homicide victims are women, and when a woman is murdered, the first likely suspect is her boyfriend or husband.

Despite the potential for arguments and occasional physical conflicts, most people get along reasonably well with their long-term partners. One study of 2,084 American adults found that 64% said they are "very happy" with their relationship, whereas only 19% said they are unhappy (and some of those were only slightly unhappy). Men are a little more happy in relationships—but only slightly: For example, 75% of men and 71% of women said they have a warm and comfortable relationship. People in couples are also less depressed and less likely to abuse drugs and alcohol, although the causal arrow is not always clear (in that being moody or abusing drugs and alcohol can also be a causal factor in breaking up a relationship, and is not just a downstream result of separating).

Just as being in a couple had numerous benefits for our ancestors, it continues to have benefits in the modern world. Couples help one another at every stage of the pyramid of life: Being in a stable long-term relationship helps you survive: Married people live longer and have fewer health problems. And a romantic partnership can help fulfill your affiliation motives: Not only are spouses often one another's best friends, but a spouse can greatly expand one's social network, as Pierre and Marie Curie did for one another. Being married can also enhance your social status and make you wealthier (you share the costs of housing, so can live in more upscale digs, and you save some of your wealth because single people pay more for many things, including health care and auto insurance). You also get to distribute the labor, so that each of you does fewer tasks than you'd have to do on your own (allowing you to work on your next Nobel Prize). The time you save by not searching for new mates is time you can spend improving your performance on the job.

And in the realm of kin care, there is pretty solid evidence that having an intact family is advantageous for your kids' mental health and their performance in school. Developmental psychologist David Geary reviewed evidence to suggest that the presence of a father dramatically increases a child's likelihood of survival in traditional environments (like those in which our ancestors lived). Even in modern Westernized societies, having a father as part of the team provides benefits, such as better housing and diet, and even reduces the likelihood of being victimized by bullies.

Just as some couples were not monogamous in the ancestral world, so some couples are nonmonogamous in modern Western society. Artists Frida Kahlo and Diego Rivera had a famously polyamorous relationship, although it was not without its trials. In line with classic sex differences, Diego had more of a roving eye but was quite jealous of Frida's affairs. Frida also found it emotionally trying to handle Diego's affairs, and the whole free love thing came to an end when she caught Diego in bed with her sister. In North America today, one survey estimated that one in 25 couples are consensually nonmonogamous. Nonmonogamy is, of course, not always consensual. Another large survey found that 28% of men and 18% of women in officially monogamous relationships had engaged in an affair. If discovered, nonconsensual infidelity can have disastrous effects. As was true for our ancestors, it is still a major factor in divorce and occasionally a contributor to violence and even homicide. Also mirroring ancestral proclivities, men are much more likely to physically assault or murder unfaithful wives than women are to commit violence against unfaithful husbands.

Whether you are inclined toward exclusive monogamy or some other variation along the Frida–Diego continuum, it is good for your health and happiness, and for that of your children, to have your relationships be as mutually supportive and conflict free as possible. But there are a couple of sets of obstacles: ancestral selfish impulses that still get us into trouble in the modern world and roboparasites that prey on those impulses. Fortunately, though, we also have an evolved attachment system that can help bind the ties a little more firmly.

SELFISH NARCISSISM IN RELATIONSHIPS: SERVE YOURSELF?

"You've got to do what's right for you" was a popular sentiment during the self-indulgent 1970s and 1980s, and it is the central tenet of the Wall Street economic/libertarian view of moral decision making. The assumption is that relationships will work like open marketplaces in the sense that the greatest good will come from letting everyone seek their own self-interest, Adam Smith style. Joseph Kennedy, a poster child for American capitalism, certainly followed his own self-interest in the marital fidelity department, having numerous affairs with beautiful actresses after he made his career move from Wall Street investor to Hollywood mogul.

The self-interest doctrine isn't the credo only for well-heeled capitalists luxuriating in their mansions on Cape Cod. It also resonates with the artistic alternative lifestyle set and is a received doctrine among the intellectual descendants of the encounter group movement who worship at the altar of self-actualization. In a recent book called *The All-or-Nothing Marriage*, Northwestern University's Eli Finkel argued that marriages over the past 2 centuries have progressed up Maslow's classic hierarchy—from a focus on survival and safety needs during our great grandparents' time (when couples worked hard to run the farm together) to a focus on social needs during the economically comfortable second half of the 20th century (when the ideal became being best friends and soul mates). Recently, we've moved on again, with marriages now being seen as crucibles for self-actualization. Postmodern 21st century marriages are now, Finkel argued, flexible arrangements in which each individual can realize their personal aspirations—even if that sometimes means finding sexual fulfillment outside the marriage.

If each individual used their personal desires as the criterion, we'd follow the powerful dictates of those selfish genes our ancestors passed on to us. Here's what that might look like:

- Each man would attempt to have as many sexual partners as he could, deserting his (first) wife and the children as soon as he found a younger or more fertile partner. All men would act like Diego Rivera, jumping into bed with any willing woman and then lying about it, and trying to keep a straight face.

- Every woman would use whatever means necessary to get a commitment from a man who was willing to pledge his time and resources to helping raise her offspring. Then she'd sneak around with a handsome symmetrical playboy who had "good genes" and cover up all the evidence. Her best-case scenario would be a committed sap of a husband at home raising children that are not his own, like a hardworking robin nurturing the offspring of some lazy fly-by-night cuckoo.

Turns out that the desire to run around on one's partner isn't a very special calling. Indeed, three out of four women, and fully 98 out of 100 men in relationships, have had a sexual fantasy about an outside partner in the past 2 months. So, you probably are not pure of motive. But would you be happy in a world in which everyone simply let their self-satisfying fantasies run their lives? If you are a man, would you want a woman who snuck around searching for a guy with better genes whenever you weren't looking? If you are a woman, would you be happy with a man who was trying to live out the life of Rajinder Singh, the maharajah with 350 wives we introduced in Chapter 6? Turns out, even if you are not prone to empathy or guilt and would feel comfortable taking a completely selfish perspective, doing what's right for you may feel good in the short run, but, in the long run, it may not be the best mantra for a happy life in the modern world.

DON'T TRUST YOUR OWN JUDGMENT

Even though we just noted that the overwhelming majority of men and women have fantasies about what biologists call "extra-pair copulations," fully 90% of those very same people simultaneously believe that extramarital sex is wrong. And 70% believe infidelity is not just wrong but unforgivable! How is it that the vast majority of us believe it is unforgivable to do the very thing that we frequently fantasize about? The answer lies in that ever-popular tendency to hold one set of standards for other people and a different set for ourselves.

Social psychologists have demonstrated in numerous experiments that people roundly condemn selfish decisions by others, even as they justify the exact same choices if they themselves made them. How does that work? Our brilliant brains do a splendid job of rationalizing our own choices. Ask 10 people who are having an extramarital affair why they are doing it, and there's a good chance you will hear a lot of reasonable-sounding explanations, such as, "My partner is deficient in meeting my needs." Ask why other people have affairs, though, and it is likely you will hear a lot of nasty words of condemnation. Turns out, our brains are as good at finding fault in others as they are at finding virtues in ourselves: "I am an unfortunate victim who doesn't get enough love and attention from my spouse, but those other people who have affairs are morally reprehensible and selfish." Of course, we don't usually put those two thoughts in the same sentence because our double-talking, double-think mechanisms realize that this does not have the ring of a good press release.

There's a popular—and dangerous—myth about marital infidelity: that having an affair is not the cause of relationship problems but the consequence. Indeed, even marital therapists perpetuate this myth, as noted by relationships guru John Gottman: "Most marital therapists who write about extramarital affairs find that these trysts are usually not about sex but about seeking friendship, support, understanding, respect, attention, caring, and concern—the kind of things that marriage is supposed to offer." In this statement, Gottman seemed to be relying on marital therapists' judgments of what they hear from their clients. No doubt marital therapists hear a lot of clients telling them that they only began having an affair *after* their partner failed in the task of providing sufficient friendship, understanding, respect, and attention. But such an explanation seems equally likely to be a rationalization concocted after the fact by the cheater's self-serving explanation modules. Indeed, when Denise Previti and Paul Amato analyzed data from a 17-year study of 1,475 married people, they found that extramarital sex was a *predictor* of later divorce, independent of how happy the couple had been before the infidelity.

A couple of different processes are at work here. First, our brains are designed to become more self-centered under the influence of sexual arousal. Dan Ariely and George Loewenstein conducted a rather edgy experiment in which they asked young men to make judgments about whether it was alright to use force to get a woman to have sex with you. Most of them said that it was entirely unacceptable under any circumstances. But other men were asked that same question after they had gotten themselves sexually aroused (via a classic "manual manipulation" manipulation). Men who were sexually aroused were now much more favorable about using physical coercion as a means to the end of self-satisfaction.

Besides the reason-warping influence of sexual arousal, a second biasing process is the powerful tendency to evaluate information in ways that make us look good. Charles Lord and his colleagues conducted a classic study with Stanford University undergraduates who were asked to evaluate a set of scientific findings on the benefits of capital punishment. Because the findings were carefully balanced to show weaknesses as well as strengths on both sides of the issue, people who started with extreme views should have moved toward the moderate center. But the results did not turn out that way at all. Instead, those who initially *favored* capital punishment came away *more convinced than ever* that they were right. Those on the other side—who initially *opposed* capital punishment—looked at the exact same body of mixed evidence and came away more convinced that *they* were correct. How was it possible that the same evidence could support opposite conclusions? Turns out, students selectively remembered the weaknesses of evidence on the other side of the argument and the strengths of evidence that favored their side. With regard to marital relationships, these self-serving biases don't come into play only to justify egregious self-indulgences, such as marital infidelity. They also regularly show up in everyday explanations about who contributes more to the household chores. Michael Ross and Fiore Sicoly asked married couples to estimate how much responsibility they bore for mundane tasks, such as washing the laundry, keeping the house clean, and taking out the trash. When the researchers summed up how much the husband attributed to himself and how much the wife attributed to herself, they found something amazing: For most of the couples, the totals came in at more than 100%. How could that be? When asked to remember their contributions versus those of their spouse, people were able to remember 11 of their own for every eight of their spouses, so the husband thought he was doing more than 50% and so did the wife (with more than 100% of the household chores being knocked off regularly, this raises the question of why the average couple's house isn't always 100% neat and clean).

Those little self-serving biases can add up over time. David Watson and John Humrichouse asked newlyweds to rate their own personality and their partner's early in the marriage and then again 2 years later. At the beginning, people in the honeymoon frame of mind viewed their partners more positively than they viewed themselves. Over time, they saw themselves as becoming more agreeable and less emotionally negative. Ratings of spouses, unfortunately, went in the opposite direction. Although most of us think we're becoming better and better all the time, our spouses think we're getting worse.

So, you're probably going to have a happier relationship if you can resist the inclination to define a good relationship in terms of your own self-fulfillment as evaluated by your own inner legal defense team.

You may be wondering: But what if I really do contribute more to the relationship? There is a 50% chance that you do (although the research leads us to guess that 95% of readers *think* they are in that overcrowded 50% even though your partner probably thinks otherwise). We'd still recommend that you try doing more nice things for your partner and griping less about how little they do. You may just find that your partner becomes happier, gets more enjoyment out of spending time with you, and might even welcome the opportunity to cook a nice dinner together and clean up afterward while listening to some of your favorite tunes from the early courtship phase. Research by Amie Gordon and her colleagues revealed that kindness and gratitude in romantic relationships fuel a self-perpetuating cycle: One partner's acts of kindness and gratitude lead the other partner to be more committed, kind, and grateful in turn.

Given that most of us are so incredibly biased to overestimate what our relationships cost us and how much those relationships benefit our partners, it helps to regularly remind yourself what your partner contributes and what you receive as benefits from the relationship. There are all those rewards from simply being in a relationship, even if your partner isn't as self-sacrificing as St. Theresa the Little Flower (or even as you). As we noted earlier in this chapter, a long-term partner can help you out at every step of life's pyramid—with basic needs (food, shelter); self-protection (another pair of eyes and ears if you're walking around at night); affiliation (your partner's friends often become your friends); status (your partner's connections and wealth can also increase yours, as happened when Franklin and Eleanor Roosevelt pooled their vast reserves of social capital); and, of course, kin care (your partner shares your powerful interest in any children you have together). Before complaining that taking out the garbage is slowing you down in your quest for a Nobel Prize, it might be worthwhile running down a checklist of all those steps in the pyramid where your partner gives you a boost.

Besides the benefits of keeping your partner happier, there are other good reasons for you to remember to count the benefits rather than just the costs in your relationships. Another study by Denise Previti and Paul Amato showed that people who focus on the rewards in their marriages are less likely to divorce later, even after correcting for how happy they were at the start.

So, it turns out that you can best serve your long-term self-interests not by following your first selfish impulses but, instead, doing what you can to serve your partner's interests.

THE ATTACHMENT SYSTEM: THE BETTER SIDE OF HUMAN NATURE

Bad news inherently gets more attention, and that makes sense. After all, our ancestors needed to be alert to potential threats and not sleep through it when the bad guys came storming over the hill to burn the village and kidnap all the women. News about sexual infidelity and violence is particularly attention grabbing. But most of the time, our ancestors were pretty congenial to one another, or we wouldn't be here to talk about it. Indeed, we are wired up with some pretty powerful bonding systems, originally designed to keep our ancestral great-great grandfathers and grandmothers teamed up. Remember, children with two parents were more likely to survive in the ancestral environment.

Although the young in 95% of other mammalian species grow up without much contribution from their fathers, humans are in the minority of species in which the father regularly hangs around. It appears that, somewhere in the past million years of evolution, our brains co-opted the same bonding system that attaches a mammalian mother to her offspring and repurposed the system for adult loving relationships. Unlike adult chimpanzees, who mate promiscuously and lose little love on their mating partners, human adults' feelings toward one another are similar to the feelings between a mother and a child: powerful emotions linked to a built-in oxytocin system. That system seems to act both to reduce stress when our partners are around and to inspire us to nurture them when they are feeling stressed.

In other mammals, the oxytocin system is triggered by close physical contact and stroking, as happens between mothers and infants. And studies of adults suggest the same is true for adult human beings. Physical contact, such as hugging or rubbing your partner's back, triggers a release of stress-buffering oxytocin, which, in turn, triggers nurturant and supportive behaviors on the partner's part in a literal positive feedback loop.

Along with Kathleen Light and several other colleagues, Karen Grewen at the University of North Carolina conducted a number of studies examining the links between physical contact, oxytocin, and stress. In one study, they brought 38 couples into the laboratory and instructed them to spend 10 minutes sitting together on a love seat. Their job description for that 10 minutes was to hold hands and discuss a time that had brought them together as a couple, and then to watch a romantic video clip. At the end of the session, they stood up and gave one another a nice long hug. The women whose partners were more supportive had higher oxytocin levels as well as lower blood pressure and lower levels of blood stress hormones. In other research, the same team found that partners who hugged one another frequently outside the lab had lower blood pressure and lower resting heart rates. They also found that higher oxytocin is linked to more positive reactions to a partner's expressions of gratitude and to a tendency to view one's partner through rose-colored glasses, interpreting their expressions in more positive, and less defensive, ways.

So, it seems like hugging your partner is part of a virtuous cycle: If you embrace your partner more, it reduces their stress hormones and triggers the release of oxytocin, which leads them to feel more

positively toward you and inclines them to make positive interpreta-
tions of the things you say, which, in turn, leads to you to want to hug
your partner more.

It doesn't take long to hug your partner, a few seconds' investment for all those physiological payoffs. Of course, given the benefits of touching, you should make time for longer periods of contact,
when you can. Christopher Moyer and his colleagues conducted
a meta-analysis of 37 studies examining the therapeutic effects of
massage. They found that a single massage session reduced anxiety,
blood pressure, and heart rate. Over the long haul, massage therapy
reduced depression and anxiety as effectively as psychotherapy. So,
when your partner is feeling down, finding the time to give them a
nice back rub will have a deeply calming effect—for both of you.
Because other research suggests that negative mood is damaging to
relationship stability, a massage is something nice you can do for
your partner that will have long-term payoffs for both of you.

ROBOPARASITES OF LOVE: CLICK HERE
AND HAVE YOUR WALLET READY!

For most of human history, our ancestors lived in small villages
where everyone knew everyone else. With the advent of agriculture,
some of our progenitors began moving into larger villages, but they
still had few encounters with strangers. In the past thousand years,
cities grew larger, but most people still lived in rural areas. The industrial revolution changed all that, and more and more people began
migrating into urban areas. Even as late as 1867, though, when Marie
Curie was born, the majority of the world's population still lived in
small villages or on farms.

But increasingly, like Marie Curie and her older sister, people
began moving to cities like Paris, London, New York, and Mexico
City, and women as well as men began entering the workforce in

those large cities. Today, more than half of the world's population lives in large cities: Eighty-three percent of Americans and 84% of people in the United Kingdom live in urban areas. In more than 90% of homes in the United States today, one of the spouses goes off to work every day, and in about half, both go away from the home. That opens up a lot of opportunities for extramarital affairs that didn't exist in the good old days. Indeed, rates of marital infidelity are highest in large cities, with Los Angeles and New York topping the list in North America.

About one in five American men will have an affair. The comparable statistic used to be about one in 10 for women, but since their entry into the workforce in greater numbers, women now have rates of infidelity approaching those of men. Even people who don't actually consummate an affair are likely to encounter plenty of temptingly attractive strangers and coworkers as they go about their daily lives in the modern world. All those salient possibilities may well increase your subjective estimate about how easy it would be to replace your spouse if they start to get on your nerves. Although married people still vow to stick it out till death do them part, as did Marie Curie in her relationship with Pierre, about 40% to 50% of marriages today will end long before the Grim Reaper comes for one of the partners. The number of divorces has been decreasing in recent years, but, alas, part of the explanation for that is that people are less likely to get married in the first place, so when unofficially cohabiting couples split (which they do at an even higher rate than married couples), it does not get recorded in the archival data base. And all those newly separated people constitute yet another tributary of temptation for people who are still married.

If industrialization made it easier to follow one's own wandering eye, everything changed again with the information revolution. Now with social media, you can reconnect with your old lovers and kindle a new flirtation over email, even with people who don't live or work nearby. With the onset of dating apps, you can also find new alternatives without all the muss and fuss of finding someone in real life. You can even filter your search for people who are willing to have a fling without strings attached. As we mentioned in Chapter 1, the Ashley Madison website showed a beautiful woman with her finger over her luscious red lips (in a "shh" gesture of secrecy) and a logo bluntly stating, "Life is short: Have an affair." The webpage claimed that "millions of people just like you are looking for a discreet connection." Other popular dating websites, such as OKCupid, also include people who describe themselves as interested in "polyamorous" involvements, and Tinder, the "hookup app" allows you to meet someone for a fling with minimal obstacles, such as actually getting to know one another before having sex.

Apps like Facebook aren't explicitly designed to facilitate affairs, but they do make it easier than ever to get in touch with your old flames and perhaps rekindle those romantic feelings if you're feeling underappreciated by your current partner.

Not only are all those apps making it infinitely easier to have an affair, turns out there are apps that help you cover your tracks by camouflaging your cheating photos as a mathematical calculator app or allowing you to instantly erase all your naughty messages by shaking your phone (in case your spouse pulls into the driveway while you are in a digitally compromised position).

Because there's a lot of sneaking around on the one side, there is also an emerging market in apps and devices to snoop on your partner, including spyware and even car-tracking devices.

To add fuel to the fires of temptation, easy access to free erotic videos can make it seem like there are hundreds of highly attractive and passionate potential alternatives to your tired and headache-prone partner.

Of course, your feelings about your mate will ebb and flow naturally as a function of whether they are under a lot of stress at work, whether they are keeping up their share of the household chores, or whether the kids are being especially cranky. Given all the temptations, what's a modern married person to do?

We have talked about the power of stimulus control in several chapters so far. It's tough to stay fit in a world full of Ben & Jerry's Chocolate Fudge Brownie ice cream and kettle-cooked, mesquite barbecue–flavored potato chips, and it's tough to stay on task and get ahead in a world full of addictive computer games and iPhone apps. So, one useful trick is preemptive stimulus control. Just as you should stay out of the supermarket aisle where they are selling potato chips and chocolate ice cream if you want to stay fit, and erase those addictive games if you want to actually get ahead at work, you should stay away from apps that keep you in touch with old lovers, Ashley Madisons, and easy imaginary sex with porn stars who look like fashion models.

Active and public commitments can help us in our quest for self-control. John Lydon and his colleagues found that people who are committed to their current relationships are likely to downgrade the attractiveness of alternative partners. And research by Jeff Simpson and Caryl Rusbult and their colleagues also found that committed partners avoid looking at alternatives in the first place. This is a good thing because other studies by our research team indicated that simply seeing highly beautiful fashion models makes the normal people around us, and even our partners, look less attractive and can even make us feel less committed. Other research by John Gonzaga and his colleagues found that thinking about sex increases our attention to alternative partners but also found another possible key to fidelity: Thinking about love has the opposite effect, making us less keen to even look at alternative possibilities.

Of course, technology isn't all bad and could be used to strengthen your relationship. John Gottman and his colleagues, who have conducted studies comparing how happy and unhappy couples act in their relationships, developed an app that consists of exercises designed to give you daily reminders to do the things that happy couples do to keep one another happy and avoid the things that unhappy couples do to get on each other's nerves.

Besides those high-end fixes, you can always make it a regular point to send your partner a virtual hug every time you take a coffee break during the day at work.

KNOWING WHEN TO WALK AWAY

We have been working on the assumption that what's right for you is to stay in a relationship. Given all the research suggesting that people in relationships are, in the long run, happier and healthier, and because of all the harmful long-run consequences of divorce for children as well as their parents, we think that the best general rule is not to head for the hills of Ashley Madisonland when you encounter inevitable everyday conflicts in your relationship. So, we've emphasized a few mental tricks that can help you avoid short-term selfish impulses and the onslaught of temptations in the modern world.

But what if you actually are in a relationship that is not helping you climb the pyramid of life but is instead hurling obstacles in your path? A bad relationship partner, like a nasty boss at work, can actually be harmful to your health. In comparing Diego Rivera to a trolley that nearly killed her and left her crippled for life, Frida Kahlo observed, "There have been two grave accidents in my life. One was the trolley, the other was Diego. Diego was by far the worst." One of Frida's most memorable paintings depicted her own face dripping tears, with a likeness of Diego on her forehead. Another, meant to reflect the depth of her pain, depicted a bloody woman murdered by her own husband.

A bad relationship can make you feel unsafe, can lose you friends, and can not only interfere with your chances of winning that Nobel Prize but also hamper your ability to hold down a regular job at the local shopping center.

Again, modern technology can enter the picture to make things worse, turning a cell phone into a weapon to keep an unpleasant argument going all through the workday. One of our close friends had a partner who would send incessant text messages during working hours of the sort, "Why didn't you respond to my text message from 10 minutes ago???" "Because I am working" should have been an acceptable answer but would only trigger another angry onslaught of digital disruptions.

There are two main pathways to take when a relationship goes into the red column. You can stick around and try to make it better, or you can walk away.

One question to ask yourself is whether the problems with this relationship are, in fact, under your control. If you are in a relationship with someone who doesn't seem as into you as you are into them, it may be a big waste of time to try to convince that person that they should love you more. Doug's friend Guy Van Orden once observed that, although a partner may look incredibly attractive on paper—the brilliant mind of a potential Nobel Laureate in the body of a movie star—it is ridiculous to feel attraction toward them if they are making you feel bad about yourself. And there's research suggesting that unrequited love is stressful not only for the would-be lover but also for the person doing the "unrequiting." The more you pressure someone to care about you, the less attractive you become. So, if there are no children involved, and a relationship is making you feel bad about yourself, it may be the right choice to take the first train out of town and not look back.

But what if you are in a long-term relationship in which there once was strong mutual love and you now have children together?

That is a different story, in which case it's wise to do everything in your power to make the relationship positive again. The first step is to stop complaining and bickering. This can be tough, but there are tricks that John Gottman and his research team discovered in comparing the way that happy and unhappy couples communicate. For example, in their book on marital conflict resolution, Gottman's colleagues Clifford Notarius and Howard Markman developed a guide to politeness in couples, which includes the following suggestions:

- If your partner invites you to do something together, respond positively. If your partner suggests a walk, don't simply snap back something like, "Can't you see how exhausted I am?!" Say instead, "I like the idea of spending some time together, but I'm really tired right now. Would you be up for taking a walk in the morning and just watching a movie now?" That's best delivered with a hug and a smile.
- If your partner does a household chore, don't find the flaw but express your thanks instead. Don't say, "You missed a spot!" but instead, "Thanks!"
- Don't psychoanalyze your partner's behavior under the pretense of helpfulness. Saying something like, "Do you know you're being clinically obsessive-compulsive when you insist on keeping the kitchen so spotlessly clean?" may reveal more about your own clinical problems than your partner's and won't help the relationship.
- Speak for yourself rather than put words into your partner's mouth. If your partner invites you to try a new Thai restaurant, don't say, "I don't think you'll enjoy that restaurant." Say instead, "I'm not quite up for Thai food, dear, but I would like to [something your partner might enjoy here]."
- If you have an opinion, say it directly rather than let your partner play a guessing game. If you really want to eat Mexican

food tonight, say that instead of asking your partner generally, "Would you like to eat out tonight?" and then being disappointed if they suggest going to that new Thai restaurant you don't particularly like.

- If you have nothing nice to say, just keep quiet.

The researchers found that unhappy couples are especially bad at communicating, and when one member of the couple says something negative, the other frequently responds with a zinger—a counterblast likely to start a war of verbal attrition ("Oh, you think *I'm* compulsive! What about your mother?!"). But good communication techniques are learnable. Indeed, couples who learned those positive communication techniques were 50% less likely to split up than a control group of couples who just ran with the standard default marital communication techniques.

More generally, it's useful to switch the focus from negative to positive. Return to doing positive things together, cooking nice dinners together, watching movies, and giving one another back rubs instead of gripe sessions.

If the problem is everyday annoying interactions, you'll do best if you assume it's *your* job to make those interactions better. Remember that you have a lot more control over your own behavior than over your partner's. If you act nice, your partner is a lot more likely to respond nicely than if you sharpen your complaining skills, in which case your partner is likely to become defensive and enjoy your company less and less. Remember those self-fulfilling prophecies: Negative expectations lead you to act in ways that trigger negative behaviors; positive expectations lead you to behave in ways that trigger positive responses.

Of course, sometimes your partner is simply set on leaving, no matter how considerate and forgiving you are. In that case, if there are no children, you'll get over it (although it may be really depressing for a few months and intermittently depressing for a year, unless you find another partner in the interim). But you will get over it. Try taking a vacation to some faraway place if you can afford it, or joining a hiking club, or volunteering at a local charity. That will keep your mind occupied during the recovery period and give you a reason to feel good about yourself.

If there are children, though, then you have a very tough job: to try to have the best possible divorce you can. Although the many stresses of divorce, and the resentments about what could have been, make it easy to keep the bickering and negativity going for years, now without any of the alleviation from happy times together, it is in your long-term best interest to forgive your partner. Those good communication techniques are especially hard to practice when you have been wronged by the other person, but if you have children in common, it becomes especially important to practice the art of not striking back.

It can help to remind yourself of the same rule you'd use in the case of unrequited love: If the other person was not helping you climb up in life but was instead throwing obstacles in your path, you will, in the long run, be better off without them. And the sooner you stop engaging in counterfactual thinking, dwelling on what might have been, the better off you will be.

BOTTOM LINES: SUGGESTIONS FOR STAYING IN ROMANTIC RELATIONSHIPS

Our ancestors, although sometimes polygynous, nevertheless stood out from the rest of the mammalian class for maintaining long-term love relationships. Those relationships, among hunter–gatherers and modern humans alike, have always involved some degree of conflict and jealousy but have also generated a lot of benefits, then and now. The modern world involves more contact with strangers who might be attractive as possible alternative partners and fewer kin nearby to monitor our potential infidelities.

Considering those similarities and differences, here are several takeaway messages:

- *Beware of self-serving biases regarding your partner's contributions versus yours.* Remember Linus Pauling's modification of the Golden Rule: "Do unto others 20-percent better than you would have them do unto you."
- *Remind yourself regularly of the benefits you get out of your relationship.* And communicate those to your partner along with your appreciation.
- *Hug frequently.*
- *Beware of technological aids to infidelity.* Remember the research that (nonmutual) infidelity is a cause of relationship deterioration (although those powerful self-serving biases lead many to claim the opposite causal sequence: "I only did it because my needs weren't being met").
- *Communicate affectionately and nondefensively with your partner.* Say positive things most of the time, even if (and perhaps especially if) you don't like the last thing your partner said.

CHAPTER 8

FAMILY VALUES

David Kaczynski was raised in a small and tightly knit Polish Catholic family in Chicago during the 1950s and 1960s. The family consisted of David, his one older brother whom he greatly admired, and their mother and father, who provided the two boys with a loving and supportive home environment. David's older brother, Theodore, was a bit socially awkward but something of a genius. Theodore finished high school at age 16, went to Harvard to study mathematics, then won an award for the best doctoral dissertation in mathematics at the University of Michigan. These stellar academic achievements led to an offer of a prestigious position as a tenure-track professor at University of California, Berkeley. Although not quite so academically gifted as his older brother, David was also quite bright, earning a degree from Columbia University, where he wrote for the university newspaper before going off to work as a schoolteacher.

William Bulger was raised in somewhat larger, but also tightly knit, Irish Catholic family in Boston during the 1940s, where he was the third of six children. William was the academically gifted one in the lot, earning both an undergraduate degree in English literature and a JD in law from Boston College. William went on to become a successful politician and academic, serving as the head of the Massachusetts state senate for more than a decade and later as president of the University of Massachusetts. Like David Kaczynski, William Bulger also had an older brother, named James. But although James was quite bright, he was not academically inclined. In fact, while his younger brother was buried in his law studies, James joined a street gang, and by age 14 had already been arrested for larceny. Over the next few years, as William continued to excel at academic pursuits, his older brother was arrested numerous times for forgery, assault, and armed robbery. Rather than finishing high school, James was hauled off to a juvenile reformatory.

Despite their differences in academic success, however, David Kaczynski and William Bulger's older brothers shared one distinction: Both spent more than a decade on the FBI's list of the 10 most wanted criminals in America, and both successfully managed to evade massive manhunts for more than 15 years. David's older brother, Ted, was more widely known as the "Unabomber." William's brother Jimmy was better known by his nickname "Whitey," and his wanted poster listed racketeering, extortion, money laundering, and 18 counts of murder as some of the reasons the FBI had placed him on their list of most-wanted fugitives.

Both those infamous older brothers also presented their younger siblings with a powerful moral dilemma: If your brother were on the FBI's most wanted list as a likely offender in multiple murders, and you knew where he was living, would you turn him in?

For David Kaczynski, the question was torturous to answer. For one thing, it was not perfectly clear that his older brother, Ted, was, in fact, the man the FBI was hunting. After quitting his professorship at Berkeley, Ted had moved to a small cabin in Montana, where he attempted to live off the grid. As time progressed, Ted sent increasingly hostile and accusatory letters to their parents.

David's wife, a philosophy professor at Union College in New York, told him that some of the content of Ted's letters bore a resemblance to the things that had been published as the "Unabomber

Manifesto" in *The New York Times*. At first, David thought the similarities a mere coincidence and protested that his brother, though a bit paranoid, would not hurt another living thing. But after several months of comparing the letters with the manifesto and after consulting with lawyers and a former FBI detective, David realized that his wife might well be right.

When David went to tell his mother that Ted might possibly the Unabomber, she responded by saying, "Oh, don't tell anyone!"

David himself was torn between powerful opposing inclinations: loyalty to his older brother, whom he still loved, combined with concern that merely being approached by the FBI would lead the emotionally imbalanced Ted to become violent or self-destructive. And David asked himself what kind of man would turn in his own brother.

Ultimately, David's reservations were outweighed by the fact that the Unabomber had already killed three people and injured more than a dozen others. There was the real possibility that if Ted was the Unabomber, he might go on to kill other innocent victims. In the end, David made the tough decision: He let the FBI have a look at Ted's letters. It turned out that when federal officers arrived at Ted's remote cabin, they found not only a typed copy of the Unabomber Manifesto but also materials for making explosive devices, and even one newly minted bomb, neatly wrapped up and ready to be mailed to his next victim.

For William Bulger, there was no ambiguity about whether his older brother was or was not a criminal. William knew Whitey had lived outside the law. Indeed, William had used his political connections to set Whitey up as an FBI informant (a connection that later helped Whitey slip out of town before his arrest). After Whitey went on the lam, William never appeared to even consider turning him in, even though the two had been in touch. When called on to testify, William pleaded the Fifth Amendment. His unwillingness to help the government find his brother led the University of Massachusetts to force him into retirement. Some defended William's decision, however, as in the case of one friend who claimed that William's silence was motivated by "love and affection for his family." A columnist for *The Boston Globe*, however, took a dimmer view: "Faced with a moral dilemma, William repeatedly made the wrong choice, putting loyalty to his felonious brother over responsibility to his neighborhood, his constituents, or the larger public community whose university he led."

The quandary faced by these two men with murderous brothers illustrates, in one way, a novel problem with family relationships in the modern world. In another way, though, it highlights an age-old dilemma.

TRADITIONAL FAMILY VALUES

When modern politicians talk about "traditional family values," they are conjuring up an idealized image of a nuclear family living in the American suburbs during the 1950s—an image captured in television shows such as *Ozzie and Harriet* or *Leave It to Beaver*. That idealized family is composed of a father who goes off to work 5 days a week to earn money, paired up with a mother who stays home and tends to household chores, such as shopping for groceries, cooking meals from recipes found in *Ladies' Home Journal*, and keeping a clean and organized home for two children, who attend public school and earn a small allowance by helping their mom wash the dishes and cleaning their room.

But such an idealized nuclear family only ever represented a small percentage of the U.S. population—and that during only a brief period in the middle of the 20th century. It hardly characterized most American families even then, and it was certainly not representative of the typical family throughout most of human history. Based on what we know about the range of societies, past and present, a small freestanding nuclear family was not, and has never been, the norm for our species. The husband-and-wife dyad has instead almost always been inextricably woven into a larger extended family network.

Cooperative Breeders

As we noted in Chapter 6, anthropologists such as Sarah Hrdy and Kim Hill argued that humans should be regarded as a *cooperative breeding species* in which the young are cared for not only by their mother but also by *alloparents*, that is, other members of the group who assist the mother. Only about 3% of mammals are cooperative breeders, which makes *Homo sapiens* a member of a relatively small club that also includes wild dogs, elephants, meerkats, and marmosets. In other mammalian species, it is more common for the mother to go it alone, with little or no parenting assistance from the father. Deadbeat dads are thus the norm among other warm-blooded creatures.

In human cooperative breeding networks, the other individuals who help the mother raise her children are most frequently relatives, linked either by blood ties or by virtue of having married into the kin network. In Chapter 4, we described how a typical girl from the Maisin group in New Guinea spent a good portion of her day helping care for her younger siblings or cousins, and she also helped her mother prepare food to share with their other relatives. Among the Maisin, a man and his wife live in a separate hut with their children; hence there is, at one level, a "nuclear family" comparable to that of the idealized 1950s suburban couple. However, that nuclear family's hut is only a few feet from that of the father's parents, and the father's brothers and their families live in that same cluster of huts. Given all the sharing of food and tasks across those families, it makes sense to think of this extended family as the reproductive unit. Indeed, when Kim Hill and his colleagues recorded the number of calories provided by young couples and their children in traditional societies, they found that those small nuclear families did not forage sufficient food to survive on their own. The extended network of alloparents was critical to survival.

Grandmothers

As mentioned in Chapter 6, *menopause*, or the termination of reproduction by older females, is a unique feature of *Homo sapiens* not found in other primates and rarely found in other animal species. The typical script for a female mammal is to keep producing offspring until she drops. Given that evolution is all about *differential reproduction*— in which the name of the game is to get genes into future generations— it makes sense to keep making babies. Why would any organism ever stop reproducing? Evolutionary anthropologists, including Kristin Hawkes, have suggested that human menopause is not some design flaw in our species, such that female reproductive capacity breaks down earlier than the male's does. They argued instead that menopause is itself an adaptation: a feature, not a bug.

In traditional societies, women who have passed menopause continue to serve their genes' self-interests. But they do so indirectly, by helping their children and grandchildren. Data from a wide range of human societies—including Hadza hunter–gatherers, West African horticulturalists, and peasant farmers in Germany, India, and Japan— indicate that children in traditional societies who have the support of grandmothers are more likely to survive and thrive. Studies of children's survival rates in German families living between 1720 and 1874, and among Oromo pastoralists in rural Ethiopia, suggested that it is input from the maternal grandma—the mother's mother— that is most important.

Grandma isn't the only critical helper; having sisters around also increases the odds of survival in traditional societies. Indeed, girls living among groups such as the Yąnomamö did not want to be married off to a man in a distant village, which would leave them without the support and protection of their families. Nearby brothers also help. For a Yąnomamö woman, as for a Mexican woman living in a more modern village, having brothers nearby reduced the likelihood that her husband would be physically abusive.

Why Harriet Needed Ozzie

So, the traditional human family, rather than being nuclear, was an extended one. One feature of the 1950s nuclear family is an accurate representation of the history of our species, however. It is a feature that differentiates Ozzie and Harriet and the rest of us from 95% of other mammals: the presence of a father who participates in the family and who provides resources that promote the children's survival. Other research with traditional societies has indicated that infants and children who have fathers around are more likely to survive than are those who are fatherless.

If the typical mammalian father is little more than a sperm donor, why is the human dad so much more involved? Evolutionary biologists have pointed out that paternal investment in children is a feature of our species that coevolved with the development of large brains. Since the time of our earliest ape ancestors, the human brain tripled in size. Those big fat brains necessitated a relatively premature birth by mammalian standards, so we are born well before our bodies have developed sufficiently to carry our big heads around.

During the time that women in hunter–gatherer groups are pregnant and nursing those highly clingy and dependent offspring, there is a dramatic reduction in the number of calories those women can provide for themselves. As a consequence, their husbands and other relatives pitch in to provide more calories for the over-extended mom.

And the dependency of human children does not end when the baby stops nursing. Humans in all societies have an extended dependency period and do not bring in sufficient calories to feed themselves until they are well into their teens. Humans are not even capable of breeding until their teenage years. After they develop to the point at which they can move around and help themselves, though, children and adolescents may begin helping to care for and babysit their siblings and cousins. Those years also provide a period of apprenticeship, when developing kids can learn the complex set of skills that characterizes our species. Weaving a good basket or making a bow and arrow or a canoe may not seem that complex, but compared with the achievements of any other primate, they are rocket science (indeed, our ancestors' ability to engineer new solutions to recurring problems and the technological know-how they passed on to future generations are the foundations of all modern achievements, including rocket science). Hence, our ancestors' long period of juvenile dependency was a catalyst to the explosive developments of technology in the past few thousand years.

Family Conflict

Family life was critically important to our ancestors, but it would be misleading to depict it as one big joyous communal picnic. In Pospisil's ethnography of the Kapauku Papuans, he described one incident in which a man had angered his fellow villagers by accumulating great wealth but refusing to share with others, violating the group's strong custom of communal sharing. The villagers persuaded the man's cousins to kill him, and the cousins, in turn, solicited the man's son to become part of the execution squad that bumped off the stingy old fellow.

In a classic paper, evolutionary biologist Robert Trivers spelled out the biological roots of family conflict. To begin with, brothers and sisters, and children and their parents, all share roughly 50% of their genes. This should, and does, lead them to have a large stake in one another's well-being. However, the wrinkle comes from the fact that each individual shares twice as many genes with themselves as they do with their closest relative (except in the rare case of identical twins). Because mom shares half of her genes with each child, she will be inclined to split any resources equally between her children. From the child's perspective, however, any benefits given to her sister are discounted by 50% compared with those same benefits given directly to her. This leads to sibling rivalry and also sets the stage for parent–child conflict because the individual child's genetic self-interest is not best served by mommy fairly distributing resources.

In other animal species, sibling rivalry often gets quite intense, and Douglas Mock has documented how newly hatched egrets sometimes kill their own nestmates. Egret siblicide is more likely to be perpetrated when the brood size is larger, and thus parental resources are stretched. In humans, siblicide is not common, but there are some historically well-known examples. Genghis Khan killed his older half-brother, for example, and Cleopatra was involved in murdering more than one of her siblings (a practice she did not introduce into the Ptolemaic line, which had, for generations, been murdering one another in pursuit of all that pharaonic wealth and power).

Much more common than siblicide, however, was infanticide. The practice of leaving unwanted infants to die was common in hunter–gatherer and horticultural societies, and it was most likely to happen when the mother was young (and could go on to have more children later). Infanticide was more likely when the infant appeared unhealthy and also when the woman did not have a husband to help care for the child. Infanticide did not disappear with the advent of agriculture; it was still commonly practiced in ancient Rome, when the paterfamilias had the right to give the thumbs-up or thumbs-down to an infant. If there was any suspicion of infidelity on the wife's part, his thumb was more likely to turn down.

Just as we don't want to view traditional family life as a picnic, though, it would also be a going too far to think it was a continual reenactment of Shakespeare's *Tragedy of Hamlet*, with jealous relatives and in-laws wantonly slaughtering one another. Alongside their selfish individual desires, our ancestors also had much to gain by getting along with one another. Brothers and sisters may have squabbled over the division of parental resources, but they also protected one another, cared for one another, taught one another, and shared with one another. And along with their cousins and in-laws, they combined their efforts to accomplish tasks that would have been impossible for isolated individuals, such as protecting their group against bands of unrelated marauders. Indeed, our ancestors' selfish genetic interests were best served—most of the time—by cooperating with those around them. And the fact that they were surrounded by brothers, sisters, and cousins, who shared a substantial portion of their genes, usually made unselfish behaviors profitable from a genetic perspective. Helping two of your siblings survive was, from the gene's perspective, equivalent to helping yourself.

MODERN FAMILY LIFE

In a quick comparison of the ancestral family and the modern household, it might seem as though almost everything has changed. We have already noted that the isolated nuclear family living in the 1950s suburbs was very unlike the traditional extended family. But between the end of the 1950s and 2016, the family got even more nuclear—with the number of children living in *single*-parent households tripling. In 2016, fully 27% of children lived with only one parent (in 85% of those cases, that single parent was the mother). At the same time, grandparents have been increasingly excluded from the domestic scene. Worldwide, only 38% of grandparents lived with their extended families in 2018, and in the United States, that number was even lower—at a mere 8%.

One of the factors that has contributed to the splintering of the extended family is geographic mobility. Hunter–gatherers, if they migrated out of their native villages, tended to move to someplace nearby, within easy walking distance. As in the case of the Maisin, one parent typically stayed close to their extended family (the father in Maisin society). Hence, children almost always had extensive contact with their grandparents, aunts, uncles, and cousins on at least one side of the family. None of this is possible if mom is single and was recently transferred by her company from her hometown of Cedar Rapids to the Los Angeles office.

After the advent of agriculture, it was common for farmland to be passed down within a family and for cultivation to require many hands, so extended families still tended to stick together. Once the industrial revolution occurred, however, many people began migrating away from their extended families to work alongside strangers in large urban areas. During the 1800s, nine out of 10 Americans lived on a farm. But only about 14% of Americans lived in rural communities in 2016. More than twice that many (31%) lived in cities, and fully 55% lived in suburbs. Although suburbs might seem like a compromise between urban and rural life, they are actually more likely to pull families apart.

Another feature of modern life that has flipped the traditional extended family model is this: Most of us now live in societies made up of people to whom we are completely unrelated. As noted earlier, many or most of the people in an ancient village were linked by blood ties or because they were in-laws. This was still true, to some extent, in very small agricultural villages. However, nine out of 10 people in the modern world now live in cities or suburbs. As a consequence, our neighbors and the people we pass every day on the street are mostly not related to us.

In large cities, some people still live in urban villages near their workplaces and within walking distance of their extended family. Doug grew up in an apartment in New York City, with his grandparents and maternal aunt living one door down, along with several cousins, and there was another maternal aunt living one door down in the other direction. His paternal grandparents lived on the next block, and his grandmother would pass by on her way back from church, dropping off a bag of rolls and jelly donuts from the nearby bakery. But as he got older, all those relatives started moving into suburbs more than an hour's travel distance away, and his own family moved to a different suburban town. People living in suburbs tend to work far away from their homes—as did Doug's stepfather, who commuted for 2 hours every day to a job on Madison Avenue in Manhattan. Thus, one or both suburban parents often spend the best part of their days separated even from their nuclear families.

Some Changes Aren't Bad

Not all the changes in family life in the modern world are problematic. Whereas a child living in an ancestral setting stood a reasonable chance of dying or being deserted at birth if they did not have a father, children of single mothers are no longer likely to starve in the modern industrialized world. Investment by fathers used to be critical for survival; it is still important but is now related to academic achievement and emotional and social competence, and is less essential for staying alive.

Also, on the positive side of the ledger, infanticide has largely, although not completely, disappeared in the developed world. Even in modern times, children who do not live with both biological parents are more likely to be neglected and abused, and those living with stepparents are statistically more likely to be murdered. But although the relative danger to children is greater in homes without two biological parents, the threats posed by violence and accidents are now much lower than they were in the ancestral world. Indeed, the majority of stepparents in the modern world have relatively positive relationships with their stepchildren. Of 2,691 adults in one Pew survey, 42% had at least one step-relative, and of those, 70% were very satisfied with their family life. This is only slightly lower than the 78% satisfaction rate in families composed of only biological relatives.

The age at which people begin their families has also changed. In the ancestral environment, women were married shortly after reaching puberty, and men typically married a few years later. Children came along very soon afterward, so that being a teenage parent was the norm for our ancestors. By 1972, though, the average age of first parenthood had jumped to 21 for American women and 27 for men. In the ensuing half century, the clock has started later and later so that American women now have their first child, on average, at age 26, and men first become fathers, on average, at age 31. For college-educated Americans and for those living in upscale urban environments, add another few years. In San Francisco and Manhattan, women have their first child at around age 33. Women living in Europe or wealthy Asian countries, such as Japan or South Korea, are also now waiting till after age 30 to have their first child.

Changes in people's relationships with kin are related to changes in their relationship with broader society. In ancestral villages, if relatives or in-laws had grievances with one another, they needed to handle it within the extended family. In modern societies, there are centralized governments that coordinate relations between unrelated individuals. As modern city-states evolved, they developed norms that encouraged a commitment to the wider community.

Athenians thought of themselves as loyal not only to their families but also to the Athenian state—likewise for Egyptians, Spartans, and Romans. Today, people grow up learning allegiances to wider collectives—to think of themselves as Australians, Americans, Brits, Brazilians, Italians, or Israelis. According to Steven Pinker, the development of such larger collectives has had one important positive consequence: It is a key factor in reducing the extremely high levels of violence that prevailed in the ancestral world. By allowing a centralized authority to enforce universally applicable laws, people were no longer expected to, or even permitted to, engage in the never-ending spirals of family-versus-family and village-versus-village vengeance that characterized groups such as the Yąnomamö. Not that our family or tribal loyalties have disappeared, but some of their dangerous consequences have been buffered in modern societies.

The stories of David Kaczynski and William Bulger demonstrate conflicts between innate loyalties to family versus acquired loyalties to a larger society. The two men came to opposite conclusions about how to handle those conflicts. It's probably important that William Bulger and his brother, Whitey, both remained connected to one another and to their local urban community: the shantytown Irish of South Boston. Besides sticking close to the family, Whitey Bulger was, like his more conventional younger brother, politically savvy and charming, and he at least claimed to constrain his violence to conflicts with other local criminals over power and territory. Indeed, William had helped Whitey become an FBI informant, further blurring the line between Whitey's involvements in the local criminal culture and the wider society. David Kaczynski and his brother, on the other hand, migrated to different parts of the country, and Ted explicitly and angrily broke ties with his parents and with society as a whole. Furthermore, Ted Kaczynski's Unabomber violence did not follow the conventions of local warfare but was instead randomly directed at other American citizens and fueled by a somewhat paranoid and antisocial philosophy. Hence, it makes sense that David Kaczynski's loyalty to society would win out over his loyalty to his antisocial and unhinged older brother.

Some Things Never Change

It's important to note that many features of family life have remained pretty much the same since ancestral times. In ancient human families, the young depended on their parents for many years. This extended juvenile dependence has not only persisted into the modern era, it has been magnified. Throughout history, it was common for a girl to leave her family soon after puberty, but girls in modern families now stay with the family until they go away to college. Even after that, young women commonly return home during school breaks and may even come back home to live for a while after college graduation. Boys follow a similar trajectory, and just as boys in ancestral villages stayed with the family even longer than girls did, boys in the modern world are still more likely than girls to live with their parents during their 20s.

Girls in the modern world are, like ancestral girls, still more interested in child care than are boys. And while boys continue to play competitive and warlike games like their male ancestors, girls continue to play with dolls and to express more of an interest in caring for babies. Although grandparents are not as involved as they once were in child care, they are still frequently involved in helping raise children. When Dave's son Finian was born, Fin's grandmothers on both sides of the family relocated from thousands of miles away to help take care of him. In one survey of retired people, 80% said they thought it important to live near their children and grandchildren. When Michelle Obama moved into the White House with her two children, her mother came along to help. And a British study found that despite the fact that many grandparents now live in a different neighborhood, a third of grandparents nevertheless provide regular care for their grandchildren.

Those numbers may not be so radically different from the ancestral environment, in which many grandparents did not survive long enough to help out, and grandparents on one side may have been unable to help if their daughter or son had moved to another village when they married. It also remains true that maternal grandmothers are more likely to help out. When young people are asked to nominate the grandparent to whom they feel closest, for example, they most frequently nominate their maternal grandmother and least frequently nominate their paternal grandfather.

Features of family life that have persisted from the ancestral environment into the modern world are the conflict of interest between siblings and parent–offspring conflict. But modern families are much smaller and have much greater wealth than traditional families, so there is more for each child, and the stakes are not as high. Remember the research on egrets: Siblicide was much less likely when the brood size was small.

FAMILY MATTERS IN THE MODERN WORLD

Despite the perennial persistence of some family strife, people's families remain centrally important in their lives. In one research program conducted across 27 societies around the globe, our research team asked people about all of the different motives we've been discussing in this book, including self-protection, affiliation, status, finding mates, keeping mates, and caring for family members. In one part of that research, we asked people what they were most concerned about right now, and then we asked them to rate how much their current concerns were related to each of the different fundamental motives. People rated caring for family members as more important than all of the other goals except keeping mates (the other family-values goal). This pattern—more emphasis on goals linked to family—held true in Bolivia, Brazil, China, and Japan, as it did in Uganda and the United States.

In another study conducted with Jaimie Krems and Becca Neel, we asked people what they would be doing if they wanted to either become self-actualized or to find meaning in their lives. When people thought about pursuing self-actualization, they imagined doing things linked to status, but if they wanted to find meaning in life, they instead chose activities related to caring for their kin. And when Catherine Salmon and Martin Daly asked Canadian women to pick the one person in the world who was closest to them, many picked their spouses or friends, but fully 55% chose a relative (and of those, mom was the primary pick 79% of the time). Men were more likely to choose their spouses, although 40% of men chose a relative as closest to them (and, again, mom topped the list).

THE BENEFITS OF KEEPING YOUR KIN CLOSE

In 1923, when Walter Elias Disney was 20 years old, his financial prospects were not promising. After having been laid off from one job, he had twice failed in his attempts to start his own business. After his second start-up went bankrupt, he moved out to California, where he joined his older brother Roy (as kids, Walt and Roy shared a paper route in Chicago). The brothers rented a room from their uncle. Times continued to be tough, and Roy often had to lend Walt the $5 he needed to pay his rent as well as cover the additional $1 they paid their uncle to rent his garage, where they worked trying to start a new business: making animated cartoons. With his older brother to help out, Walt's luck began to turn. The brothers' upstart business had some success with a new character they called Mickey Mouse, and they used their profits to hire more artists to produce the first full-length animated movie, *Snow White and the Seven Dwarfs.* Walt continued to have problems managing his finances, but Roy managed the books and helped keep the company on an even keel. Although Walt and his brother, Roy, didn't always get along, they stayed in business together, and today, the $1 per week they invested in renting their uncle's garage has grown into a staggering $130 billion. Its assets include Pixar, Hulu, 20th Century Studios, Marvel Studios, Disneyland, and Walt Disney World.

The Disney brothers aren't the only family members who helped one another along to great success. The Winkelvoss twins, who became well known after the movie *Social Network* depicted their lawsuit against Mark Zuckerberg, and who famously did everything together, jointly made more than a billion dollars from investment in Bitcoin, not to mention rowing their way into a prominent spot on the U.S. Olympic team in Beijing. The brothers John F. Kennedy, Robert Kennedy, and Ted Kennedy became major political leaders in the United States with their help of one another and their wealthy father, who had himself been U.S. ambassador to England. And Venus and Serena Williams trained together to win Olympic Gold medals and multiple Grand Slam titles.

Despite the splintering of modern families, close relatives are still likely to give one another not only the shirts off their back but even the body parts underneath. Of 5,396 kidney donors in 2014, fully 63% were relatives. Of those, 80% were blood relatives (the other 20% were spouses). And of the blood relatives, 86% were first-degree relatives who share 50% of their genes (brothers, sisters, children, or parents).

In the chapter on friendship (see Chapter 4), we talked about a study in which students tried to answer tough GRE questions as part of a team with a friend, a relative, or a stranger, and they were told that their pair had performed exceptionally well. The men paired with friends gave themselves more credit, whereas the women gave more credit to their friends. But when they were paired with a relative, both the men and women tended to give more credit to their family member than to themselves. This is more evidence for the argument that it pays to keep your family close. Besides giving you the odd internal organ when you really need it, your relatives are also more likely to give you credit for your accomplishments, even when you don't necessarily deserve it.

Just because your relatives are more likely to cut you slack doesn't mean you should take them for granted. Remember, unless you are one of the small percentage of people with an identical twin (three in 1,000), even your siblings only share 50% of their genes with you, but 100% with themselves. So, it's a good policy to thank your family members every time they do you a favor.

Speaking of shared genes, you should really avoid the tendency to take your steprelatives for granted. If Doug could advise his younger self, he'd counsel himself to expect less of his stepfather and to explicitly thank him more for all he did.

Some people worry that an understanding of genetic selfishness will make people more openly selfish. That is a good example of the familiar naturalistic fallacy: the misconception that what is natural is therefore good. On the contrary, an understanding of selfish genes can help us take a Zen perspective in the face of inevitable sibling rivalry and the conflicts between children and stepparents. If you appreciate that your family members' interests sometimes conflict with yours, it is easier to make compromises and to forgive them for not always prioritizing your needs above all other considerations. Indeed, if you truly understand how it works, you'll realize, as we've noted before, that it was in our ancestors' genetic selfish interest to be less explicitly selfish toward the other members of their groups. Without their relatives, steprelatives, and in-laws, a totally self-centered early human would have been out on the plains of Africa trying to fend for themselves against lions and leopards and buzzards. Oh, my. Then, as now, there were self-centered individualists who couldn't get along with their groups. But they probably didn't become anybody's ancestor.

PARASITIZING FAMILIAL INSTINCTS IN THE MODERN WORLD

In August 2020, as the Republican Party's U.S. presidential convention was about to unfold, a visit to the party's main website revealed the following statement: "Our country should value the traditions of family, life, religious liberty, and hard work." That list thus places "family" first in the list of values the party's leaders felt were important to represent. A visit to the Democratic Party's home page at the same time revealed a picture of a young girl that, if clicked, started a cascade of touching images of children and families, and the question: "As Democrats, what are we fighting for?" Among the answers: "for the mothers, for the fathers, for the daughters. . . ." During the presidential convention, Joseph R. "Joe" Biden, Jr., christened Kamala Harris, his running mate, and her husband, as honorary members of the Biden family, and the former president, Barack Obama, referred to Biden as his "brother."

It is informative that, during a contentious election, both major political parties agreed on the importance of family values. But when you hear the term "family" in a communication from any political party, reach for your checkbook because a request for a contribution is soon to follow. Before you write the check, though, you might want to take a quick look not at the eloquence of their spin but at what legislation the requesting candidate or organization has actually passed to help ensure a better life for the members of your family.

Politicians aren't alone in exploiting family imagery to induce you to part with your hard-earned dollars, pounds, or Euros. Medical advertisements often suggest that you should call your doctor and get a prescription for the latest drug that a major pharmaceutical company is hawking: Don't do it for yourself, you are counseled. Do it "because you care about them." Such a communication is typically accompanied by a collage of images depicting a middle-aged man with his loving wife, children, and grandchildren.

For years, the telecommunication and photography industries also joined forces with Madison Avenue advertising corporations to provide thousands of jobs for big-eyed children and kindly looking elderly models, who appeared in endless ads reminding you how important it is to "stay in touch with your loved ones" by enrolling for a new phone service and "capture those fleeting and priceless family memories" by buying a new camera.

Politicians, drug companies, and manufacturers of phones and cameras can at least claim that it's fair to use family imagery in their advertising and fundraising efforts. Consider however, some of the other megacorporations that exploit family imagery to help peddle their merchandise. One classic Coca-Cola advertisement declares "It's a family affair" and depicts a smiling and sharply dressed couple at a table with half-empty Coke bottles while junior voraciously chugs down his bottle of Coke. The fine print argues, "Happy moments make a happy family. Ice-cold Coca-Cola makes *the pause that refreshes* a happy moment the whole family can share." An insert shows a whole full case of Cokes and suggests "order a case" so that you can serve Coke to your family "from your own refrigerator." Several decades later, the descendant of that classic ad shows a gleefully smiling African American family seated behind a table containing a half-empty gallon bottle of Coke, with the caption: "Family time is the best time." Other soda pop pushers have also poured millions of dollars into advertisements associating their beverages with family. For years, 7Up ads showed happy smiling families at picnics, on beaches, and even doing homework, under the caption

"The 'Fresh Up' Family Drink!" Given that research in recent years suggests a 26% boost in the odds of getting diabetes from drinking one or two cans of soda daily and given the dramatic increases in childhood diabetes, stuffing the refrigerator with cases of sugary beverages might not actually be the best thing you could do for your family.

Besides the relatively benign mainstream exploitation of family imagery to sell products or raise political contributions, there are much more malicious ways for modern criminals to exploit family love. Roberto Primero Luis had borrowed $10,000 from his father-in-law, Tomás, to pay a "coyote" to smuggle him from Guatemala across the U.S. border. When Roberto went missing just after reaching the U.S. border, Tomás called the coyote's number and was told that his son-in-law had been kidnapped and was injured. The supposed kidnapper informed Tomás that he would release Roberto if Tomás could send $3,600 to cover Roberto's medical expenses. Tomás sent the money but later learned that his son-in-law had not been kidnapped. Instead, Roberto's body was discovered by U.S. Border Patrol in Arizona's desert, where the young man had gotten stranded without water while attempting to find his way over a remote mountain pass between Mexico and the United States. Tomás never saw his $3,600 again, but he was not alone in having been maliciously exploited by this scam.

Modern technology has made another version of this scam remarkably easy to pull off. One elderly couple got a call from someone who identified himself as Sergeant Charles Johnson from the United States Embassy in the Dominican Republic. Sergeant Johnson informed the couple that their grandson was in the Dominican Republic for a wedding but had gotten into a car accident. The elderly couple later got a follow-up call from someone impersonating their grandson, who explained that drugs had been found in the car. He had tested negative for drugs but needed them to send him

$9,600 cash so he could appear in court that day instead of having to wait 2 to 3 weeks. After dropping off the cash at a FedEx location, the elderly couple decided to try to call their grandson's number. He answered the phone and informed them that he was not in jail in the Dominican Republic but safe at home in Colorado. This particular couple managed to stop the delivery. Unfortunately, a visit to the Federal Trade Commission's webpage on "family emergency scams" (see https://www.consumer.ftc.gov/scams/family-emergency-scams) reveals other stories of elders who have fallen for the same trick and lost a substantial amount of money.

Apparently, the scam typically involves a call from someone claiming to be a police officer or a lawyer, followed by a call from someone impersonating the grandchild, who apologizes that his voice sounds funny because his mouth was injured in "the accident." The scammers use social media sites to obtain information about grandparents and their traveling grandchildren, and the request always involves an urgent plea for the grandparents to immediately wire money or send cash cards. This allows the elders' money to be stolen with no trace. The family emergency scam suggests caution about the information you make public on social media, and it warns you to be absolutely sure that when you hope to help someone in your family, you're really helping someone in your family. More broadly, such exploitations counsel us to think carefully and check with others before responding to requests that might be exploiting our most powerful motivations.

BOTTOM LINES: SUGGESTIONS FOR FURTHERING FAMILY VALUES

Compared with traditional small-scale societies, modern urban cultures involve much smaller families and geographic mobility that often separates family members and places most of us in close proximity to nonrelatives. But family-related motives nevertheless continue to rank high among people living in modern societies. Considering those continuities, we suggest some potentially useful advice:

- *Keep your kin as close as possible.* When it comes to extremely costly benefits, such as donating body organs, family members are most likely to pitch in.
- *Maintain virtual contact with kin if you are geographically separated.* You can't share a turkey dinner over Zoom, but you can share a laugh or some social support.
- *Don't take helpful steprelatives for granted.* Most stepparents are not like Cinderella's stepmom, so if you have a stepparent who has helped you out, remember that, from their genes' perspective, they are going above and beyond the call of duty. Be sure to express your appreciation.
- *While you're at it, be sure to explicitly and regularly express your gratitude to any biological relatives who have helped you out.* Grandma will probably help anyway, but she might be pleasantly surprised at a nice note thanking her for all she's done.
- *Beware of those who use modern technology to parasitize familial instincts.* The geographic dispersal of families, the ease of gaining access to social networks, and our natural inclination to respond quickly to close relatives in need can be used against us.

CHAPTER 9

BACK TO THE FUTURE

As we were finishing this book in October 2020, the modern world was facing some serious problems. The daily headlines were full of stories about a viral pandemic that had killed more than a million people worldwide, with the highest per capita death toll in the United States of America. That pandemic led to massive unemployment and political unrest, as well as radical alterations in people's everyday lives. In late 2020, the United States Census Bureau reported that 8.3 million Americans were behind in their rent, and that number had increased to 20 million by December 2020. Millions were expecting to be evicted—put out into the street—in the next few months. During the past year, applications for marriage licenses were down, and unmarried people found it especially difficult to even begin new romantic connections. Rates of murder, aggravated assault, arson, and car theft had all jumped since the beginning of the pandemic.

But the news was not all bad. Rates of rape and burglary also dropped during the pandemic. People started getting more flu vaccinations, cooking healthy food at home, and eating more meals with their family members. One large survey found that 78% of people thought the pandemic had made them value their family relationships more, and another found that 58% said they appreciated their marital partner more. Overall, almost 60% of people thought the pandemic had changed their lives for the better.

Both authors of this book have occupations that normally involve a lot of contact with other people, and the pandemic forced us to adjust to virtual meetings instead of real face-to-face contact. But, at the same time, the crisis allowed us to spend more time with our children and other family members. Whereas Doug usually spent the summer with Dave's younger brother in British Columbia, with an occasional short visit from Dave and his kids, in 2020, we all got to hang out together for several weeks at our family getaway in the local mountains, hiking and kayaking with the three younger Kenricks. In one sense, the pandemic forced us back into life in a small kin group, more like that experienced by our hunter–gatherer ancestors. That part was not bad.

The time together also gave us an opportunity to finish up this book and to look back on what we'd learned from comparing the Yąnomamö, Maisin, Aché, and !Kung San to our own lives in the 21st century. What follows is an aerial map of the ground we've covered.

STAYING ALIVE

Back in Chapter 2, we told the story of Brooklyn-born adventurer Helen Klaben, who almost starved to death in the Alaskan wilderness but went on to live a long and interesting life. We contrasted her story with that of another person born in Brooklyn—Walter Hudson—who did not get to travel much, partly because he reached 1,197 pounds and was unable to fit through the door to leave his room. Hudson's story could not have happened in the past because our ancestors had to work hard for every ounce of fat or sugar in their diets. But despite living in a very different world, Walter Hudson, like the rest of us, had inherited our ancestors' proclivity to eat rich foods whenever possible and get all the rest they could in between. Because our hunter–gatherer ancestors had to work so hard for calories, overeating just wasn't a problem, and they did not die of heart attacks, cancer, or diabetes.

In the modern world, though, the food and beverage industry caters masterfully to our ancestral craving for fats and sugars. In so doing, though, it leaves us vulnerable to obesity and several novel diseases. To combat this fatal mismatch problem, we discussed psychological research showing that it is much easier to control your environment than to resist temptation. The bottom line is that if you want to stay fit, set up your personal world so that you don't have easy access to Ben & Jerry's and bags of potato chips—and so you have to exercise before getting your calories.

PROTECTING OURSELVES FROM THE BAD GUYS

We opened Chapter 3 with two stories about self-protection: one a harrowing encounter between the young anthropologists Kim Hill and Hillard Kaplan and a group of armed Yora tribesmen wearing helmets taken from several recently killed telephone line workers, and the other about Samantha Power's scary encounters with sexually predatory Bosnian leaders. Those stories illustrated a continuing legacy of conflict and threat similar to that faced by our ancestors, but we also reviewed evidence suggesting how far we have come in the modern world. The fierce Yanomamö and even the peaceful !Kung Bushmen had much higher rates of violence than we have today, and intergroup conflict back then was more likely to turn violent.

Despite being safer, though, we don't feel safe, because the news media and politicians parasitize our fears of other groups. And in the modern world, there's a whole new set of threats from microplunderers who rob you not with six-guns but with fountain pens and hidden fees. Our ancestors protected themselves by pulling together with the other members of their groups, a tactic that can still be a useful defense against both microplunderers and larger scale human parasites. We also suggested an individual tactic for avoiding being exploited by microplunderers: Unsubscribe from political and news sources that regularly take your money by arousing your fears.

GETTING ALONG

The chapter on getting along (see Chapter 4) began with the story of Danny Kahneman, who went from a friendless child in Nazi-occupied France to the developer, with close buddy Amos Tversky, of the field of behavioral economics. Looking back at ancestral comradeship, we described how the members of the Maisin and Aché shared food and information with people they knew throughout their lives, and we contrasted that with the impermanence and lack of depth in many friendships in the modern mobile and digital world.

What remains the same is that we are still inclined to befriend those who are nearby, who share resources with us, and who are similar to us (although that similarity is now based on common interests and not solely on family ties). Comparing friendship in the ancient world and the modern world suggests several useful bits of advice: Base your friendships on real commonalities, hang on to the people you really know and trust, and make yourself useful to them.

GETTING AHEAD

In Chapter 5, we opened our discussion of the status motive with the story of Robert Cialdini, who had to choose between working his way through college and an offer to play on a minor league professional baseball team. Cialdini took the college route, which removed the very tiny possibility of becoming Willie Mays but opened the door to a stable career and to later international recognition as the "guru of social influence." As we observed, our ancestors did not have many rungs on the social ladder, but now, some wealthy individuals earn thousands of times as much income as regular wage earners do. We also talked about roboparasites, such as addictive computer games that yield unending opportunities to win more digital points but distract us from gaining points in real life.

Besides the novel problems of wealth inequality and electronic status parasites, though, modern life also offers unique opportunities. There are now many different ladders instead of only one to climb, and this offers us the option to choose a career well matched to our skills and interests. One major piece of advice from considering both hunter–gatherers and modern organizations is to strive for prestige rather than compete for dominance. By becoming an expert and using your expertise to help your team, rather than trying to gain power to exploit others, you generate respect instead of resentment.

FINDING TRUE LOVE

Our discussion of modern love began in Chapter 6 with the tale of Sharon Clark, who was swept off her feet by a sweet-talking stranger named Giovanni Vigliotto, married him in a heartbeat, and then found herself wondering where he'd gone with all her worldly possessions. When she finally tracked him down, she discovered he was already married—and not to one woman but to 105 of them. In the hunter–gatherer world, it was rare to even meet 100 potential mates over the course of your lifetime, much less marry them all. Our ancestors only encountered a small pool of possible mates: people known to them and their relatives.

In the modern world, people are more likely to meet strangers online or in bars, and there are hundreds of possibilities. But like Giovanni Vigliotto, some of those charming strangers may not be what they seem to be. We suggested that, besides being nice and working out, which increases mating options for both sexes, it pays to be deliberate in choosing your mating strategy and to look for true signals that your potential partner is offering what you are looking for. To be sure your potential partner is the real thing, it pays to shop locally. And while you're carefully shopping around, it makes sense to enjoy the pleasures of being single.

STAYING IN LOVE

Chapter 7's guest star was Marya Skłodowska, a bookish young Polish woman who moved to Paris after one failed relationship, shunning romantic attachments so she could pursue her scientific studies. While Marya was hard at work studying physics and chemistry at the University of Paris, though, she met a fellow researcher named Pierre Curie and ended up marrying him. They stuck together until his untimely death in a horse carriage accident did them part. Before his death, though, they won a Nobel Prize and produced two daughters, both of whom went on to their own accomplishments.

We observed that our ancestors, though sometimes polygynous, nevertheless stood out from the rest of the mammalian class for maintaining long-term love relationships. We described how marriages among hunter–gatherers and among modern humans have always involved some degree of conflict and jealousy but also have generated a lot of benefits. The takeaways from the research on successful relationships are these: Put your partner's interests ahead of your own, hug them frequently, and avoid modern technological aids to infidelity.

TAKING CARE OF FAMILY

In discussing the kin care motive (see Chapter 8), we contrasted David Kaczynski and William Bulger, both of whom had brothers on the FBI's most wanted list. David and William came to different conclusions about whether to help their family versus society at large. We discussed how the extended and lifelong family ties of hunter–gatherers have been replaced by smaller and often geographically isolated single-parent and two-parent nuclear families, and how young people now spend even longer periods dependent on their families.

Our powerful family instincts are artfully parasitized today by political parties, drug companies, phone manufacturers, sugary beverage manufacturers, and family emergency scammers. One takeaway from the research in the chapter is that it still pays to keep your kin close: They will give you a kidney and more credit than you deserve. It also pays not to take them for granted (even though they'll tolerate it more than will nonrelatives) but, instead, to thank them when they help you. And because many of us have step-relatives and in-laws, who only indirectly share our genetic interests, it pays to thank them twice as much.

PUTTING OURSELVES IN THE PICTURE

We wrote this book because we are convinced that evolutionary psychology, which started as a purely theoretical enterprise, has begun to reveal a wealth of very practical implications—insights well worth sharing with our children, our students, and the general public. We decided to end with an exercise that brings those practical implications all the way home: to ask ourselves how the two of us were faring on the ancestral to-do list—to frankly confront where we were succeeding and where we most needed work.

We could have assigned Dave to tell Doug where he was failing, and Doug to detail Dave's shortcomings, but we thought it might be better for the long-term future of our little team to do it a different way: for each of us to look at the ancestral to-do list and tell the other one three ways in which he was doing well. We both also thought about three ways in which we ourselves could improve. And we tried to draw a few general lessons we could apply not only to our future lives but also as a few potentially useful tips for our kids, and for you, the reader.

Doug's Take on Three of Dave's Strengths

In Doug's opinion, Dave deserves kudos for his accomplishments in caring for his family, staying alive, and getting ahead.

CARING FOR FAMILY MEMBERS

Dave wisely ignored my advice to move to Australia when he was having a terrible, horrible, no good, very bad day during an otherwise not so delightful divorce. As a consequence, 10 years later, Dave has a great relationship with his kids. He chose to stay near his ex-wife, and the two of them share parenting responsibilities. He takes plenty of time to give his son and daughter guidance, and they really love him. Indeed, his ex-wife just publicly thanked him on Facebook for his help in caring for the kids during the pandemic. And despite Grandpa Doug's occasional failings in the advice department, Dave has helped out the old man in ways he couldn't have done from the outback, mate.

STAYING ALIVE

Dave is 42, and he's stayed in great shape by rock climbing, biking to work, and even hiking down to the bottom of the Grand Canyon recently. When Dave saw how the lure of alcohol was messing up the lives of a couple of people he knew, despite having inherited his father's Irish genes to enjoy the taste of beer, he decided to just quit completely.

240

GETTING AHEAD

Dave went to film school at New York University, which is a status symbol in the cinematic community but doesn't translate as well into a day job. But he has managed to earn a living by putting his cinematic production skills to work making educational videos, many of them applying psychology to everyday life problems. Dave is also continually learning something new: how to do digital animation, how to create apps for the iPhone, how to set up websites, and how to start a business and manage employees. Most of his projects include lifting up his team members, and when our social psychology textbook released an interactive digital version, Dave became a coauthor (and created an engaging series of 3-minute animated videos in which psychologists from around the globe describe their most interesting research).

Doug's Take on Three of Doug's Areas for Improvement

Doug thinks he himself could use some work in the categories of staying alive, protecting himself from the bad guys, and getting ahead.

STAYING ALIVE

Despite knowing about the dangers of overindulgence, it's tough to avoid bringing home chocolate-covered treats from the supermarket and putting them in glass jars on the kitchen counter. I could do a much better job setting up my environment so that I have to work for those calories, ancestral style, rather than dangling temptations in front of myself, Elvis Presley style.

PROTECTING MYSELF FROM THE BAD GUYS

Another goal is to stop compulsively reading the daily headlines about the scary things politicians are saying and to stay off social media, where my friends often post items about the scary things politicians are saying.

With the time saved by not going online to read about the scary political events, I could begin my next book project: about the greatest discoverers in psychophysics, behavior genetics, evolutionary psychology, ethology, and cognitive science, with the title *Discovery of Human Nature*. Learning about all that should keep me out of trouble, as my mother would have said, at least for a couple of years.

Dave's Take on Three of Doug's Strengths

Dave thought that his old man deserved praise for getting ahead, caring for his kin, and surviving.

GETTING AHEAD

When it comes to work, my dad is a guy who shows up and works hard, and he also helps the people around him succeed. As a professor, he understands that an important part of his job is helping his students get jobs and gain status. He takes that aspect of his job very seriously, and it's reflected in the success of his students, several of whom are now eminent professors at top-notch universities around the world.

KIN CARE

My dad has helped me out in a bunch of big ways throughout my life, providing social and emotional support, not to mention a few bucks whenever I needed them during my years as a starving artist. But one of the things I've really appreciated is his willingness to come over and help me out with projects around the house. As a workaholic college professor, my dad has often encouraged me to hire professionals to fix things so I could focus on writing. I really like taking care of my house myself, though, so I usually ignore that advice. But then I often end up getting overwhelmed—trying to fix the plumbing, trim the trees, and still find time to take care of my kids and do some writing. Again and again, my dad has come over at 6 a.m. to help me cut down tree limbs, rewire lights, or fix a leaky sink. I really appreciate that, even though he initially encouraged me not to take this all on, he's still willing to show up to help me trim the trees and haul them out into the alley.

SURVIVAL

For a professor in his 70s, my dad can carry a heck of a lot of tree branches. Unlike his friend, Bob Cialdini, my dad never had the sort of athletic prowess it would take to get a minor league baseball contract. But he has made a few lifestyle choices that have really helped him stay fit over the years. He quit smoking before I was born. He always bikes to work, he's an avid hiker, and when he golfs, he refuses to rent a cart (and even gets some extra exercise because, being so athletically ungifted, he hits a few wild shots). And over the past 20 years, I've seen him (mostly) put aside his love of pizza and ice cream in favor of homemade, low carb dinners with a bowl of fruit for dessert. My grandparents smoked themselves to death before I got to know them, but my dad may even get to meet his great-grandkids.

Dave's Take on Three of Dave's Areas for Improvement

In Dave's self-assessment, he is still a work in progress when it comes to staying alive, getting along, and getting a mate.

STAYING ALIVE

Several of the suggestions in this book involve using ancestral solutions to solve modern problems, and I've used that strategy for several years. When I'm trying to lose weight, rather than switching from Coke to Diet Coke, I switch from soda to water. My biggest battle throughout life has been a struggle with depression. For years, I relied on natural, tried-and-true methods to keep my depression under control. I would hike 5 miles every day. I made sure I got enough sleep. I completely quit drinking. But sometimes things got worse despite all those healthy choices. I would get so overwhelmed with panic it was physically painful, and my anxieties could lead me to have trouble paying attention to a normal conversation. My therapist kept pushing me to try antidepressants, but I was convinced I just needed better habits and a little mental fortitude. I wanted the status of being a guy who solved his own problems, and like so many people, I was willing to sacrifice my relationships, my job, and my family for that status. But then I realized something: I pay my therapist because she's spent her life scouting around for ways to help people move to better places in life. So, I promised her I would try antidepressants and stay on them for at least a year.

Now, 6 months in, I wish I had been on these since I was 20. Getting through life is a thousand times easier. I can still write (or, I should say, I can actually write again), and it has improved my friendships and my relationship with my kids. So now, my big goal is to listen to the experts. Heck, maybe I'll even listen to my dad when he tells me to hire a plumber.

GETTING ALONG

A few months back, my daughter convinced me to get TikTok. At first, it was really fun. I had a profile called "AdvicewithDave" on which I gave silly recommendations, and I used a filter that made my head look giant. But then, after 3 weeks, I got into a flame war with people on some atheist TikTok page. Of course, such battles won't make me any friends, so I'm going to try to do two things differently. One: I'm going to try not to tell other people how to live their lives. Two: I'm going to mind my own business on the internet and not be a jerk. I deleted my (many) Reddit logins, and I deleted TikTok.

GETTING A MATE

I'm going to get a puppy.

IS THERE ONE BIG LESSON FROM THE PAST 200,000 YEARS?

This question brings us back to our opening example of the person we regard as a shining role model for a life well lived: Osceola McCarty. As we described in the Introduction, this remarkable woman dropped out of school in the seventh grade but took pleasure in her half century of working every day to clean and press other people's laundry. All the while, Osceola saved her pennies. Eventually, she spent her substantial life savings not on herself but on a fund dedicated to helping young African American women get a college education.

What is it about Osceola that makes her life a central lesson about how to live a meaningful and fulfilling life?

Before beginning this book, Doug asked a group of his respected colleagues for a few bits of wisdom he could pass on to his other son, Liam, then 10 years old. The sample included a number of people who had lived fulfilling lives: several prominent positive psychologists, a few authors of well-known books on human behavior, a couple of especially insightful clinical psychologists, a handful of pioneering researchers who have pondered human behavior in light of evolutionary biology, and several nonacademic friends whose personalities and sense of humor have had an inspiring and positive effect on those around them. He also asked a similar question of readers of his *Psychology Today* blog, and several were nice enough to pass on thoughtful advice from elders who'd grown up in places as scattered as Bulgaria, Ireland, New Zealand, and the rural American heartland.

The search netted more than 100 gems of sagacity, but the most frequently mentioned gem of wisdom was simply: "Be kind to others."

And as we were completing the final revisions on this book, we asked Sonja Lyubomirsky (a prominent positive psychologist) to nominate a finding or two from that field that has practical application to people's lives. Her first response was: "Do acts of kindness for others (for example, make someone else happier)." In support of this suggestion, she pointed to abundant research evidence, much of which she reviewed in her book *The How of Happiness*.

Sounds easy enough, but most of us could use a few specific tactics to really pull it off. David Myers, another prominent positive psychologist and a notoriously positive human being who wrote *The Pursuit of Happiness*, gave us one: "Spend more time asking people about themselves than talking about yourself." Myers noted that "every person is, in some way, your superior" and pointed out that by taking an interest in everyone you meet, you can learn a lot of things that can help you understand yourself. And besides taking a sincere interest in hearing what other people have to say about themselves, there are lots and lots of everyday kindnesses you can practice—like buying a coworker a cup of coffee and writing a thank-you note when someone does something nice for you.

There are a few obstacles to being nice, though. Other people aren't always nice to us. Some may exploit our niceness. Our self-serving cognitive biases lead us all to overvalue our own contributions and underestimate those of others. But there are ways around those obstacles.

To deal with the problem of exploitation, game theorists have come up with the *tit-for-tat strategy*, which works like this: If you and I have repeated interactions, I start out being nice, and I am always nice when you are nice. Given that people usually reciprocate kindness, that gets people trapped in a virtuous cycle. But what if the other person exploits me? If you are playing the tit-for-tat strategy, and the other person is nasty or uncooperative, you immediately reciprocate with an uncooperative response. That could, and often does, get people trapped in a vicious cycle of retaliation. But the critical trick with the tit-for-tat strategy is this: After showing that you won't suffer exploitation, you then switch back to being nice and repeat that until the other person understands the contingency: You be nice, and I will, too. Practiced in this way, the tit-for-tat strategy tends to promote prolonged cooperative relationships, which are a lot more rewarding than prolonged competitive hostilities.

To deal with the problem of self-serving biases, there is Linus Pauling's correction factor, which we mention in Chapter 7 but which bears repeating: "Do unto others twenty-five percent better than you expect them to do unto you. [Adding:] The twenty-five percent is for error."

It can be an especially useful tool to do nice unto others when you feel yourself hovering on the verge of being nasty. When a colleague with a proclivity for stirring up online controversy recently attacked Doug on Facebook, Doug was about to respond with a righteous defensive counterattack. But by instead taking a few deep breaths and then saying two (honest) positive things about this colleague and his work, the response was quite polite, and the imminent battle passed.

If we look at our modern-world selves through the long lens of human evolution, one thing is clear: Our selfish genes got us to this point in history not by encouraging us to be narrowly selfish in the economic rationalist's sense. Our ancestors survived because they cooperated with their groups, which allowed them to accomplish things that no scrawny naked hominin could ever have accomplished on their own in a world filled with lions, tigers, and rhinos. We are designed to cooperate, so go ahead: Let yourself be kind. It's not only natural, it is, in the longer perspective, completely rational.

POSTSCRIPT: TO-DO TOMORROW

Thinking about the infinite number of ways you could improve your life can be exhausting. All those possibilities could motivate you to take a nap or play a video game. But there's a lot of research suggesting that setting small, immediately achievable goals is a better way to motivate yourself. So, here's our attempt to do just that, using the ancestral to-do list as a guide to the immediate future.

TOMORROW'S TO-DO LIST (DOUG)

- *Survive.* Go to the supermarket (on my bike), purchase blueberries; raspberries; strawberries; swiss chard; garlic; plain, unsweetened yogurt; seltzer; tofu; eggplant; a single bar of 90% chocolate (to be doled out in small chunks over the next week as rewards for daily bouts of aerobic exercise).
- *Protect myself from the bad guys.* Skip all the daily news headlines, unsubscribe from any political group that sends me a scary message.
- *Get along.* Write a blog post for *Psychology Today* plugging an interesting research finding from one of the colleagues on my team.

- *Get ahead.* Spend an extra hour at the end of the day helping one of my students revise a paper for publication.
- *Find a mate.* I already have a mate. So: Make a note about one of the things that initially attracted me to my wife and skip to the next category.
- *Keep my mate.* Hug my wife 10 times over the course of the day. Give her my note about what attracted me to her.
- *Care for family members.* Make dinner, invite Dave and his kids. Don't turn Dave in to the FBI (unless he really deserves it).

TOMORROW'S TO-DO LIST (DAVE)

- *Survive.* Oops. I've gained 20 pounds in quarantine. I guess it's time to go off carbs, so I can be ready for the rock gym and keep up with my old man on our next hike in the mountains.
- *Protect myself from the bad guys.* I really need to avoid arguing with people on Reddit. I'll stay completely off social media for the whole day. I'll also try to be friendly to a person with different political views from mine.
- *Get along.* I'll send a text to my cousins. I'll also invite one person to work on a project together.
- *Get ahead.* I really just need to focus on the three simple tasks I promised my boss I would have done by Monday. If I complete those, I can work on big, lofty goals.
- *Find a mate.* So, for me, I think it's important to date carefully. Shortly after I got divorced, I pursued a bunch of online relationships that were all incredibly unstable and not the best thing for my kids. One thing that I've come to terms with is that I'm not going to ever be the cool, tough, bad boy. I'm back to volunteering with people with special needs, and I'm getting a puppy. In the past, my best relationships have all started in real life. And if I don't end up finding someone, oh, well—at least I'll have a puppy.

- *Keep a mate.* Um . . . I don't think this one is applicable. If I end up meeting someone tomorrow, I guess I'll offer to help her with the dishes or something.
- *Care for family members.* I'm going to try to get my kids to play ping-pong together. It's a silly little thing, but it seems fun.

TOMORROW'S TO-DO LIST (YOU)

- *Survive.* _____
- *Protect myself from the bad guys.* _____
- *Get along.* _____
- *Get ahead.* _____
- *Find a mate.* _____
- *Keep a mate.* _____
- *Care for family members.* _____

NOTES

INTRODUCTION: EVOLUTIONARY PSYCHOLOGY AS A GUIDE TO SELF-ACTUALIZATION

Research showing negative consequences of seeking happiness was presented in Gruber et al. (2011) and Mauss et al. (2011).

EVOLUTIONARY POSITIVE PSYCHOLOGY AND THE SEVEN FUNDAMENTAL MOTIVES

Discussions of the advances made in the understanding of human nature from an evolutionary perspective can be found in Doug's book *Sex, Murder, and the Meaning of Life: A Psychologist Investigates How Evolution, Cognition, and Complexity Are Revolutionizing Our View of Human Nature* (Kenrick, 2011) and in Steven Pinker's (2002) book, *The Blank Slate: The Modern Denial of Human Nature*. For a more detailed look at some of the research and theory generated by this perspective, see the collections of articles edited by Charles Crawford and Dennis Krebs (2008), Robin Dunbar and Louise Barrett (2007), or David Buss (D. M. Buss, 2015, 2016).

The revised pyramid of human motives (see Figure 1) was first presented in a paper by Kenrick et al. (2010).

Maslow's hierarchy was presented in his classic 1943 paper in *Psychological Review*. His research on self-actualized people was described in his 1954 book *Motivation and Personality*.

For some of the many developments in modern positive psychology, see Lyubomirsky et al. (2005); Myers (2000), Seligman et al. (2005), Allen (2018), and Geher and Wedberg (2020). Sonja Lyubomirsky's (2007) *The How of Happiness: A Scientific Approach to Getting the Life You Want* is rich with research-based suggestions to improve your well-being. Lani Shiota and her colleagues (2014, 2017) have extended the modular approach to distinguishing several distinct positive emotions.

THE CLASSIC PYRAMID GETS AN UPDATE

The research connecting self-actualization to status and affiliation motives, as well as between parenting and meaning in life, was described in Krems et al. (2017).

For a broad discussion of human life history, see Del Giudice et al. (2016).

For an interesting and generally less known history of how organizational psychologists developed the famous pyramid from Maslow's original hierarchy, see Bridgman et al. (2019).

THE NATURALISTIC FALLACY: OSCEOLA McCARTY VERSUS GENGHIS KHAN

For Osceola McCarty's story, see Bragg (1995) or Zinsmeister (n.d.). The quote "I loved the work . . ." came from Zinsmeister (n.d., para. 7). The quote "People tell me now that I am a hero . . ." came from McCarty (1996, p. 48).

CHAPTER 1. MODERN PROBLEMS MEET ANCIENT HUMAN MOTIVES

ANCESTRAL PROBLEMS

Some of the research examining fundamental motives in different countries around the world was described in Ko et al. (2020). As noted in the Introduction, Maslow's hierarchy was presented in his 1943 paper in *Psychological Review*. The revised pyramid is described in Kenrick et al. (2010).

2. *Protect yourself from attackers and plunderers.* Evidence of high homicide rates in traditional societies is presented in numerous anthropological reports (e.g., Chagnon, 1968; Hill et al., 2007). Reviewing data across 13 different hunter–gatherer societies, Gurven and Kaplan (2007) found that 12.5% had died violent deaths either from homicide (6.3%) or war (5.2%).

3. *Make and keep friends.* Kim Hill and Magdalena Hurtado described their research with the Aché in their 1996 book, *Aché Life History: The Ecology and Demography of a Foraging People.*

4. *Get some respect.* The relative sex differences in reproductive payoffs associated with status were reviewed in Sadalla et al. (1987) and M. Wilson and Daly (1985).

5. *Find a mate.* The evolutionary arguments for sex differences in mate selection criteria were reviewed by Trivers (1972). Data supporting Trivers's theory have been presented in numerous research papers, including Kenrick et al. (1990).

6. *Hang on to that mate.* The evidence regarding the advantages of having two parents for human survival in traditional societies was reviewed by Geary (2000). Flinn et al. (2007) present a

good review of the evolution of the human family. The evidence for love across the range of human societies is reviewed by Jankowiak and Fischer (1992).

7. *Care for your family members.* Evidence that parents alone do not produce enough calories to support children was reviewed in Hill and Hurtado (2009). Evidence of the importance of grandparents was presented in Gibson and Mace (2005) and Hawkes et al. (1997), and additional evidence is reviewed by Hrdy (2007).

MODERN PROBLEMS

1. *Survive.* For changing death rates linked to obesity versus starvation, see World Health Organization (2021). For obesity rates in European women and men, see World Health Organization (n.d.). For American rates, see Centers for Disease Control and Prevention (n.d.-a). For a discussion of the mismatch between our evolved hunger mechanisms and the modern environment, see Pinel et al. (2000). See Saad (2014) for data on the number of hours worked by the average American; the estimates of foragers are based on Sackett (1996; see also Dyble et al., 2019, who compared a group of traditional Filipinos, some of whom were engaged in agriculture and others who were still living a preagricultural lifestyle). For discussions of the various implications of evolutionary mismatch, see D. M. Buss (2000), Maner and Kenrick (2010), Nesse and Berridge (1997), or Li et al. (2018).

2. *Protect yourself from the bad guys.* For a comparison of modern and past homicide rates, see Pinker (2011). For the analysis of interest in bad news, see Rosentiel (2007).

3. *Make and keep friends.* For a discussion of the number of people living alone, see Byron (2019), or check out the United States Census Bureau (2000). Florida (2019) discussed the number of people who were born in, versus migrated to, different states. Country of birth data for Sydney can be found in .id (n.d.). For an analysis of the historical trends in people's membership in social groups, see Putnam (2000). Holt-Lunstad (2017) and Holt-Lunstad et al. (2015) presented the arguments for an epidemic of loneliness. Jean Twenge and her colleagues tracked the effects of decreases in face-to-face contact among adolescents (e.g., Twenge & Campbell, 2019).

4. *Get some respect.* The discussion of wealth inequality in hunter–gatherers is based on Smith et al. (2010). For one discussion of economic inequality in the modern United States, see Horowitz et al. (2020). For a discussion of American household debt, see H. Johnson (2020). Dittmar et al. (2014) reviewed the links between materialism and diminished well-being. The harmful effects of inequality are discussed in Daly (2017). Deaths of despair are discussed in A. Case and Deaton (2020).

5. *Find a mate.* For a discussion of decreased dating in modern adolescents, see Twenge and Park (2019). For a discussion of similar trends in other countries, see Ortiz-Ospina and Roser (2020).

6. *Hang on to that mate.* Swanson (2015) discussed trends in divorce in the United States based on data from Olson (2015). Amato and James (2010) discussed increasing divorce rates in Europe and findings that poverty are associated with divorce in both Europe and the United States.

7. *Care for my family members.* For a discussion of the percentage of children being cared for by nonrelatives, see Laughlin (2013). The estimate of 37 minutes of quality time came from a study

of 2,000 U.S. parents commissioned by Visit Anaheim (and was widely advertised to imply that the amount of family time would increase if the family decided to visit Disneyland, bypassing discussion of whether standing in long lines would constitute "quality time"; Visit Anaheim, 2018). The comparisons of different countries in this regard came from Henry and Bartos (2018) and Porter (2018).

CHAPTER 2. THE PSYCHOLOGY OF BASIC SURVIVAL

The story of Helen Klaben is told in her book *Hey, I'm Alive!* (Klaben & Day, 1963) and in Sandomir (2018).

The story of Walter Hudson can be found in Plummer (1987).

WHAT KILLED WALTER HUDSON AND ELVIS PRESLEY IS MOST LIKELY GOING TO KILL YOU, TOO

Annual statistics for deaths from various causes can be found by searching for "leading causes of death" on the Centers for Disease Control and Prevention's National Center for Health Statistics website (see https://www.cdc.gov/nchs/).

WHY DON'T WE PANIC AT THE SIGHT OF CHEESESTEAKS?

See Marks (1969) for a description of his work and the related work of G. Stanley Hall (1897). For further discussion of our bias to learn certain fears and not others, see Öhman and Mineka (2003) and Marks and Nesse (1994).

The "intensity of many fears, especially in youth" quote came from Hall (1897, pp. 246–247).

WHAT KILLED OUR ANCESTORS?

The article in *The New England Journal of Medicine* comparing causes of death in 1910 and 2010 is by D. S. Jones et al. (2012).

The statistics on COVID-19 and the 1918 flu pandemic are from the National Center for Immunization and Respiratory Diseases (n.d.) and *The New York Times* (2021), respectively.

The data from archaeological sites are discussed by Acsádi and Nemeskéri (1970) and by S. H. Preston (1995).

The research on deaths in Hiwi hunter–gatherers came from Hill et al. (2007), and the data on Aka deaths are from Hewlett et al. (1986).

A review of causes of death in several hunter–gatherer groups can be found in Gurven and Kaplan (2007).

The statistics on deaths from snakebites came from "Epidemiology of Snakebites" (2021).

The gripping account of the man-eating Siberian tiger is found in Vaillant (2010).

A review of the evidence on cooking food and survival can be found in Wrangham (2009).

The program Michelle Obama launched as First Lady is described in Obama (2018).

OUR POWERFUL APPETITES OPEN THE DOOR FOR MODERN PARASITES

For a discussion of the nutritional content of food in school vending machines, see Rovner et al. (2011). See Pinel et al. (2000) for a good treatment of the mismatch between our evolved hunger mechanisms and the modern culinary environment.

IS THERE ANY WAY TO ESCAPE THE TRAP OF IMMEDIATE GRATIFICATION?

The quote "later prove to be unpleasant or lethal" from Platt's (1973) article on the concept of social traps is on page 641.

The study of how groups of friends and family increase success at weight-loss programs was reported by Wing and Jeffery (1999).

The study of stimulus control and stale popcorn is described in Wansink and Kim (2005).

SUICIDE: WHY YOU DON'T WANT TO DIE

Statistics on suicide prevalence can be found on the National Institute of Mental Health (n.d.) *Suicide* webpage.

Freud proposed the death instinct in his book *Beyond the Pleasure Principle* (Freud, 1915/2015).

D. M. Buss (2018) laid out his reasoning about the evolutionary advantages of remaining undead at the Zombie Apocalypse Medicine Meeting (which included a number of talks, such as D. M. Buss's, that were more serious than the title might imply).

Denys deCatanzaro's evolutionary analysis of suicide was presented in his 1980 article.

A discussion of the risk factors for suicide can be found at Centers for Disease Control and Prevention (n.d.-b).

For a discussion of the sex differences in suicide attempts, see Schumacher (2019).

FEAR OF FALLING AND THE LACK THEREOF

The statistics on climbing deaths in the United States and Canada are compiled annually by the American Alpine Club (see Caroom, 2020).

See "Free Solo Climbing" (2021) in *Wikipedia* for a list of well-known free climbers.

The research on testosterone and risky behavior among skateboarders was described in Ronay and von Hippel (2010).

The story of Petit's tightrope walk between New York's Twin Towers is told in the documentary film *Man on Wire* (Marsh, 2008).

CHAPTER 3. AVOIDING BULLIES, BARBARIANS, AND MICROPLUNDERERS

The story about Hill and Kaplan's visit to the Yora was a personal communication (March 14, 2021) from Kim Hill, who is a professor of anthropology at Arizona State University.

The recent book exploring Fawcett's disappearance is Grann (2010). The quote from Sydney Possuelo came from Vardi (2020).

Samantha Power's story came from her 2019 memoir, *The Education of an Idealist.*

THE BAD GUYS IN THE GOOD OLD DAYS

See Weatherford (2004) for a detailed history of Genghis Khan's life. Strong (2019) described the long history of violence in British history.

Chagnon (1968) contains the original description of the Yąnomamö tribe. Pospisil's (1963) description of the Kapauku Papuans and Hoebel's (1960) description of the Cheyenne are part of the same classic series of anthropological ethnographies as Chagnon's (1968) book.

Elizabeth Marshall Thomas's description of the Kalahari !Kung San was originally published in 1959. Richard Borshay Lee's account was published 2 decades later, in 1979.

VIOLENT INCLINATIONS IN THE MODERN WORLD

For a discussion of the original research on homicidal fantasies, see Kenrick and Sheets (1993). For a discussion of the replication revealing even higher numbers, see D. M. Buss and Duntley (2006).

Ramirez (1993) compared the justifications for homicide in Spain, Finland, and Poland, and found that "self-defense" and "protecting others" topped the list in all of these countries. In comparing moral judgments about violent acts across eight small-scale societies, Clark Barrett and his colleagues (2016) found that self-defense was one of the few factors that counted as a mitigating factor universally.

Misha Glenny (2008) detailed the extensiveness of organized crime in the modern world. Glenny's quote about the expansion of organized crime is from his TED Talk on global crime networks (TED, 2009, 00:50).

Pinker (2011) contains extensive data comparing homicide rates in the modern world with those in earlier historical periods and in non-European groups.

Wrangham's arguments about male intergroup aggression in humans and other primates are summarized in Wrangham and Peterson (1996).

Our conversation with Kim Hill was on March 14, 2021 (personal communication).

THE PSYCHOLOGICAL LEGACY OF OUR VIOLENT PAST

The research demonstrating people's proclivity to recognize anger more quickly in a man's face was described in Becker et al. (2007).

The research on fear conditioning and race was presented in Olsson et al. (2005) and in Phelps et al. (2000).

The research on ovulation effects on perceptions of men's sexual coerciveness was reported by Garver-Apgar et al. (2007). Melissa McDonald, Carlos Navarrete, and Jim Sidanius (2011) provided an overview of several lines of research on different threats by outgroup members toward men and women (see also McDonald et al., 2012).

The research indicating that people pay more attention to team alliance than to race was described in Kurzban et al. (2001).

NEW BAD GUYS IN THE 21ST CENTURY: *HOMO PREDATORIUS* AND *HOMO PARASITARIIS*

The definition of *predator* is from Merriam-Webster (n.d.).

The quote about parasites consuming their prey in units less than one can be found in E. O. Wilson (2014, p. 112).

An important qualification is in order here: Historically, the words "predator" and "parasite" have been applied to human beings to promote harmful stereotypes. Applying such terms to whole groups can contribute to dehumanization, a serious problem that only exaggerates threats between the members of different groups, as we discuss later in the chapter. It can be useful to think about how particular types of actions or communications from other people can exploit our fundamental motives to induce us to act in ways that do not help us achieve the goals those motives were designed to achieve. However, applying the term "parasite" to other individuals, or groups of individuals, can be used to justify harmful and dangerous intergroup behaviors, and transform us from unwitting victims into self-righteous bad guys.

SIX-GUNS VERSUS FOUNTAIN PENS

James B. Stewart's detailing of the financial dishonesty on Wall Street can be found in his 1992 book, *Den of Thieves*.

THE MICROPLUNDERERS

The implications of excessive fees on economic inequality were detailed by Fergus (2018).

The *Consumer Reports* survey of hidden fees was described by Wang (2019).

For a discussion of the "pink tax," see Bessendorf (2015) and Hoffman (2021).

SELF-PROTECTION MASTER LEVEL: FEAR THYSELF

For examples of research suggesting that people reciprocate both hostility and cooperativeness, see A. H. Buss (1963), Komorita et al. (1991), and Sheldon (1999).

THE AVENGERS

The classic research on drivers' self-serving attributions was conducted by Svenson (1981) and C. E. Preston and Harris (1965). Williams and Gilovich (2008) reviewed some of the research on self-serving biases and also presented evidence that people are not just trying to put on a good face but are actually willing to bet money that they are better than average.

Kteily's thought-provoking research on dehumanization was presented in Kteily et al. (2014, 2015).

The research demonstrating that dehumanization could be reduced by learning that members of another group experienced the same emotions as oneself is reported in McDonald et al. (2017).

BOTTOM LINES: SUGGESTIONS FOR AVOIDING BULLIES AND MICROPLUNDERERS

The research on how people present themselves to minimize the extent to which other people perceive them as threats was reported in Neel et al. (2013).

CHAPTER 4. GETTING ALONG

The biographical information about Daniel Kahneman and Amos Tversky came from Lewis (2017). The quote "he had no friends" is from Lewis (2017, p. 57). Shamir's quote about Kahneman's outsider status is from Lewis (2017, p. 63).

ROLLING WITH THE HOMIES IN OLD-STYLE HOOD

The description of adolescent social relationships among the Maisin came from Tietjen (1994).

The data on food sharing among the Aché were reported in Gurven et al. (2000) and in Allen-Arave et al. (2008).

Sugiyama (2004) described the data suggesting that the Shiwiar experience illnesses and injuries that would be fatal without social support.

Von Hippel (2018) reviewed some of the work suggesting a central role for group hunting in human evolution.

The data on infant survival and baboon friendships were presented in Silk et al. (2003).

For a discussion of human calorie production over the lifespan, see Kaplan et al. (2009).

Boyd's observations came from a personal communication (February 11, 2019) to Doug's class.

The story of the Arctic explorer John Rae can be found in McGoogan (2001).

Hruschka (2010) contains a wealth of information about friendship across cultures, such as the description of the friendships (*lopai*) among the Turkana.

For evidence that humans began trading more than 100,000 years before the advent of agriculture, see Brooks et al. (2018).

KAHNEMAN'S NOBEL PRIZE–WINNING FRIENDSHIP

Besides Lewis's (2017) book, Kahneman (2011) also provided some of the details about his friendship with Amos Tversky.

Kahneman and Tversky's finding that "even statisticians are not very good intuitive statisticians" is from Kahneman (2011, p. 5). Kahneman's realization that he enjoyed working with Tversky is from Kahneman (2011, pp. 5–6).

The opening quote from Kahneman's acceptance speech can be heard on The Nobel Prize website (The Nobel Prize, 2002, 00:24).

FRIENDSHIPS IN THE MODERN WORLD

For some of the diverse findings on virtual versus real contact with friends, see Kraut et al. (1998), Kross et al. (2013), Deters and Mehl (2013), Steinfield et al. (2008), and Twenge (2017).

For a discussion of decreasing social participation in the last century, see Putnam (2000).

SOME FEATURES OF FRIENDSHIP THAT TRAVELED OVER THE CENTURIES

There is half a century of research demonstrating liking for other people who are similar to us in attitudes, habits, physical characteristics, group memberships, and even musical preferences (e.g., Boer et al., 2011; Byrne, 1971; Hilmert et al., 2006).

Park and Schaller (2005) conducted the research suggesting that people infer kinship from similarity.

Some of the research suggesting that people like and trust facial photographs that have been morphed with their own picture was reported in DeBruine (2002, 2004).

The research suggesting that people would likely vote for an unfamiliar candidate if that person's face were morphed with theirs was conducted by Bailenson et al. (2008).

See J. T. Jones et al. (2004) for research suggesting that we prefer people whose names have similar letters to ours.

The research suggesting that attitude similarity overrides racial differences was done by Byrne and Wong (1962). See Chen and Kenrick (2002) for research finding that sharing similar attitudes counts for more if people initially expect to disagree with one another.

The study of friendship formation in MIT dormitories was reported by Festinger et al. (1950). The research on seating arrangement and friendship in police academy students was conducted by Segal (1974).

Dan Hruschka (2010) described his sample of 60 societies from around the world.

The study in which students were asked about meaning in life, self-actualization, and well-being was reported by Krems et al. (2017).

See Dunbar (2018) for his discussion of the health effects of friendships. His quote about the influence of friendship on "health, well-being, and happiness" is on page 32 in Dunbar (2018).

FRIENDSHIP STYLES: HIS, HERS, AND THEIRS

In his own work, such as Thaler (2015), Nobel Prize–winning Richard Thaler often warmly referred to Kahneman.

See McWilliams and Howard (1993) and David-Barrett et al. (2015) regarding sex differences in friendship styles.

See Taylor (2006) for a review of research related to the "tend and befriend" hypothesis.

The research on patterns of friendship jealousy is reported in Krems et al. (2021).

The research on friendships in gay, lesbian, heterosexual, and bisexual men and women can be found in Gillespie et al. (2015).

Make Yourself Useful

Tooby and Cosmides (1996) discussed the benefits of friendship from an evolutionary perspective.

Examples of papers with Doug's friends Rich Keefe and Ed Sadalla are Kenrick and Keefe (1992), Kenrick et al. (1990), and Sadalla et al. (1987).

Focus on Real Commonalities

The information about Michelle Obama's friendship with Santita Jackson came from Obama's 2018 memoir, *Becoming*.

Frederick Douglass's friendships are described in detail in Blight's (2018) Pulitzer Prize–winning biography.

Rosenbaum (1986) reported findings suggesting that the repulsion power of attitudinal disagreement is stronger than the attraction power of agreement.

The latest edition of our social psychology text with Steve Neuberg is Kenrick et al. (2020).

Beware of Fast but False Friends

Bob Cialdini's analysis of the social psychology of persuasion heuristics can be found in Cialdini (2021).

D. T. Regan (1971) described the research on the effects of buying a Coke on later compliance. For findings on mimicry and liking, see Chartrand and Bargh (1999) and van Baaren et al. (2003).

Give Your Friends the Credit and Gratitude They Deserve

Ackerman et al. (2007) described the study in which students were asked to recruit either a close friend or a family member.

The study of tip size and thank-you notes was conducted by Rind and Bordia (1995).

McCullough et al. (2008) discussed the multiple benefits of gratitude.

Ohtsubo et al. (2014) discussed the importance of paying attention in friendships.

CHAPTER 5. GETTING AHEAD

The latest edition of his influence book is Cialdini (2021). Both of these stories are from a personal communication to Doug Kenrick (R. B. Cialdini, February 15, 2019).

The book that refers to Cialdini as the "guru of social influence" (p. 67) is Thaler and Sunstein (2008).

GETTING AHEAD IN THE YEARS BEHIND

The !Kung San were described by Marshall (1958) and Lee (1979).

Von Rueden and Van Vugt (2015) provided an overview of research on leadership in small-scale societies and comparing it with leadership in modern societies.

GETTING BEHIND IN THE YEARS AHEAD

Douglas McMillon was Walmart's CEO in 2019 with the staggering annual income. His base salary was $1,276,892, but he earned another $22 million in stock awards, incentives, pension increases, and various other forms of compensation, such as use of the company's aircraft for his own personal travel. For a comparison of McMillon's salary with that of a typical employee, see Myerson (2019). For the comparison of salaries across 350 other companies, see Mishel and Kandra (2020).

For statistics on changes in unemployment at the onset of the coronavirus pandemic, see Bennett (2021), Congressional Research Service (2021), and Michigan Coronavirus Racial Disparities Task Force (2020) interim report.

The different occupational groupings came from the U.S. Bureau of Labor Statistics (2018).

The gender breakdown of government leaders in the United States and Sweden is reported by the Rutgers Eagleton Institute of Politics (Center for American Women and Politics, n.d.).

CHOOSING THE RIGHT CAREER: FOLLOW YOUR DREAM?

Cialdini's career advice came from a personal communication to the authors on February 15, 2019.

For a discussion of the odds of high school athletes in different sports making it into professional sports, see Manfred (2012).

See Menyes (2014) for a discussion of the odds of making it in the music industry.

Finding Out Which Day Jobs Are in Demand

The ratings of "best jobs" are from Koenig (2018).

Matching Your Personality to Your Chosen Occupation

See Holland (1992) for an in-depth review of the evidence that contributed to his theory of occupational choice.

Hogan (2007) is an excellent review of the evidence regarding the connections between personality and behavior in organizations.

Showing Up

The quote from Angela Duckworth is from Duckworth (2016, p. 34). The Ben Hogan quote is from Carville and Begala (2002, p. 118). For the Edison quote, see Oxford Reference (n.d., quote 3).

GETTING BY VERSUS GETTING IN THE GROOVE

A discussion of the research linking happiness and poverty can be found in Diener (2000).

Research suggesting that men gain most in attractiveness in going from poverty to middle incomes came from Kenrick et al. (2001).

The meta-analysis of the links between job satisfaction and job performance was done by Judge et al. (2002).

Brown and Peterson (1993) conducted the analysis of job effort and job satisfaction in salespeople.

EMBRACING FAILURE

For the Edison quote, which, though often cited, may be a slight improvement on his exact words, see Oxford Reference (n.d., quote 4).

Souder (2004) detailed the financial ups and downs of John James Audubon's life.

For information on Stacey Abrams, see Hakim et al. (2020) and Rothberg (2021).

PACING YOURSELF

Goodwin (2018) discussed the details of the sometimes extreme disappointments and successes of Abraham Lincoln and Teddy Roosevelt.

Simon's notion of "satisficing" derives from his theory of *bounded rationality,* which presumes that decisions must be constrained by trade-offs based on the limits of human cognitive capacity and the time and effort required to make a satisfactory decision (Gigerenzer & Goldstein, 1996; Simon, 1956).

Ericsson's work on deliberate practice and expertise was summarized in Ericsson and Charness (1994) and Ericsson and Ward (2007).

ROBOPARASITES IN THE WORKPLACE

The "some workers work indoors" quote is from Scarry (1968, p. 4). The study of British workers' daily work habits was reported in *How Many Productive Hours in a Work Day? Just 2 Hours, 23 Minutes . . .* (Vouchercloud, n.d.). The statistics for American workers came from Robert Half (2017).

Research on cell-phone addiction and its impact on grades can be found in Lepp et al. (2014) and J. A. Roberts et al. (2014).

The American Academy of Pediatrics recommendation about limiting screen time for children is from Ghose (2013). See also Pappas (2020).

According to Forbes Quotes, Andrew Carnegie said:

> The average person puts only 25% of his energy and ability into his work. The world takes off its hat to those who put in more than 50% of their capacity, and stands on its head for those few and far between souls who devote 100%. (Forbes Quotes, n.d., top of page).

BEING A TEAM PLAYER

Simonton (1994) reviewed evidence about the various factors that contribute to success, including working with others who are themselves successful. The 10 rules for winning a Nobel Prize came from

R. J. Roberts (2015). The statistics on the impact of papers written by teams came from Wuchty et al. (2007).

The classic study involving the economic game in which economics students had to choose to compete or cooperate is described in Frank et al. (1993).

DRIVING FOR DOMINANCE VERSUS WINNING PRESTIGE

Hogan began to study the influence of personality traits on job performance; he reported the findings in his book *Personality and the Fate of Organizations* (Hogan, 2007). The quotation is from Cramer (2005, para. 13).

The discussion of the "Dark Triad" of narcissism, Machiavellianism, and psychopathy is in Paulhus (2014). The quotation describing narcissists is on page 421.

COERCION VERSUS EXPERTISE

The two paths to status in human groups were described by Joe Henrich and Francisco Gil-White (2001) and Joey Cheng et al. (2013).

The findings on dominance-oriented group leaders came from Charleen Case and Jon Maner (2014).

Leaders' losing their grip on leadership—and their prioritization of their own power—was described by Maner and Nicole Mead (2010).

Wrangham talks about continual intergroup warfare in human groups in Wrangham and Peterson (1996).

CHAPTER 6. FINDING TRUE LOVE

For the story of Giovanni Vigliotto and Sharon Clark, see Fitzpatrick (1991), Neuhaus (1982), and Walsh (1983).

ANCESTRAL ROMANCE

Marlowe (2004) described mate choice among the Hadza of Tanzania.

E. M. Thomas (1959) described her observations of nomadic Kalahari Bushmen.

Chagnon (1968) discussed polygyny among the Yạnomamö.

An account of the maharajah with 365 wives can be found in Collins and Lapierre (1975).

See Pospisil (1963) for his ethnography of the Kapauku Papuans.

Pilling and Hart (1960) is the classic ethnography of the Tiwi society of North Australia.

MATE SELECTION IN OTHER SPECIES

Trivers (1972) is the classic analysis of the links between parental investment and sexual selection. Gould and Gould (1989) provided an excellent overview of the comparative evidence for the theory of sexual selection.

Muller et al. (2006) described chimpanzee male preference for older females.

See Euler (2011), Gibson and Mace (2005), and Hawkes and Coxworth (2013) for evidence about the importance of grandparents in human evolution and see Geary (2000) for a review of evidence for the importance of fathers to human survival and reproduction.

See Hill et al. (2011) and Hrdy (2007) for reviews of evidence that humans are a group breeding species. Hill's suggestion that humans are like "cooperative breeders" is in Hill et al. (2011, p. 1286).

MODERN LOVE

Rosenfeld et al. (2019) described the big changes in how people met their spouses between 1940 and 2020.

Goetz et al. (2019) described the various mismatches involved in modern mating.

The research on minimal intelligence required for dates, sexual partners, and marriage partners was reported in Kenrick et al. (1990, 1993).

The comparison of interracial marriages in Honolulu and other cities can be found in Livingston (2017). For a discussion of the importance of status in men's attracting mates in modern societies, see Townsend and Levy (1990) and Li et al. (2002).

Norm Li's research on mating budgets was reported in Li et al. (2002) and in Li and Kenrick (2006).

The research on income and attractiveness was reported in Kenrick et al. (2001).

The research on age preferences across societies was reported in Kenrick and Keefe (1992). The data on prostitute age and income were reported in Sohn (2016). The data from OKCupid are reported by Rudder (2014).

Gottschall et al. (2004) reported the analysis of romantic themes in 658 folktales from traditional societies.

D. Jones and Hill (1993) reported the analysis of facial attractiveness across five different cultures.

SEX, ATTRACTION, AND REPRODUCTION

The social lives of bonobos were discussed by De Waal and Lanting (1997).

Vasey and VanderLaan (2009) reported on their studies of Samoan *fa'afafine*. Bailey et al. (1994) reported data on similarities and differences between heterosexual and homosexual mate choice. Kenrick et al. (1995) reported on age preferences in people with different sexual orientations.

SHOPPING ON THE MATING MARKET: A FEW CONSUMER TIPS

Theory and research on the "paradox of choice" were reviewed by Schwartz (2004).

Research on arranged marriages was reported by Gupta and Singh (1982), Epstein et al. (2013), and P. C. Regan et al. (2012).

The data about people lying about themselves on dating sites came from Anderson et al. (2020).

FINDING MR. RIGHT

For a discussion of statistics on marriage and cohabitation, see Horowitz et al. (2019).

For links between personality traits and relationship stability, see Kelly and Conley (1987), Caughlin et al. (2000), and McNulty (2013).

For the links between dorm rooms and personality characteristics, see Gosling et al. (2002).

For the research on the effects of saying, "I love you," see Ackerman et al. (2011).

For links between mating strategies and automobile choices, see Sundie et al. (2011).

FINDING MR. RIGHT NOW

For evidence that divorce may be linked to heritable personality traits such as neuroticism and conscientiousness, see Jocklin et al. (1996). Of course, it is important not to infer that there is some gene or set of genes that inevitably determines divorce. Genetic tendencies always interact with the environment. For example, if you inherit genes that incline you to be tall, you have a built-in advantage on the basketball court, but as the two authors of this book can attest, that alone isn't going to lead you to be a good basketball player if you don't have other critical life experiences.

FINDING MR. EVERY-OTHER-WEEKEND

The research suggesting that ovulation biases women's perceptions of cads as good dads was reported in Durante et al. (2012).

Some of the research related to the dual-mating strategy hypothesis was presented in Pillsworth and Haselton (2006), and the larger body of literature on this topic, which has been controversial, was reviewed in a meta-analysis by Gildersleeve et al. (2014).

FINDING A GOOD WIFE

Research indicating that women looking for a mate show off their kindness and cooperativeness was presented in Griskevicius et al. (2007).

The evidence on changing dress styles across the ovulatory cycle was presented by Durante et al. (2008).

FINDING A GOOD TIME

The OKCupid question predicting whether a woman would have sex on the first date came from Rudder (2014). The links between unrestricted mating orientation and marijuana use were reported by Kurzban et al. (2010).

DON'T PROJECT

The research finding that men project their own sexual feelings onto attractive women was reported by Maner et al. (2005). The original research on sexual overperception by men was conducted by Antonia Abbey (1982).

MARKETING YOURSELF

The research demonstrating college men and women's responses to a stranger's overtures was reported by Clark and Hatfield (1989).

Cunningham (1989) described his research on different types of opening lines.

The research on the way men's and women's friends help them in dating contexts was reported in Ackerman and Kenrick (2009).

The research examining how men versus women show off their kindness, creativity, and willingness to spend conspicuously was reported in Griskevicius, Cialdini, and Kenrick (2006); Griskevicius et al. (2007); Griskevicius, Goldstein, et al. (2006); and Sundie et al. (2011).

The research on sex ratios and mating strategies was reported in Guttentag and Secord (1983) and Griskevicius et al. (2012).

Norm Li's suggestion about searching for appropriate sex ratios came from a personal communication (May 16, 2018) to Doug Kenrick.

The research on status and physical attractiveness was reported in Townsend and Levy (1990).

The research suggesting that being nice counts for more than social dominance was reported in Jensen-Campbell et al. (1995). See also Green and Kenrick (1994).

TWO OTHER OPTIONS: SIMPLY BEING YOURSELF AND SIMPLY BEING ALONE

For world population statistics over time, see Worldometer (n.d.).

For a perspective on the advantages of remaining single, see DePaulo and Morris (2005).

CHAPTER 7: HOW DO FOOLS STAY IN LOVE?

The classic biography of Madame Curie was written by her daughter Eve Curie (1938). The quote "ruled love and marriage out of her life's program" is from page 199 in that biography. The block quote is from page 279 of that book.

STAYING TOGETHER FOR THE FIRST FEW MILLION YEARS

Opie et al. (2013) reviewed the literature on the relative rarity of monogamy in mammals compared with birds.

Marriage patterns among the Aché foragers were described in Hill and Hurtado (1996). Mating arrangements among the !Kung San were described in Lee (1979) and Marshall (1958). Tiwi marriage patterns were described by Pilling and Hart (1960). Marital relationships among the Yąnomamö were discussed by Chagnon (1968).

STAYING TOGETHER IN THE MODERN WORLD

Swanson (2015) presented a graphic overview of 144 years of marriage and divorce in the United States.

Reviews of findings on partner abuse can be found in Archer (2000) and Hamel (2012).

The study of relationship happiness in 2,084 American adults can be found at eHarmony (2018).

For research on the benefits of marriage, see Diener (2000), Kaprio et al. (1987), Kiecolt-Glaser and Newton (2001), and Myers (2000).

See Geary (2000) for a review of evidence on the benefits of paternal investment.

Research on nonmonogamous relationships was reported by Haupert et al. (2017) and Conley et al. (2017).

SELFISH NARCISSISM IN RELATIONSHIPS: SERVE YOURSELF?

Finkel (2017) presented his case for self-fulfillment in and outside marriage.

Hicks and Leitenberg (2001) presented data on sexual fantasies about people other than one's current partner.

DON'T TRUST YOUR OWN JUDGMENT

The statistics on numbers of people finding infidelity wrong were reported by Fincham and May (2017).

An example suggesting that people are willing to forgive themselves for the same behaviors that they condemn in others is from Valdesolo and DeSteno (2008). For a review of evidence on this topic, see DeSteno and Valdesolo (2011).

Gottman's arguments about extramarital affairs not being about sex are from Gottman and Silver (1999), and the quote is from page 16 in that work. The data suggesting that affairs are a cause—rather than an effect—of marital unhappiness came from Previti and Amato (2003).

The experiment examining sexual arousal and attitudes about the use of force to have sex was conducted by Ariely and Loewenstein (2006).

The study of Stanford students' biased processing of new evidence was done by Lord et al. (1979).

The study of biased estimations of housework was conducted by Ross and Sicoly (1979).

The study of newlyweds' perceptions of one another's personalities was conducted by Watson and Humrichouse (2006).

The research suggesting a self-perpetuating cycle of forgiveness in relationships is reported in Gordon et al. (2012).

The research suggesting the importance of focusing on rewards in a marriage was conducted by Previti and Amato (2003).

THE ATTACHMENT SYSTEM: THE BETTER SIDE OF HUMAN NATURE

The links between oxytocin and physical contact were presented by Light et al. (2005).

Moyer et al. (2004) conducted the meta-analysis of massage therapy research.

ROBOPARASITES OF LOVE: CLICK HERE AND HAVE YOUR WALLET READY!

Statistics on urbanization in the United States and Britain came from O'Neill (2021a, 2021b). Comparisons of infidelity rates in different cities came from Lampen (2017). Statistics on percentage of couples with one or both partners working outside home came from the U.S. Bureau of Labor Statistics (2021).

See Moore (2015) for survey results on men and women's probabilities of having an affair.

Research on commitment and avoiding temptation from alternative partners was presented by Lydon et al. (2003), D. J. Johnson and Rusbult (1989), and Simpson et al. (1990).

Research on the influence of seeing beautiful fashion models came from Kenrick and Gutierres (1980) and Kenrick et al. (1989, 1994; but see also Balzarini et al., 2017). Research on the effects of thinking about love came from Gonzaga et al. (2008).

The Gottman app with exercises for strengthening relationships was described by Russo (2013).

KNOWING WHEN TO WALK AWAY

The source of the quote about the two grave accidents in Frida's life came from Herrera (1983, p. 107).

The research suggesting that unrequited love is unpleasant on both sides was reported by Baumeister et al. (1993).

Research by Gottman and colleagues on relationship maintenance was described in Gottman and Levenson (1992), Gottman and Silver (1999), and Notarius and Markman (1993).

The Pauling quote is from the report of the Subcommittee to Investigate the Administration of the Internal Security Act and Other Internal Security Laws (Committee on the Judiciary, United States Senate, 1960, p. 666).

CHAPTER 8. FAMILY VALUES

The story of the Kaczynski brothers is told in Kaczynski (2016). The story of the Bulger brothers is told in Lehr and O'Neill (2000).

The quote that William Bulger's silence was motivated by "love and affection for his family" was by Robert H. Quinn, former speaker of the Massachusetts State House of Representatives, and can be found in Seelye (2013, para. 17). The quote from *The Boston Globe* columnist can be found in Lehigh (2011, para. 1).

Cooperative Breeders

Evidence for humans as "cooperative breeders" was reviewed in Hrdy (2007) and in Hill and Hurtado (2009).

The Maisin culture was described by Tietjen (1994).

Grandmothers

The evidence regarding the importance of grandmothers was reviewed by Hawkes and Coxworth (2013). See also Gibson and Mace (2005), Lahdenperä et al. (2004), and Beise and Voland (2002).

Figueredo et al. (2001) reported on the importance of brothers for women living in Mexico.

Why Harriet Needed Ozzie

Geary (2000) reviewed the evidence on the importance of fathers.

See Flinn et al. (2007) for a discussion of family ties and brain development.

Family Conflict

See Pospisil (1963) for his description of the incident of cousin-killing in the Kapauku Papuans.

See the classic paper on family conflict by Trivers (1974).

See Mock (1984, 1987) for descriptions of the work on siblicide in birds. Weatherford (2004) detailed the early life of Genghis Khan and his conflict with his brother. Schiff (2010) is a good recent biography of Cleopatra.

Garland (2009, 2013) described the practice of infanticide in ancient Greece and Rome.

The Tragedy of Hamlet can be found in Shakespeare (circa 1599–1601/1899).

MODERN FAMILY LIFE

Some statistics on children living with single parents can be found in Kramer (2019). For data on grandparental contact, see AARP (2002, 2019) and Tan et al. (2010).

For the percentage living in rural communities and cities in 2016, see Parker et al. (2018a). For the percentage living on farms in the 1800s, see Waterhouse (n.d.).

Comparisons of rural and suburban patterns were discussed in Parker et al. (2018b). Bui and Miller (2015) discussed the geographical distances between family members.

Some Changes Aren't Bad

The results of the Pew survey were reported by Pew Research Center (2011).

Some statistics on age at parenthood can be found in Bui and Miller (2018) and the United States Census Bureau (2016).

Garland (2013) discussed citizens' connections to the state in traditional civilizations, and Pinker (2011) and Fukuyama (2011) discussed the relationship between the development of the state, the rule of law, and the reduction of within-group violence levels.

Some Things Never Change

The extended human period of juvenile dependence was discussed by Gardiner and Bjorklund (2007).

Michelle Obama (2018) discussed in detail the importance of her mother in terms of taking care of the grandchildren. Data from British grandparents were reported in Tan et al. (2010). Preferential links to maternal grandparents were presented in Laham et al. (2005).

FAMILY MATTERS IN THE MODERN WORLD

The research on fundamental motives across 27 societies was presented in Ko et al. (2020).

Data on the links between fundamental motives and meaning in life were presented in Krems et al. (2017). Data on Canadian women's felt proximity to their mothers were presented in Salmon and Daly (1998).

THE BENEFITS OF KEEPING YOUR KIN CLOSE

Sources for the Walt Disney story are Stewart (2005) and B. Thomas (1976, 1998).

Statistics on kidney donor relationships were reported by the National Kidney Foundation (2021).

The study finding that men and women gave more credit to relatives than to themselves was reported in Ackerman et al. (2007).

PARASITIZING FAMILIAL INSTINCTS IN THE MODERN WORLD

The Coca-Cola family time ad can be seen at Mad Men Art (n.d.), and the later ad featuring an African American family can be seen at Coca-Cola Africa (2018). One of the various 7Up family drink posters can be seen at VintagePostersNYC (n.d.).

The story of Roberto Primero Luis came from Verini (2020).

The grandparent scams were described by Kando-Pineda (2018).

CHAPTER 9. BACK TO THE FUTURE

See Long (2020) for statistics on numbers of people behind in their rent (which were based on a November 2020 survey by the United States Census Bureau, 2020). Decreases in applications for marriage licenses were reported by the Institute for Family Studies (2020).

Edwards (2020) summarized changes in crime rates during the pandemic. Vanderveele (2020) described a survey of people's flourishing before and during the pandemic. See also the Institute for Family Studies (2020). The improvements in family relationships and other behaviors during the pandemic were reported by Evans (2020) and CISION PR Newswire (2020).

IS THERE ONE BIG LESSON FROM THE PAST 200,000 YEARS?

For the responses to the *Psychology Today* question, see Kenrick (2014a, 2014b).

The quote is from Sonja Lyubomirsky to Doug Kenrick (personal communication, May 16, 2020).

See Myers (1992) for his book on happiness. He also had an excellent article on happiness in *American Psychologist* (Myers, 2000). His comments came from a personal communication to Doug Kenrick (October 24, 2014).

The tit-for-tat strategy was described in Axelrod (1984).

The Pauling quote is from the report of the Subcommittee to Investigate the Administration of the Internal Security Act and Other Internal Security Laws (Committee on the Judiciary, United States Senate, 1960, p. 666).

REFERENCES

AARP. (2002, May). *The Grandparent Study 2002 report.* https://assets. aarp.org/rgcenter/general/gp_2002.pdf

AARP. (2019). *2018 Grandparents Today National Survey: General population report.* https://www.aarp.org/content/dam/aarp/research/surveys_ statistics/life-leisure/2019/aarp-grandparenting-study.doi.10.26419-2Fres.00289.001.pdf

Abbey, A. (1982). Sex differences in attributions for friendly behavior: Do males misperceive females' friendliness? *Journal of Personality and Social Psychology, 42*(5), 830–838. https://doi.org/10.1037/0022-3514.42.5.830

Ackerman, J. M., Griskevicius, V., & Li, N. P. (2011). Let's get serious: Communicating commitment in romantic relationships. *Journal of Personality and Social Psychology, 100*(6), 1079–1094. https://doi.org/10.1037/a0022412

Ackerman, J. M., & Kenrick, D. T. (2009). Cooperative courtship: Helping friends raise and raze relationship barriers: How men and women cooperate in courtship. *Personality and Social Psychology Bulletin, 35*(10), 1285–1300. https://doi.org/10.1177/0146167209335640

Ackerman, J. M., Kenrick, D. T., & Schaller, M. (2007). Is friendship akin to kinship? *Evolution and Human Behavior, 28*(5), 365–374. https://doi.org/10.1016/j.evolhumbehav.2007.04.004

Acsádi, G., & Nemeskéri, J. (1970). *History of human life span and mortality.* Akademiai Kiado.

Allen, J. B. (2018). *The psychology of happiness in the modern world: A social psychological approach.* Springer Publishing Company.

Allen-Arave, W., Gurven, M., & Hill, K. (2008). Reciprocal altruism, rather than kin selection, maintains nepotistic food transfers on an Aché reservation. *Evolution and Human Behavior, 29*(5), 305–318. https://doi.org/10.1016/j.evolhumbehav.2008.03.002

Amato, P. R., & James, S. (2010). Divorce in Europe and the United States: Commonalities and differences across nations. *Family Science, 1*(1), 2–13. https://doi.org/10.1080/19424620903381583

Anderson, M., Vogels, E. A., & Turner, E. (2020, February 6). *Users of online dating platforms experience both positive—and negative—aspects of courtship on the web.* Pew Research Center. https://www.pewresearch.org/internet/2020/02/06/users-of-online-dating-platforms-experience-both-positive-and-negative-aspects-of-court-ship-on-the-web/

Archer, J. (2000). Sex differences in aggression between heterosexual partners: A meta-analytic review. *Psychological Bulletin, 126*(5), 651–680. https://doi.org/10.1037/0033-2909.126.5.651

Ariely, D., & Loewenstein, G. (2006). The heat of the moment: The effect of sexual arousal on sexual decision making. *Journal of Behavioral Decision Making, 19*(2), 87–98. https://doi.org/10.1002/bdm.501

Axelrod, R. (1984). *The evolution of cooperation.* Basic Books.

Bailenson, J. N., Iyengar, S., Yee, N., & Collins, N. A. (2008). Facial similarity between voters and candidates causes influence. *Public Opinion Quarterly, 72*(5), 935–961. https://doi.org/10.1093/poq/nfn064

Bailey, J. M., Gaulin, S., Agyei, Y., & Gladue, B. A. (1994). Effects of gender and sexual orientation on evolutionarily relevant aspects of human mating psychology. *Journal of Personality and Social Psychology, 66*(6), 1081–1093. https://doi.org/10.1037/0022-3514.66.6.1081

Balzarini, R. N., Dobson, K., Chin, K., & Campbell, L. (2017). Does exposure to erotica reduce attraction and love for romantic partners in men? Independent replications of Kenrick, Gutierres, and Goldberg (1989) Study 2. *Journal of Experimental Social Psychology, 70*, 191–197. https://doi.org/10.1016/j.jesp.2016.11.003

Barrett, H. C., Bolyanatz, A., Crittenden, A. N., Fessler, D. M. T., Fitzpatrick, S., Gurven, M., Henrich, J., Kanovsky, M., Kushnick, G., Pisor, A., Sceiza, B. A., Stich, S., von Rueden, C., Zhao, W., & Laurence, S. (2016). Small-scale societies exhibit fundamental variation in the role of intentions in moral judgment. *Proceedings of the National*

Academy of Sciences, *113*(17), 4688–4693. https://doi.org/10.1073/pnas.1522070113

Baumeister, R. F., Wotman, S. R., & Stillwell, A. M. (1993). Unrequited love: On heartbreak, anger, guilt, scriptlessness, and humiliation. *Journal of Personality and Social Psychology*, *64*(3), 377–394. https://doi.org/10.1037/0022-3514.64.3.377

Becker, D. V., Kenrick, D. T., Neuberg, S. L., Blackwell, K. C., & Smith, D. M. (2007). The confounded nature of angry men and happy women. *Journal of Personality and Social Psychology*, *92*(2), 179–190. https://doi.org/10.1037/0022-3514.92.2.179

Beise, J., & Voland, E. (2002). A multilevel event history analysis of the effects of grandmothers on child mortality in a historical German population: Krummhörn, Ostfriesland, 1720–1874. *Demographic Research*, *7*(Article 13), 469–498. https://doi.org/10.4054/DemRes.2002.7.13

Bennett, J. (2021, April 15). *Fewer jobs have been lost in the EU than in the U.S. during the COVID-19 downturn*. Pew Research Center. https://www.pewresearch.org/fact-tank/2021/04/15/fewer-jobs-have-been-lost-in-the-eu-than-in-the-u-s-during-the-covid-19-downturn/

Bessendorf, A. (2015, December). *From cradle to cane: The cost of being a female consumer—A study of gender pricing in New York City*. New York City Department of Consumer Affairs. https://www1.nyc.gov/assets/dca/downloads/pdf/partners/Study-of-Gender-Pricing-in-NYC.pdf

Blight, D. W. (2018). *Frederick Douglass: Prophet of freedom*. Simon and Schuster.

Boer, D., Fischer, R., Strack, M., Bond, M. H., Lo, E., & Lam, J. (2011). How shared preferences in music create bonds between people: Values as the missing link. *Personality and Social Psychology Bulletin*, *37*(9), 1159–1171. https://doi.org/10.1177/0146167211407521

Bragg, R. (1995, August 13). All she has, $150,000, is going to a university. *The New York Times*. https://www.nytimes.com/1995/08/13/us/all-she-has-150000-is-going-to-a-university.html

Bridgman, T., Cummings, S., & Ballard, J. (2019). Who built Maslow's pyramid? A history of the creation of managements studies' most famous symbol and its implications for management education. *Academy of Management Learning & Education*, *18*(1), 81–98.

Brooks, A. S., Yellen, J. E., Potts, R., Behrensmeyer, A. K., Deino, A. L., Leslie, D. E., Ambrose, S. H., Ferguson, J. R., d'Errico, F., Zipkin, A. M.,

Whittaker, S., Post, J., Veatch, E. G., Foecke, K., & Clark, J. B. (2018). Long-distance stone transport and pigment use in the earliest Middle Stone Age. *Science, 360*(6384), 90–94. https://doi.org/10.1126/science.aao2646

Brown, S. P., & Peterson, R. A. (1993). Antecedents and consequences of salesperson job satisfaction: Meta-analysis and assessment of causal effects. *Journal of Marketing Research, 30*(1), 63–77. https://doi.org/10.1177/002224379303000106

Bui, Q., & Miller, C. C. (2015, December 23). The typical American family lives only 18 miles from mom. *The New York Times.* https://www.nytimes.com/interactive/2015/12/24/upshot/24up-family.html

Bui, Q., & Miller, C. C. (2018, August 4). The age that women have babies: How a gap divides America. *The New York Times.* https://www.nytimes.com/interactive/2018/08/04/upshot/up-birth-age-gap.html#:~:text=The%20average%20age%20of%20first%2Dtime%20mothers%20is%2026%2C%20up,of%20first%20birth%20is%2031

Buss, A. H. (1963). Physical aggression in relation to different frustrations. *The Journal of Abnormal and Social Psychology, 67*(1), 1–7. https://doi.org/10.1037/h0040505

Buss, D. M. (2000). The evolution of happiness. *American Psychologist, 55*(1), 15–23. https://doi.org/10.1037/0003-066X.55.1.15

Buss, D. M. (2015). *Evolutionary psychology: The new science of the mind* (5th ed.). Psychology Press. https://doi.org/10.4324/9781315663319

Buss, D. M. (Ed.). (2016). *The handbook of evolutionary psychology* (2nd ed., Vols. 1-2). Wiley.

Buss, D. M. (2018, October 18–21). *The evolutionary psychology of zombies: Better off dead or undead?* [Conference session]. Zombie Apocalypse Medicine Meeting, Tempe, AZ, United States.

Buss, D. M., & Duntley, J. D. (2006). The evolution of aggression. In M. Schaller, J. A. Simpson, & D. T. Kenrick (Eds.), *Evolution and social psychology* (pp. 263–285). Psychology Press.

Byrne, D. (1971). *The attraction paradigm.* Academic Press.

Byrne, D., & Wong, T. J. (1962). Racial prejudice, interpersonal attraction, and assumed dissimilarity of attitudes. *Journal of Abnormal and Social Psychology, 65*(4), 246–253. https://doi.org/10.1037/h0047299

Byron, E. (2019, June 2). More Americans are living solo, and companies want their business. *The Wall Street Journal.* https://www.wsj.com/

articles/more-americans-are-living-solo-and-companies-want-their-business-11559497606

Caroom, E. (2020, September 30). 30 years of climbing accident data: An investigative report. *Outside*. https://www.rockandice.com/climbing-accidents/30-years-of-climbing-accident-data-an-investigative-report/

Carville, J., & Begala, P. (2002). *Buck up, suck up . . . and come back when you foul up: 12 winning secrets from the war room*. Simon & Schuster.

Case, A., & Deaton, A. (2020). *Deaths of despair and the future of capitalism*. Princeton University Press. https://doi.org/10.2307/j.ctvpr7rb2

Case, C. R., & Maner, J. K. (2014). Divide and conquer: When and why leaders undermine the cohesive fabric of their group. *Journal of Personality and Social Psychology*, *107*(6), 1033–1050. https://doi.org/10.1037/a0038201

Caughlin, J. P., Huston, T. L., & Houts, R. M. (2000). How does personality matter in marriage? An examination of trait anxiety, interpersonal negativity, and marital satisfaction. *Journal of Personality and Social Psychology*, *78*(2), 326–336. https://doi.org/10.1037/0022-3514.78.2.326

Center for American Women and Politics. (n.d.). *Women in the U.S. Congress 2020*. Rutgers Eagleton Institute of Politics. https://cawp.rutgers.edu/women-us-congress-2020

Centers for Disease Control and Prevention. (n.d.-a). *Adult obesity facts*. https://www.cdc.gov/obesity/data/adult.html

Centers for Disease Control and Prevention. (n.d.-b). *Suicide prevention: Risk and protective factors*. https://www.cdc.gov/suicide/factors/index.html

Chagnon, N. A. (1968). *Yąnomamö: The fierce people*. Holt, Rinehart and Winston.

Chartrand, T. L., & Bargh, J. A. (1999). The chameleon effect: The perception–behavior link and social interaction. *Journal of Personality and Social Psychology*, *76*(6), 893–910.

Chen, F. F., & Kenrick, D. T. (2002). Repulsion or attraction? Group membership and assumed attitude similarity. *Journal of Personality and Social Psychology*, *83*(1), 111–125. https://doi.org/10.1037/0022-3514.83.1.111

Cheng, J. T., Tracy, J. L., Foulsham, T., Kingstone, A., & Henrich, J. (2013). Two ways to the top: Evidence that dominance and prestige are distinct yet viable avenues to social rank and influence. *Journal of Personality and Social Psychology, 104*(1), 103–125. https://doi.org/10.1037/a0030398

Cialdini, R. B. (1985). *Influence: Science and practice.* Scott, Foresman and Company.

Cialdini, R. B. (2021). *Influence: The psychology of persuasion* (3rd ed.). Allyn & Bacon.

CISION PR Newswire. (2020, September 25). *Parade/Cleveland Clinic "Healthy Now" survey reveals positive long-term effects of COVID-19 pandemic: Embracing healthy lifestyle changes, valuing personal relationships, finding meaning, remaining hopeful.* https://www.prnewswire.com/news-releases/paradecleveland-clinic-healthy-now-survey-reveals-positive-long-term-effects-of-covid-19-pandemic-embracing-healthy-lifestyle-changes-valuing-personal-relationships-finding-meaning-remaining-hopeful-301137946.html

Clark, R. D., & Hatfield, E. (1989). Gender differences in receptivity to sexual offers. *Journal of Psychology & Human Sexuality, 2*(1), 39–55. https://doi.org/10.1300/J056v02n01_04

Coca-Cola Africa. (2018, October 6). *Family time is the best time.* [Twitter post]. Twitter. Retrieved August 8, 2021, from https://twitter.com/cocacolaafrica/status/1048437701966487553

Collins, L., & Lapierre, D. (1975). *Freedom at midnight.* Simon & Schuster.

Committee on the Judiciary, United States Senate. (1960, October 11). *Testimony of Dr. Linus Pauling: Hearing before the Subcommittee to Investigate the Administration of the Internal Security Act and Other Internal Security Laws—Part 2* [Report]. U.S. Government Printing Office.

Congressional Research Service. (2021, June 15). *Unemployment rates during the COVID-19 pandemic* (Report No. R46554). https://fas.org/sgp/crs/misc/R46554.pdf

Conley, T. D., Matsick, J. L., Moors, A. C., & Ziegler, A. (2017). Investigation of consensually nonmonogamous relationships: Theories, methods, and new directions. *Perspectives on Psychological Science, 12*(2), 205–232. https://doi.org/10.1177/1745691616667925 (Erratum published 2017, *Perspectives on Psychological Science, 12*(3), p. 548)

Cramer, J. J. (2005, June 17). Phil Purcell's people problem. *New York.* https://nymag.com/nymetro/news/bizfinance/columns/bottomline/12072/

Crawford, C., & Krebs, D. (Eds.). (2008). *Foundations of evolutionary psychology*. Taylor & Francis Group/Lawrence Erlbaum Associates.

Cunningham, M. R. (1989). Reactions to heterosexual opening gambits: Female selectivity and male responsiveness. *Personality and Social Psychology Bulletin*, *15*(1), 27–41. https://doi.org/10.1177/0146167289151003

Curie, E. (1938). *Madame Curie*. Doubleday.

Daly, M. (2017). *Killing the competition: Economic inequality and homicide*. Routledge. https://doi.org/10.4324/9780203787748

David-Barrett, T., Rotkirch, A., Carney, J., Behncke Izquierdo, I., Krems, J. A., Townley, D., McDaniell, E., Byrne-Smith, A., & Dunbar, R. I. M. (2015). Women favour dyadic relationships, but men prefer clubs: Cross-cultural evidence from social networking. *PLOS ONE*, *10*(3), Article e0118329. https://doi.org/10.1371/journal.pone.0118329

De Waal, F., & Lanting, F. (1997). *Bonobo: The forgotten ape*. University of California Press.

DeBruine, L. M. (2002). Facial resemblance enhances trust. *Proceedings of the Royal Society B: Biological Sciences*, *269*(1498), 1307–1312. https://doi.org/10.1098/rspb.2002.2034

DeBruine, L. M. (2004). Facial resemblance increases the attractiveness of same-sex faces more than other-sex faces. *Proceedings of the Royal Society B: Biological Sciences*, *271*(1552), 2085–2090. https://doi.org/10.1098/rspb.2004.2824

deCatanzaro, D. (1980). Human suicide: A biological perspective. *Behavioral and Brain Sciences*, *3*(2), 265–272. https://doi.org/10.1017/S0140525X0000474X

Del Giudice, M., Gangestad, S. W., & Kaplan, H. S. (2016). Life history theory and evolutionary psychology. In D. M. Buss (Ed.), *The handbook of evolutionary psychology: Foundations* (pp. 88–114). John Wiley & Sons.

DePaulo, B. M., & Morris, W. L. (2005). Singles in society and in science. *Psychological Inquiry*, *16*(2–3), 57–83. https://doi.org/10.1080/1047840X.2005.9682918

DeSteno, D., & Valdesolo, P. (2011). *Out of character: Surprising truths about the liar, cheat, sinner (and saint) lurking in all of us*. Crown Publishing Group/Random House.

Deters, F. G., & Mehl, M. R. (2013). Does posting Facebook status updates increase or decrease loneliness? An online social networking experiment.

Social Psychological & Personality Science, 4(5), 579–586. https://doi.org/10.1177/1948550612469233

Diener, E. (2000). Subjective well-being. The science of happiness and a proposal for a national index. *American Psychologist, 55*(1), 34–43. https://doi.org/10.1037/0003-066X.55.1.34

Dittmar, H., Bond, R., Hurst, M., & Kasser, T. (2014). The relationship between materialism and personal well-being: A meta-analysis. *Journal of Personality and Social Psychology, 107*(5), 879–924. https://doi.org/10.1037/a0037409

Duckworth, A. (2016). *Grit: The power of passion and perseverance.* Scribner.

Dunbar, R. I. M. (2018). The anatomy of friendship. *Trends in Cognitive Sciences, 22*(1), 32–51. https://doi.org/10.1016/j.tics.2017.10.004

Dunbar, R. I. M., & Barrett, L. (2007). *Oxford handbook of evolutionary psychology.* Oxford University Press.

Durante, K. M., Griskevicius, V., Simpson, J. A., Cantú, S. M., & Li, N. P. (2012). Ovulation leads women to perceive sexy cads as good dads. *Journal of Personality and Social Psychology, 103*(2), 292–305. https://doi.org/10.1037/a0028498

Durante, K. M., Li, N. P., & Haselton, M. G. (2008). Changes in women's choice of dress across the ovulatory cycle: Naturalistic and laboratory task-based evidence. *Personality and Social Psychology Bulletin, 34*(11), 1451–1460. https://doi.org/10.1177/0146167208323103

Dyble, M., Thorley, J., Page, A. E., Smith, D., & Migliano, A. B. (2019). Engagement in agricultural work is associated with reduced leisure time among Agta hunter-gatherers. *Nature Human Behaviour, 3*(8), 792–796. https://doi.org/10.1038/s41562-019-0614-6

Edwards, R. (2020, December 4). *Crime and the coronavirus: What you need to know.* Safewise. https://www.safewise.com/blog/covid-19-crimes/

eHarmony. (2018). *64 percent of Americans say they're happy in their relationships.* CISION PR Newswire. https://www.prnewswire.com/news-releases/64-percent-of-americans-say-theyre-happy-in-their-relationships-300595502.html#:~:text=A%20new%20national%20report%20%22The,happy%20with%20their%20sex%20lives

Epidemiology of snakebites. (2021, July 22). In *Wikipedia.* https://en.wikipedia.org/w/index.php?title=Epidemiology_of_snakebites&oldid=1034939642

Epstein, R., Pandit, M., & Thakar, M. (2013). How love emerges in arranged marriages: Two cross-cultural studies. *Journal of Comparative Family Studies, 44*(3), 341–360. https://doi.org/10.3138/jcfs.44.3.341

Ericsson, K. A., & Charness, N. (1994). Expert performance: Its structure and acquisition. *American Psychologist, 49*(8), 725–747. https://doi.org/10.1037/0003-066X.49.8.725

Ericsson, K. A., & Ward, P. (2007). Capturing the naturally occurring superior performance of experts in the laboratory: Toward a science of expert and exceptional performance. *Current Directions in Psychological Science, 16*(6), 346–350. https://doi.org/10.1111/j.1467-8721.2007.00533.x

Euler, H. A. (2011). Grandparents and extended kin. In C. Salmon & T. K. Shackleford (Eds.), *Oxford handbook of evolutionary family psychology* (pp. 181–207). Oxford University Press.

Evans, E. (2020, September 22). Surprise! Families have grown stronger during COVID-19, not weaker. *Deseret News.* https://www.deseret.com/indepth/2020/9/21/21436378/byu-afs-2020-covid-19-families-relationships-grow-stronger-not-weaker-pandemic-coronavirus

Fergus, D. (2018). *Land of the fee: Hidden costs and the decline of the American middle class.* Oxford University Press.

Festinger, L., Schachter, S., & Back, K. (1950). *Social pressures in informal groups.* Stanford University Press. https://doi.org/10.2307/3707362

Figueredo, A. J., Corral-Verdugo, V., Frías-Armenta, M., Bachar, K. J., White, J., McNeill, P. L., Kirsner, B. R., & del PilarCastell-Ruiz, I. (2001). Blood, solidarity, status, and honor: The sexual balance of power and spousal abuse in Sonora, Mexico. *Evolution and Human Behavior, 22*(5), 295–328. https://doi.org/10.1016/S1090-5138(01)00067-8

Fincham, F. D., & May, R. W. (2017). Infidelity in romantic relationships. *Current Opinion in Psychology, 13*, 70–74. https://doi.org/10.1016/j.copsyc.2016.03.008

Finkel, E. J. (2017). *The all-or-nothing marriage: How the best marriages work.* Dutton.

Fitzpatrick, T. (1991, February 6). The lover. *Phoenix New Times.* https://www.phoenixnewtimes.com/news/the-lover-6411973

Flinn, M. V., Quinlan, R. J., Coe, K., & Ward, C. V. (2007). Evolution of the human family: Cooperative males, long social childhoods, smart mothers, and extended kin networks. In C. A. Salmon &

T. K. Shackelford (Eds.), *Family relationships: An evolutionary perspective* (pp. 16–38). Oxford University Press. https://doi.org/10.1093/acprof:oso/9780195320510.003.0002

Florida, R. (2019, March 5). *The geography of America's mobile and "stuck," mapped.* Bloomberg City Lab. https://www.bloomberg.com/news/articles/2019-03-05/mobile-vs-stuck-who-lives-in-their-u-s-birth-state

Forbes Quotes: Thoughts on the Business of Life. (n.d.). *The average person puts only 25% of his energy and ability into his work. The world takes off its hat to those who put in more than 50% of their capacity, and stands on its head for those few and far between souls who devote 100%* [Quotation]. Forbes. https://www.forbes.com/quotes/466/

Frank, R. H., Gilovich, T., & Regan, D. T. (1993). Does studying economics inhibit cooperation? *Journal of Economic Perspectives, 7*(2), 159–171. https://doi.org/10.1257/jep.7.2.159

Free solo climbing. (2021, June 26). In *Wikipedia.* https://en.wikipedia.org/w/index.php?title=Free_solo_climbing&oldid=1030596014

Freud, S. (2015). *Beyond the pleasure principle.* Dover Publications. (Original work published 1915)

Fukuyama, F. (2011). *The origins of political order: From prehuman times to the French revolution.* Farrar, Straus and Giroux.

Gardiner, A., & Bjorklund, D. F. (2007). All in the family: An evolutionary developmental perspective. In C. A. Salmon & T. K. Shackelford (Eds.), *Family relationships: An evolutionary perspective* (pp. 337–358). Oxford University Press. https://doi.org/10.1093/acprof:oso/9780195320510.003.0015

Garland, R. (2009). *Daily life of the ancient Greeks.* Greenwood Press.

Garland, R. (2013). *The other side of history: Daily life in the ancient world.* The Great Courses: Ancient History. The Teaching Company.

Garver-Apgar, C. E., Gangestad, S. W., & Simpson, J. A. (2007). Women's perceptions of men's sexual coerciveness change across the menstrual cycle. *Acta Psychologica Sinica, 39*(3), 536–540.

Geary, D. C. (2000). Evolution and proximate expression of human paternal investment. *Psychological Bulletin, 126*(1), 55–77. https://doi.org/10.1037/0033-2909.126.1.55

Geher, G., & Wedberg, N. (2020). *Positive evolutionary psychology: Darwin's guide to living a richer life.* Oxford University Press.

Ghose, T. (2013, October 28). Pediatricians: No more than 2 hours screen time daily for kids. *Scientific American*. https://www.scientificamerican.com/article/pediatricians-no-more-than-2-hour-screen-time-kids/

Gibson, M. A., & Mace, R. (2005). Helpful grandmothers in rural Ethiopia: A study of the effect of kin on child survival and growth. *Evolution and Human Behavior*, *26*(6), 469–482. https://doi.org/10.1016/j.evolhumbehav.2005.03.004

Gigerenzer, G., & Goldstein, D. G. (1996). Reasoning the fast and frugal way: Models of bounded rationality. *Psychological Review*, *103*(4), 650–669. https://doi.org/10.1037/0033-295X.103.4.650

Gildersleeve, K., Haselton, M. G., & Fales, M. R. (2014). Do women's mate preferences change across the ovulatory cycle? A meta-analytic review. *Psychological Bulletin*, *140*(5), 1205–1259. https://doi.org/10.1037/a0035438

Gillespie, B. J., Frederick, D., Harari, L., & Grov, C. (2015). Homophily, close friendship, and life satisfaction among gay, lesbian, heterosexual, and bisexual men and women. *PLOS ONE*, *10*(6), Article e0128900. https://doi.org/10.1371/journal.pone.0128900

Glenny, M. (2008). *McMafia: A journey through the global criminal underworld*. Alfred A. Knopf.

Goetz, C. D., Pillsworth, E. G., Buss, D. M., & Conroy-Beam, D. (2019). Evolutionary mismatch in mating. *Frontiers in Psychology*, *10*, Article 2709. https://doi.org/10.3389/fpsyg.2019.02709

Gonzaga, G. C., Haselton, M. G., Smurda, J., Davies, M. S., & Poore, J. C. (2008). Love, desire, and the suppression of thoughts of romantic alternatives. *Evolution and Human Behavior*, *29*, 119–126. https://doi.org/10.1016/j.evolhumbehav.2007.11.003

Goodwin, D. K. (2018). *Leadership in turbulent times*. Simon & Schuster.

Gordon, A. M., Impett, E. A., Kogan, A., Oveis, C., & Keltner, D. (2012). To have and to hold: Gratitude promotes relationship maintenance in intimate bonds. *Journal of Personality and Social Psychology*, *103*(2), 257–274. https://doi.org/10.1037/a0028723

Gosling, S. D., Ko, S. J., Mannarelli, T., & Morris, M. E. (2002). A room with a cue: Personality judgments based on offices and bedrooms. *Journal of Personality and Social Psychology*, *82*(3), 379–398. https://doi.org/10.1037/0022-3514.82.3.379

Gottman, J. M., & Levenson, R. W. (1992). Marital processes predictive of later dissolution: Behavior, physiology, and health. *Journal of*

Personality and Social Psychology, 63(2), 221–233. https://doi.org/10.1037/0022-3514.63.2.221

Gottman, J. M., & Silver, N. (1999). *The seven principles for making marriage work.* Three Rivers Press.

Gottschall, J., Martin, J., Quish, H., & Rea, J. (2004). Sex differences in mate choice criteria are reflected in folktales from around the world and in historical European literature. *Evolution and Human Behavior, 25*(2), 102–112. https://doi.org/10.1016/S1090-5138(04)00007-8

Gould, J. L., & Gould, C. G. (1989). *Sexual selection.* Scientific American Library.

Grann, D. (2010). *The lost city of Z: A tale of deadly obsession in the Amazon.* Vintage Departures.

Green, B. L., & Kenrick, D. T. (1994). The attractiveness of gender-typed traits at different relationship levels: Androgynous characteristics may be desirable after all. *Personality and Social Psychology Bulletin, 20*(3), 244–253. https://doi.org/10.1177/0146167294203002

Griskevicius, V., Cialdini, R. B., & Kenrick, D. T. (2006). Peacocks, Picasso, and parental investment: The effects of romantic motives on creativity. *Journal of Personality and Social Psychology, 91*(1), 63–76. https://doi.org/10.1037/0022-3514.91.1.63

Griskevicius, V., Goldstein, N. J., Mortensen, C. R., Cialdini, R. B., & Kenrick, D. T. (2006). Going along versus going alone: When fundamental motives facilitate strategic (non)conformity. *Journal of Personality and Social Psychology, 91*(2), 281–294. https://doi.org/10.1037/0022-3514.91.2.281

Griskevicius, V., Tybur, J. M., Ackerman, J. M., Delton, A. W., Robertson, T. E., & White, A. E. (2012). The financial consequences of too many men: Sex ratio effects on saving, borrowing, and spending. *Journal of Personality and Social Psychology, 102*(1), 69–80. https://doi.org/10.1037/a0024761

Griskevicius, V., Tybur, J. M., Sundie, J. M., Cialdini, R. B., Miller, G. F., & Kenrick, D. T. (2007). Blatant benevolence and conspicuous consumption: When romantic motives elicit strategic costly signals. *Journal of Personality and Social Psychology, 93*(1), 85–102. https://doi.org/10.1037/0022-3514.93.1.85

Gruber, J., Mauss, I. B., & Tamir, M. (2011). A dark side of happiness? How, when, and why happiness is not always good. *Perspectives on Psychological Science, 6*(3), 222–233. https://doi.org/10.1177/1745691611406927

Gupta, U., & Singh, P. (1982). An exploratory study of love and liking and types of marriages. *Indian Journal of Applied Psychology, 19*, 92–97.

Gurven, M., Allen-Arave, W., Hill, K., & Hurtado, M. (2000). "It's a Wonderful Life": Signaling generosity among the Aché of Paraguay. *Evolution and Human Behavior, 21*(4), 263–282. https://doi.org/10.1016/S1090-5138(00)00032-5

Gurven, M., & Kaplan, H. (2007). Longevity among hunter-gathers: A cross-cultural examination. *Population and Development Review, 33*(2), 321–365. https://doi.org/10.1111/j.1728-4457.2007.00171.x

Guttentag, M., & Secord, P. F. (1983). *Too many women? The sex ratio question.* SAGE Publications.

Hakim, D., Saul, S., & Thrush, G. (2020, November 6). As Biden inches ahead in Georgia, Stacey Abrams draws recognition and praise. *The New York Times.* https://www.nytimes.com/2020/11/06/us/politics/stacey-abrams-georgia.html

Hall, G. S. (1897). A study of fears. *The American Journal of Psychology, 8*(2), 147–249.

Hamel, J. (2012, November). *Partner Abuse State of Knowledge Project: Findings at-a-glance.* http://www.domesticviolenceresearch.org/pdf/FindingsAt-a-Glance.Nov.23.pdf

Haupert, M. L., Gesselman, A. N., Moors, A. C., Fisher, H. E., & Garcia, J. R. (2017). Prevalence of experiences with consensual nonmonogamous relationships: Findings from two national samples of single Americans. *Journal of Sex & Marital Therapy, 43*(5), 424–440. https://doi.org/10.1080/0092623X.2016.1178675

Hawkes, K., & Coxworth, J. E. (2013). Grandmothers and the evolution of human longevity: A review of findings and future directions. *Evolutionary Anthropology, 22*(6), 294–302. https://doi.org/10.1002/evan.21382

Hawkes, K., O'Connell, J. F., & Jones, N. G. B. (1997). Hadza women's time allocation, offspring provisioning, and the evolution of long postmenopausal life spans. *Current Anthropology, 38*(4), 551–577. https://doi.org/10.1086/204646

Henrich, J., & Gil-White, F. J. (2001). The evolution of prestige: Freely conferred deference as a mechanism for enhancing the benefits of cultural transmission. *Evolution and Human Behavior*, 22(3), 165–196. https://doi.org/10.1016/S1090-5138(00)00071-4

Henry, E., & Bartos, S. (2018). *Report card 2018: The wellbeing of young Australians*. Australian Research Alliance for Children and Youth. https://www.aracy.org.au/publications-resources/command/download_file/id/361/filename/ARACY_Report_Card_2018.pdf

Herrera, H. (1983). *Frida: A biography of Frida Kahlo*. New York, Harper-Collins Publishers.

Hewlett, B. S., Van De Koppel, J. M., & Van De Koppel, M. (1986). Causes of death among Aka pygmies of the Central African Republic. In L. L. Cavalli-Sforza (Ed.), *African pygmies* (pp. 45–63). Academic Press.

Hicks, T. V., & Leitenberg, H. (2001). Sexual fantasies about one's partner versus someone else: Gender differences in incidence and frequency. *Journal of Sex Research*, 38(1), 43–50. https://doi.org/10.1080/00224490109552069

Hill, K., & Hurtado, A. M. (1996). *Aché life history: The ecology and demography of a foraging people*. Aldine de Gruyter.

Hill, K., & Hurtado, A. M. (2009). Cooperative breeding in South American hunter–gatherers. *Proceedings of the Royal Society B: Biological Sciences*, 276(1674), 3863–3870. https://doi.org/10.1098/rspb.2009.1061

Hill, K., Hurtado, A. M., & Walker, R. S. (2007). High adult mortality among Hiwi hunter-gatherers: Implications for human evolution. *Journal of Human Evolution*, 52(4), 443–454. https://doi.org/10.1016/j.jhevol.2006.11.003

Hill, K. R., Walker, R. S., Božičević, cM., Eder, J., Headland, T., Hewlett, B., Hurtado, A. M., Marlowe, F., Wiessner, P., & Wood, B. (2011). Co-residence patterns in hunter-gatherer societies show unique human social structure. *Science*, 331(6022), 1286–1289. https://doi.org/10.1126/science.1199071

Hilmert, C. J., Kulik, J. A., & Christenfeld, N. J. S. (2006). Positive and negative opinion modeling: The influence of another's similarity and dissimilarity. *Journal of Personality and Social Psychology*, 90(3), 440–452. https://doi.org/10.1037/0022-3514.90.3.440

Hoebel, E. A. (1960). *The Cheyennes: Indians of the Great Plains*. Holt, Rinehart and Winston.

Hoffman, M. (2021, January 11). *The Pink tax: How women pay more for pink*. Bankrate. https://www.bankrate.com/finance/credit-cards/pink-tax-how-women-pay-more/

Hogan, R. (2007). *Personality and the fate of organizations.* Psychology Press.

Holland, J. L. (1992). *Making vocational choices. A theory of vocational personalities and work environments* (2nd ed.). Psychological Assessment Resources.

Holt-Lunstad, J. (2017). The potential public health relevance of social isolation and loneliness: Prevalence, epidemiology, and risk factors. *Public Policy and Aging Report, 27*(4), 127–130. https://doi.org/10.1093/ppar/prx030

Holt-Lunstad, J., Smith, T. B., Baker, M., Harris, T., & Stephenson, D. (2015). Loneliness and social isolation as risk factors for mortality: A meta-analytic review. *Perspectives on Psychological Science, 10*(2), 227–237. https://doi.org/10.1177/1745691614568352

Horowitz, J. M., Graf, N., & Livingston, G. (2019, November 6). *How married and cohabiting adults see their relationships.* https://www.pewresearch.org/social-trends/2019/11/06/how-married-and-cohabiting-adults-see-their-relationships/

Horowitz, J. M., Igielnik, R., & Kochhar, R. (2020, January 9). *Trends in income and wealth inequality.* Pew Research Center Social and Demographic Trends. https://www.pewsocialtrends.org/2020/01/09/trends-in-income-and-wealth-inequality/

Hrdy, S. B. (2007). Evolutionary context of human development: The cooperative breeding model. In C. A. Salmon & T. K. Shackelford (Eds.), *Family relationships: An evolutionary perspective* (pp. 39–68). Oxford University Press.

Hruschka, D. J. (2010). *Friendship: Development, ecology, and evolution of a relationship.* University of California Press. https://doi.org/10.1525/california/9780520265462.001.0001

.id. (n.d.). *Greater Sydney: Birthplace.* https://profile.id.com.au/australia/birthplace?WebID=250

Institute for Family Studies. (2020, September 22). *The good and bad news about marriage in the time of COVID-19.* https://www.aei.org/articles/the-good-and-bad-news-about-marriage-in-the-time-of-covid/

Jankowiak, W. R., & Fischer, E. F. (1992). A cross-cultural perspective on romantic love. *Ethnology, 31*(2), 149–155. https://doi.org/10.2307/3773618

Jensen-Campbell, L. A., Graziano, W. G., & West, S. G. (1995). Dominance, prosocial orientation, and female preferences: Do nice guys really finish last? *Journal of Personality and Social Psychology, 68*(3), 427–440. https://doi.org/10.1037/0022-3514.68.3.427

Jocklin, V., McGue, M., & Lykken, D. T. (1996). Personality and divorce: A genetic analysis. *Journal of Personality and Social Psychology, 71*(2), 288–299. https://doi.org/10.1037/0022-3514.71.2.288

Johnson, D. J., & Rusbult, C. E. (1989). Resisting temptation: Devaluation of alternative partners as a means of maintaining commitment in close relationships. *Journal of Personality and Social Psychology, 57*(6), 967–980. https://doi.org/10.1037/0022-3514.57.6.967

Johnson, H. (2020, July 16). *Here's how much the average American pays in interest each year.* The Simple Dollar. https://www.thesimpledollar.com/loans/personal/heres-how-much-the-average-american-pays-in-interest-each-year/

Jones, D., & Hill, K. (1993). Criteria of facial attractiveness in five populations. *Human Nature, 4*(3), 271–296. https://doi.org/10.1007/BF02692202

Jones, D. S., Podolsky, S. H., & Greene, J. A. (2012). The burden of disease and the changing task of medicine. *The New England Journal of Medicine, 366*(25), 2333–2338. https://doi.org/10.1056/NEJMp1113569

Jones, J. T., Pelham, B. W., Carvallo, M., & Mirenberg, M. C. (2004). How do I love thee? Let me count the Js: Implicit egotism and interpersonal attraction. *Journal of Personality and Social Psychology, 87*(5), 665–683. https://doi.org/10.1037/0022-3514.87.5.665

Judge, T. A., Bono, J. E., Ilies, R., & Gerhardt, M. W. (2002). Personality and leadership: A qualitative and quantitative review. *Journal of Applied Psychology, 87*(4), 765–780. https://doi.org/10.1037/0021-9010.87.4.765

Kaczynski, D. (2016). *Every last tie.* Duke University Press. https://doi.org/10.1215/9780822375005

Kahneman, D. (2011). *Thinking, fast and slow.* Farrar, Straus, & Giroux.

Kando-Pineda, C. (2018, July 3). *Scammers create fake emergencies to get your money.* Federal Trade Commission Consumer Information. https://www.consumer.ftc.gov/blog/2018/07/scammers-create-fake-emergencies-get-your-money

Kaplan, H., Gurven, M., & Winking, J. (2009). An evolutionary theory of human life span: Embodied capital and the human adaptive complex. In V. L. Bengston, D. Gans, N. M. Pulney, & M. Silverstein (Eds.),

Handbook of theories of aging (pp. 39–60). Springer Publishing Company.

Kaprio, J., Koskenvuo, M., & Rita, H. (1987). Mortality after bereavement: A prospective study of 95,647 widowed persons. *American Journal of Public Health, 77*, 283–287. https://doi.org/10.2105/AJPH.77.3.283

Kelly, E. L., & Conley, J. J. (1987). Personality and compatibility: A prospective analysis of marital stability and marital satisfaction. *Journal of Personality and Social Psychology, 52*(1), 27–40. https://doi.org/10.1037/0022-3514.52.1.27

Kenrick, D. T. (2011). *Sex, murder, and the meaning of life: A psychologist investigates how evolution, cognition, and complexity are revolutionizing our view of human nature.* Basic Books.

Kenrick, D. T. (2014a, December 11). How to overcome the 6 obstacles to kindness. *Psychology Today.* https://www.psychologytoday.com/us/blog/sex-murder-and-the-meaning-life/201412/want-go-far-make-your-goal

Kenrick, D. T. (2014b). How to survive as a hominid, part II: 10 Gems of wisdom for life on earth. *Psychology Today: Sex, murder and the meaning of life.* https://www.psychologytoday.com/us/blog/sex-murder-and-the-meaning-life/201411/how-survive-hominid-part-ii

Kenrick, D. T., Griskevicius, V., Neuberg, S. L., & Schaller, M. (2010). Renovating the pyramid of needs: Contemporary extensions built upon ancient foundations. *Perspectives on Psychological Science, 5*(3), 292–314. https://doi.org/10.1177/1745691610369469

Kenrick, D. T., Groth, G. R., Trost, M. R., & Sadalla, E. K. (1993). Integrating evolutionary and social exchange perspectives on relationships: Effects of gender, self-appraisal, and involvement level on mate selection criteria. *Journal of Personality and Social Psychology, 64*(6), 951–969. https://doi.org/10.1037/0022-3514.64.6.951

Kenrick, D. T., & Gutierres, S. E. (1980). Contrast effects and judgments of physical attractiveness: When beauty becomes a social problem. *Journal of Personality and Social Psychology, 38*(1), 131–140. https://doi.org/10.1037/0022-3514.38.1.131

Kenrick, D. T., Gutierres, S. E., & Goldberg, L. L. (1989). Influence of erotica on ratings of strangers and mates. *Journal of Experimental Social Psychology, 25*(2), 159–167. https://doi.org/10.1016/0022-1031(89)90010-3

Kenrick, D. T., & Keefe, R. C. (1992). Age preferences in mates reflect sex differences in mating strategies. *Behavioral and Brain Sciences, 15*(1), 75–91. https://doi.org/10.1017/S0140525X00067595

Kenrick, D. T., Keefe, R. C., Bryan, A., Barr, A., & Brown, S. (1995). Age preferences and mate choice among homosexuals and heterosexuals: A case for modular psychological mechanisms. *Journal of Personality and Social Psychology, 69*(6), 1166–1172. https://doi.org/10.1037/0022-3514.69.6.1166

Kenrick, D. T., Neuberg, S. L., Cialdini, R. B., & Lundberg-Kenrick, D. E. (2020). *Social psychology: Goals in interaction* (7th ed.). Pearson.

Kenrick, D. T., Neuberg, S. L., Zierk, K. L., & Krones, J. M. (1994). Evolution and social cognition: Contrast effects as a function of sex, dominance, and physical attractiveness. *Personality and Social Psychology Bulletin, 20*(2), 210–217. https://doi.org/10.1177/0146167294202008

Kenrick, D. T., Sadalla, E. K., Groth, G., & Trost, M. R. (1990). Evolution, traits, and the stages of human courtship: Qualifying the parental investment model. *Journal of Personality, 58*(1), 97–116. https://doi.org/10.1111/j.1467-6494.1990.tb00909.x

Kenrick, D. T., & Sheets, V. (1993). Homicidal fantasies. *Ethology and Sociobiology, 14*(4), 231–246. https://doi.org/10.1016/0162-3095(93)90019-E

Kenrick, D. T., Sundie, J. M., Nicastle, L. D., & Stone, G. O. (2001). Can one ever be too wealthy or too chaste? Searching for nonlinearities in mate judgment. *Journal of Personality and Social Psychology, 80*(3), 462–471. https://doi.org/10.1037/0022-3514.80.3.462

Kiecolt-Glaser, J. K., & Newton, T. L. (2001). Marriage and health: His and hers. *Psychological Bulletin, 127*(4), 472–503. https://doi.org/10.1037/0033-2909.127.4.472

Klaben, H., & Day, B. F. (1963). *Hey, I'm alive!* McGraw-Hill Books Company.

Ko, A., Pick, C. M., Kwon, J. Y., Barlev, M., Krems, J. A., Varnum, M. E. W., Neel, R., Peysha, M., Boonyasiriwat, W., Brandstätter, E., Crispim, A. C., Cruz, J. E., David, D., David, O. A., de Felipe, R. P., Fetvadjiev, V. H., Fischer, R., Galdi, S., Galindo, O., . . . Kenrick, D. T. (2020). Family matters: Rethinking the psychology of human social motivation. *Perspectives on Psychological Science, 15*(1), 173–201. https://doi.org/10.1177/1745691619872986 (Corrigendum published 2021, *Perspectives on Psychological Science, 16*[2], pp. 473–476. https://doi.org/10.1177%2F1745691621995517)

Koenig, R. (2018, May 16). Hot jobs for college grads. *U.S. News & World Report*. https://money.usnews.com/careers/best-jobs/articles/2018-05-16/hot-jobs-for-college-grads

Komorita, S. S., Hilty, J. A., & Parks, C. D. (1991). Reciprocity and cooperation in social dilemmas. *Journal of Conflict Resolution, 35*(3), 494–518. https://doi.org/10.1177/0022002791035003005

Kramer, S. (2019, December 12). *U.S. has world's highest rate of children living in single-parent households*. Pew Research Center. https://www.pewresearch.org/fact-tank/2019/12/12/u-s-children-more-likely-than-children-in-other-countries-to-live-with-just-one-parent/

Kraut, R., Patterson, M., Lundmark, V., Kiesler, S., Mukopadhyay, T., & Scherlis, W. (1998). Internet paradox. A social technology that reduces social involvement and psychological well-being? *American Psychologist, 53*(9), 1017–1031. https://doi.org/10.1037/0003-066X.53.9.1017

Krems, J. A., Kenrick, D. T., & Neel, R. (2017). Individual perceptions of self-actualization: What functional motives are linked to fulfilling one's full potential? *Personality and Social Psychology Bulletin, 43*(9), 1337–1352. https://doi.org/10.1177/0146167217713191

Krems, J. A., Williams, K. E. G., Aktipis, C. A., & Kenrick, D. T. (2021). Friendship jealousy: One tool for maintaining friendships in the face of third-party threats? *Journal of Personality and Social Psychology, 120*(4), 997–1012. https://doi.org/10.1037/pspi0000311

Kross, E., Verduyn, P., Demiralp, E., Park, J., Lee, D. S., Lin, N., Shablack, H., Jonides, J., & Ybarra, O. (2013). Facebook use predicts declines in subjective well-being in young adults. *PLOS ONE, 8*(8), Article e69841. https://doi.org/10.1371/journal.pone.0069841

Kteily, N., Bruneau, E., Waytz, A., & Cotterill, S. (2015). The ascent of man: Theoretical and empirical evidence for blatant dehumanization. *Journal of Personality and Social Psychology, 109*(5), 901–931. https://doi.org/10.1037/pspp0000048

Kteily, N., Cotterill, S., Sidanius, J., Sheehy-Skeffington, J., & Bergh, R. (2014). "Not one of us": Predictors and consequences of denying ingroup characteristics to ambiguous targets. *Personality and Social Psychology Bulletin, 40*(10), 1231–1247. https://doi.org/10.1177/0146167214539708

Kurzban, R., Dukes, A., & Weeden, J. (2010). Sex, drugs and moral goals: Reproductive strategies and views about recreational drugs. *Proceedings* of the *Royal Society B: Biological Sciences, 277*(1699), 3501–3508. https://doi.org/10.1098/rspb.2010.0608

Kurzban, R., Tooby, J., & Cosmides, L. (2001). Can race be erased? Coalitional computation and social categorization. *Proceedings of the National Academy of Sciences, 98*(26), 15387–15392. https://doi.org/10.1073/pnas.251541498

Laham, S. M., Gonsalkorale, K., & von Hippel, W. (2005). Darwinian grandparenting: Preferential investment in more certain kin. *Personality and Social Psychology Bulletin, 31*(1), 63–72. https://doi.org/10.1177/0146167204271318

Lahdenperä, M., Lummaa, V., Helle, S., Tremblay, M., & Russell, A. F. (2004). Fitness benefits of prolonged post-reproductive lifespan in women. *Nature, 428*(6979), 178–181. https://doi.org/10.1038/nature02367

Lampen, C. (2017, December 14). This is the city with the fastest growing population of cheaters. *Women's Health.* https://www.womenshealthmag.com/sex-and-love/a19974454/city-with-the-most-cheaters/

Laughlin, L. (2013). *Who's minding the kids?* United States Census Bureau. https://www.census.gov/library/publications/2013/demo/p70-135.html

Lee, R. B. (1979). *The !Kung San: Men, women, and work in a foraging society.* Cambridge University Press.

Lehigh, S. (2011, June 29). What is William Bulger's obligation? *The Boston Globe.* http://archive.boston.com/bostonglobe/editorial_opinion/oped/articles/2011/06/29/william_bulgers_loyalty_trumps_morality/

Lehr, D., & O'Neill, G. (2000). *Black mass: Whitey Bulger, the FBI, and a devil's deal.* PublicAffairs.

Lepp, A., Barkley, J. E., & Karpinski, A. C. (2014). The relationship between cell phone use, academic performance, anxiety, and satisfaction with life in college students. *Computers in Human Behavior, 31*, 343–350. https://doi.org/10.1016/j.chb.2013.10.049

Lewis, M. (2017). *The undoing project: A friendship that changed our minds.* W. W. Norton & Co.

Li, N. P., Bailey, J. M., Kenrick, D. T., & Linsenmeier, J. A. (2002). The necessities and luxuries of mate preferences: Testing the tradeoffs. *Journal of Personality and Social Psychology, 82*(6), 947–955. https://doi.org/10.1037/0022-3514.82.6.947

Li, N. P., & Kenrick, D. T. (2006). Sex similarities and differences in preferences for short-term mates: What, whether, and why. *Journal of*

Personality and Social Psychology, 90(3), 468–489. https://doi.org/
10.1037/0022-3514.90.3.468

Li, N. P., van Vugt, M., & Colarelli, S. M. (2018). The evolutionary mismatch hypothesis: Implications for psychological science. *Current Directions in Psychological Science, 27*(1), 38–44. https://doi.org/
10.1177/0963721417731378 (Corrigendum published 2019, *Current Directions in Psychological Science, 28*[6], p. 626. https://doi.org/
10.1177/0963721419885877)

Light, K. C., Grewen, K. M., & Amico, J. A. (2005). More frequent partner hugs and higher oxytocin levels are linked to lower blood pressure and heart rate in premenopausal women. *Biological Psychology, 69*(1), 5–21. https://doi.org/10.1016/j.biopsycho.2004.11.002

Livingston, G. (2017, May 18). *In U.S. metro areas, huge variation in intermarriage rates.* Pew Research Center. https://www.pewresearch.
org/fact-tank/2017/05/18/in-u-s-metro-areas-huge-variation-in-intermarriage-rates/

Long, H. (2020, December 7). Millions of Americans are heading into the holidays unemployed and over $5,000 behind on rent. *The Washington Post.* https://www.washingtonpost.com/business/2020/12/07/unemployed-debt-rent-utilities/

Lord, C. G., Ross, L., & Lepper, M. R. (1979). Biased assimilation and attitude polarization: The effects of prior theories on subsequently considered evidence. *Journal of Personality and Social Psychology, 37*(11), 2098–2109. https://doi.org/10.1037/0022-3514.37.11.2098

Lydon, J. E., Fitzsimons, G. M., & Naidoo, L. (2003). Devaluation versus enhancement of attractive alternatives: A critical test using the calibration paradigm. *Personality and Social Psychology Bulletin, 29*(3), 349–359. https://doi.org/10.1177/0146167202250202

Lyubomirsky, S. (2007). *The how of happiness: A scientific approach to getting the life you want.* The Penguin Press.

Lyubomirsky, S., King, L., & Diener, E. (2005). The benefits of frequent positive affect: Does happiness lead to success? *Psychological Bulletin, 131*(6), 803–855. https://doi.org/10.1037/0033-2909.131.6.803

Mad Men Art. (n.d.). *Consumer goods.* https://www.madmenart.com/vintage-advertisement/coca-cola-its-a-family-affair-1937/

Maner, J. K., & Kenrick, D. T. (2010). When adaptations go awry: Functional and dysfunctional aspects of social anxiety. *Social Issues and*

Policy Review, 4(1), 111–142. https://doi.org/10.1111/j.1751-2409.2010.01019.x

Maner, J. K., Kenrick, D. T., Becker, D. V., Robertson, T. E., Hofer, B., Neuberg, S. L., Delton, A. W., Butner, J., & Schaller, M. (2005). Functional projection: How fundamental social motives can bias interpersonal perception. *Journal of Personality and Social Psychology, 88*(1), 63–78. https://doi.org/10.1037/0022-3514.88.1.63

Maner, J. K., & Mead, N. L. (2010). The essential tension between leadership and power: When leaders sacrifice group goals for the sake of self-interest. *Journal of Personality and Social Psychology, 99*(3), 482–497. https://doi.org/10.1037/a0018559

Manfred, T. (2012, February 10). Here are the odds that your kid becomes a professional athlete (hint: They're small). *Business Insider.* https://www.businessinsider.com/odds-college-athletes-become-professionals-2012-2

Marks, I. M. (1969). *Fears and phobias.* Academic Press.

Marks, I. M., & Nesse, R. M. (1994). Fear and fitness: An evolutionary analysis of anxiety disorders. *Ethology and Sociobiology, 15*(5–6), 247–261. https://doi.org/10.1016/0162-3095(94)90002-7

Marlowe, F. W. (2004). Mate preferences among Hadza hunter-gatherers. *Human Nature, 15*(4), 365–376. https://doi.org/10.1007/s12110-004-1014-8

Marsh, J. (Director). (2008). *Man on wire* [Video trailer]. https://www.youtube.com/watch?v=Cz6oddi0mts

Marshall, E. M. (1958). *The harmless people.* Vintage/Random House.

Maslow, A. H. (1943). A theory of human motivation. *Psychological Review, 50*(4), 370–396. https://doi.org/10.1037/h0054346

Maslow, A. H. (1954). *Motivation and personality.* Harper & Row.

Mauss, I. B., Tamir, M., Anderson, C. L., & Savino, N. S. (2011). Can seeking happiness make people unhappy? Paradoxical effects of valuing happiness. *Emotion, 11*(4), 807–815. https://doi.org/10.1037/a0022010

McCarty, O. (1996). *Simple wisdom for rich living.* Longstreet Press.

McCullough, M. E., Kimeldorf, M. B., & Cohen, A. D. (2008). An adaptation for altruism? The social causes, social effects, and social evolution of gratitude. *Current Directions in Psychological Science, 17*(4), 281–285. https://doi.org/10.1111/j.1467-8721.2008.00590.x

McDonald, M. M., Navarrete, C. D., & Sidanius, J. (2011). Developing a theory of gendered prejudice: An evolutionary and social dominance perspective. In R. M. Kramer, G. J. Leonardelli, & R. W. Livingston (Eds.), *Social cognition, social identity, and intergroup relations: A Festschrift in Honor of Marilynn B. Brewer* (pp. 192–223). Psychology Press.

McDonald, M. M., Navarrete, C. D., & Van Vugt, M. (2012). Evolution and the psychology of intergroup conflict: The male warrior hypothesis. *Philosophical Transactions of the Royal Society, B: Biological Sciences*, 367(1589), 670–679. https://doi.org/10.1098/rstb.2011.0301

McDonald, M. M., Porat, R., Yarkoney, A., Reifen Tagar, M., Kimel, S., Saguy, T., & Halperin, E. (2017). Intergroup emotional similarity reduces dehumanization and promotes conciliatory attitudes in prolonged conflict. *Group Processes & Intergroup Relations*, 20(1), 125–136. https://doi.org/10.1177/1368430215595107

McGoogan, K. (2001). *Fatal Passage*. Carroll & Graf.

McNulty, J. K. (2013). Personality and relationships. In J. A. Simpson & L. Campbell (Eds.), *Oxford handbook of close relationships* (pp. 535–552). Oxford University Press.

McWilliams, S., & Howard, J. A. (1993). Solidarity and hierarchy in cross-sex friendships. *Journal of Social Issues*, 49(3), 191–202. https://doi.org/10.1111/j.1540-4560.1993.tb01176.x

Menyes, C. (2014, January 21). If you're a musician, chances are you're totally undiscovered, says a new study. *Music Times*. https://www.musictimes.com/articles/3563/20140121/youre-musician-chances-totally-undiscovered-new-study.htm

Merriam-Webster. (n.d.). Predator. In *Merriam-Webster.com dictionary*. Retrieved July 19, 2021, from https://www.merriam-webster.com/dictionary/predator

Michigan Coronavirus Racial Disparities Task Force. (2020, November). *Interim report*. https://www.michigan.gov/documents/coronavirus/Interim_Report_Final_719168_7.pdf

Mishel, L., & Kandra, J. (2020, August 18). *CEO compensation surged 14% in 2019 to $21.3 million*. Economic Policy Institute. https://www.epi.org/publication/ceo-compensation-surged-14-in-2019-to-21-3-million-ceos-now-earn-320-times-as-much-as-a-typical-worker/

Mock, D. W. (1984). Siblicidal aggression and resource monopolization in birds. *Science*, 225(4663), 731–733. https://doi.org/10.1126/science.225.4663.731

Mock, D. W. (1987). Siblicide, parent–offspring conflict, and unequal parental investment by egrets and herons. *Behavioral Ecology and Sociobiology, 20*(4), 247–256. https://doi.org/10.1007/BF00292177

Moore, P. (2015, June 2). *One in five Americans say they've been unfaithful.* YouGovAmerica. https://today.yougov.com/topics/lifestyle/articles-reports/2015/06/02/men-more-likely-think-cheating

Moyer, C. A., Rounds, J., & Hannum, J. W. (2004). A meta-analysis of massage therapy research. *Psychological Bulletin, 130*(1), 3–18. https://doi.org/10.1037/0033-2909.130.1.3

Muller, M. N., Thompson, M. E., & Wrangham, R. W. (2006). Male chimpanzees prefer mating with old females. *Current Biology, 16*(22), 2234–2238. https://doi.org/10.1016/j.cub.2006.09.042

Myers, D. G. (1992). *The pursuit of happiness: Who is happy—and why.* William Morrow and Company.

Myers, D. G. (2000). The funds, friends, and faith of happy people. *American Psychologist, 55*(1), 56–67. https://doi.org/10.1037/0003-066X.55.1.56

Myerson, N. (2019, April 23). *Walmart CEO Doug McMillon's total pay was nearly $24 million last year.* CNN Business. https://www.cnn.com/2019/04/23/business/walmart-ceo-doug-mcmillon-pay-retail/index.html

National Center for Immunization and Respiratory Diseases. (n.d.). *1918 pandemic (H1N1 virus).* Centers for Disease Control and Prevention. https://www.cdc.gov/flu/pandemic-resources/1918-pandemic-h1n1.html

National Institute of Mental Health. (n.d.). *Suicide.* https://www.nimh.nih.gov/health/statistics/suicide

National Kidney Foundation. (2021). *Organ donation and transplantation statistics.* https://www.kidney.org/news/newsroom/factsheets/Organ-Donation-and-Transplantation-Stats

Neel, R., Neufeld, S. L., & Neuberg, S. L. (2013). Would an obese person whistle Vivaldi? Targets of prejudice self-present to minimize appearance of specific threats. *Psychological Science, 24*(5), 678–687. https://doi.org/10.1177/0956797612458807

Nesse, R. M., & Berridge, K. C. (1997). Psychoactive drug use in evolutionary perspective. *Science, 278*(5335), 63–66. https://doi.org/10.1126/science.278.5335.63

Neuhaus, C. (1982, April 12). Scorned and swindled by her bigamist husband, Sharon Vigliotto got mad, then got even. *People*. https://people.com/archive/scorned-and-swindled-by-her-bigamist-husband-sharon-vigliotto-got-mad-then-got-even-vol-17-no-14/

The New York Times. (2021, August 3). *Coronavirus in the U.S.: Latest map and case count*. https://www.nytimes.com/interactive/2021/us/covid-cases.html

The Nobel Prize. (2002, December 8). *Daniel Kahneman prize lecture: Prize lecture—Maps of bounded rationality* [Video]. https://www.nobelprize.org/prizes/economic-sciences/2002/kahneman/lecture/

Notarius, C., & Markman, J. (1993). *We can work it out: Making sense of marital conflict*. Putnam.

Obama, M. (2018). *Becoming*. Crown.

Öhman, A., & Mineka, S. (2003). The malicious serpent: Snakes as a prototypical stimulus for an evolved module of fear. *Current Directions in Psychological Science, 12*(1), 5–9. https://doi.org/10.1111/1467-8721.01211

Ohtsubo, Y., Matsumura, A., Noda, C., Sawa, E., Yagi, A., & Yamaguchi, M. (2014). It's the attention that counts: Interpersonal attention fosters intimacy and social exchange. *Evolution and Human Behavior, 35*(3), 237–244. https://doi.org/10.1016/j.evolhumbehav.2014.02.004

Olson, R. S. (2015, June 15). *144 years of marriage and divorce in 1 chart*. Randal S. Olson. http://www.randalolson.com/2015/06/15/144-years-of-marriage-and-divorce-in-1-chart/

Olsson, A., Ebert, J. P., Banaji, M. R., & Phelps, E. A. (2005). The role of social groups in the persistence of learned fear. *Science, 309*(5735), 785–787. https://doi.org/10.1126/science.1113551

O'Neill, A. (2021a, July 21). *Degree of urbanization in the United States from 1970 to 2020*. Stastista. https://www.statista.com/statistics/269967/urbanization-in-the-united-states/

O'Neill, A. (2021b, July 21). *United Kingdom: Degree of urbanization from 2010 to 2020*. Statista. https://www.statista.com/statistics/270369/urbanization-in-the-united-kingdom/

Opie, C., Atkinson, Q. D., Dunbar, R. I. M., & Shultz, S. (2013). Male infanticide leads to social monogamy in primates. *Proceedings of the National Academy of Sciences, 110*(33), 13328–13332. https://doi.org/10.1073/pnas.1307903110

Ortiz-Ospina, E., & Roser, M. (2020). *Marriages and divorces*. Our World in Data. https://ourworldindata.org/marriages-and-divorces

Oxford Reference. (n.d.). *Thomas Alva Edison 1847–1931: American inventor.* https://www.oxfordreference.com/view/10.1093/acref/9780191826719.001.0001/q-oro-ed4-00003960

Pappas, S. (2020, April 1). What do we really know about kids and screens? *APA Monitor on Psychology.* https://www.apa.org/monitor/2020/04/cover-kids-screens

Park, J. H., & Schaller, M. (2005). Does attitude similarity serve as a heuristic cue for kinship? Evidence of an implicit cognitive association. *Evolution and Human Behavior, 26*(2), 158–170. https://doi.org/10.1016/j.evolhumbehav.2004.08.013

Parker, K., Horowitz, J. M., Brown, A., Fry, R., Cohn, D., & Igielnik, R. (2018a, May 22). *Demographic and economic trends in urban, suburban and rural communities.* Pew Research Center. https://www.pewresearch.org/social-trends/2018/05/22/demographic-and-economic-trends-in-urban-suburban-and-rural-communities/

Parker, K., Horowitz, J. M., Brown, A., Fry, R., Cohn, D., & Igielnik, R. (2018b, May 22). *What unites urban, suburban, and rural communities.* Pew Research Center. https://www.pewsocialtrends.org/2018/05/22/what-unites-and-divides-urban-suburban-and-rural-communities/

Paulhus, D. L. (2014). Toward a taxonomy of dark personalities. *Current Directions in Psychological Science, 23*(6), 421–426. https://doi.org/10.1177/0963721414547737

Pew Research Center. (2011, January 13). *A portrait of stepfamilies.* https://www.pewsocialtrends.org/2011/01/13/a-portrait-of-stepfamilies/

Phelps, E. A., O'Connor, K. J., Cunningham, W. A., Funayama, E. S., Gatenby, J. C., Gore, J. C., & Banaji, M. R. (2000). Performance on indirect measures of race evaluation predicts amygdala activation. *Journal of Cognitive Neuroscience, 12*(5), 729–738. https://doi.org/10.1162/089892900562552

Pilling, A. R., & Hart, C. W. M. (1960). *The Tiwi of North Australia.* Holt, Rinehart and Winston.

Pillsworth, E. G., & Haselton, M. G. (2006). Male sexual attractiveness predicts differential ovulatory shifts in female extra-pair attraction and male mate retention. *Evolution and Human Behavior, 27*(4), 247–258. https://doi.org/10.1016/j.evolhumbehav.2005.10.002

Pinel, J. P., Assanand, S., & Lehman, D. R. (2000). Hunger, eating, and ill health. *American Psychologist, 55*(10), 1105–1116. https://doi.org/10.1037/0003-066X.55.10.1105

Pinker, S. (2002). *The blank slate: The modern denial of human nature.* Viking/Penguin.

Pinker, S. (2011). *The better angels of our nature: Why violence has declined.* Viking.

Platt, J. (1973). Social traps. *American Psychologist, 28*(8), 641–651. https://doi.org/10.1037/h0035723

Plummer, W. (1987, October 26). After 27 years in his bedroom, 1,200-lb. Walter Hudson decides to take a load off. *People Magazine, 28*(17), p. 60.

Porter, M. (2018, March 16). *Australian parents rank first for time spent with children.* Essential Kids. http://www.essentialkids.com.au/health/relationships/australian-parents-rank-first-for-time-spent-with-children-20180315-h0xigc

Pospisil, L. (1963). *The Kapauku Papuans of West New Guinea.* Holt, Rinehart and Winston.

Power, S. (2019). *The education of an idealist: A memoir.* Dey Street Books.

Preston, C. E., & Harris, S. (1965). Psychology of drivers in traffic accidents. *Journal of Applied Psychology, 49*(4), 284–288. https://doi.org/10.1037/h0022453

Preston, S. H. (1995). Human mortality throughout history and prehistory. In J. L. Simon (Ed.), *The state of humanity* (pp. 30–36). Basil Blackwell.

Previti, D., & Amato, P. R. (2003). Why stay married? Rewards, barriers, and marital stability. *Journal of Marriage and the Family, 65*(3), 561–573. https://doi.org/10.1111/j.1741-3737.2003.00561.x

Putnam, R. P. (2000). *Bowling alone: The collapse and revival of American community.* Simon & Schuster.

Ramirez, J. M. (1993). Acceptability of aggression in four Spanish regions and a comparison with other European countries. *Aggressive Behavior, 19*(3), 185–197. https://doi.org/10.1002/1098-2337(1993)19:3%3C185::AID-AB2480190304%3E3.0.CO;2-T

Regan, D. T. (1971). Effects of a favor and liking on compliance. *Journal of Experimental Social Psychology, 7*(6), 627–639. https://doi.org/10.1016/0022-1031(71)90025-4

Regan, P. C., Lakhanpal, S., & Anguiano, C. (2012). Relationship outcomes in Indian-American love-based and arranged marriages. *Psychological Reports, 110*(3), 915–924. https://doi.org/10.2466/21.02.07.PR0.110.3.915-924

Rind, B., & Bordia, P. (1995). Effect of server's "thank you" and personalization on restaurant tipping. *Journal of Applied Social Psychology, 25*(9), 745–751. https://doi.org/10.1111/j.1559-1816.1995.tb01772.x

Robert Half. (2017, July 19). *Working hard or hardly working? Employees waste more than one day a week on non-work activities.* https://rh-us.mediaroom.com/2017-07-19-WORKING-HARD-OR-HARDLY-WORKING-Employees-Waste-More-Than-One-Day-a-Week-on-Non-Work-Activities

Roberts, J. A., Yaya, L. H., & Manolis, C. (2014). The invisible addiction: Cell-phone activities and addiction among male and female college students. *Journal of Behavioral Addictions, 3*(4), 254–265. https://doi.org/10.1556/JBA.3.2014.015

Roberts, R. J. (2015). Ten simple rules to win a Nobel Prize. *PLOS Computational Biology, 11*(4), Article e1004084. https://doi.org/10.1371/journal.pcbi.1004084

Ronay, R., & von Hippel, W. (2010). The presence of an attractive woman elevates testosterone and physical risk taking in young men. *Social Psychological & Personality Science, 1*(1), 57–64. https://doi.org/10.1177/1948550609352807

Rosenbaum, M. E. (1986). The repulsion hypothesis: On the nondevelopment of relationships. *Journal of Personality and Social Psychology, 51*(6), 1156–1166. https://doi.org/10.1037/0022-3514.51.6.1156

Rosenfeld, M. J., Thomas, R. J., & Hausen, S. (2019). Disintermediating your friends: How online dating in the United States displaces other ways of meeting. *Proceedings of the National Academy of Sciences, 116*(36), 17753–17758. https://doi.org/10.1073/pnas.1908630116

Rosentiel, T. (2007, August 22). *Two decades of American news preferences.* Pew Research Center. https://www.pewresearch.org/2007/08/22/two-decades-of-american-news-preferences-2/

Ross, M., & Sicoly, F. (1979). Egocentric biases in availability and attribution. *Journal of Personality and Social Psychology, 37*(3), 322–336. https://doi.org/10.1037/0022-3514.37.3.322

Rothberg, E. (2021). *Stacey Abrams*. National Women's History Museum. https://www.womenshistory.org/education-resources/biographies/stacey-abrams

Rovner, A. J., Nansel, T. R., Wang, J., & Iannotti, R. J. (2011). Food sold in school vending machines is associated with overall student dietary intake. *Journal of Adolescent Health, 48*(1), 13–19. https://doi.org/10.1016/j.jadohealth.2010.08.021

Rudder, C. (2014). *Dataclysm: Love, sex, race, and identity—What our online lives tell us about our offline selves*. Crown.

Russo, F. (2013, February 13). Want a better relationship? There's an app for that. *Time*. https://healthland.time.com/2013/02/13/want-a-better-relationship-theres-an-app-for-that/

Saad, L. (2014, August 29). *The "40-hour" workweek is actually longer—by seven hours*. Gallup. https://news.gallup.com/poll/175286/hour-workweek-actually-longer-seven-hours.aspx

Sackett, R. (1996). *Time, energy, and the indolent savage. A quantitative cross-cultural test of the primitive affluence hypothesis* [Unpublished doctoral dissertation]. University of California, Los Angeles.

Sadalla, E. K., Kenrick, D. T., & Vershure, B. (1987). Dominance and heterosexual attraction. *Journal of Personality and Social Psychology, 52*(4), 730–738. https://doi.org/10.1037/0022-3514.52.4.730

Salmon, C. A., & Daly, M. (1998). Birth order and familial sentiment: Middleborns are different. *Evolution and Human Behavior, 19*(5), 299–312. https://doi.org/10.1016/S1090-5138(98)00022-1

Sandomir, R. (2018, December 11). Helen Klaben Kahn, survivor of a 49-day Yukon ordeal, dies at 76. *The New York Times*. https://www.nytimes.com/2018/12/11/obituaries/helen-kleban-kahn-dead.html

Scarry, R. (1968). *What do people do all day?* Random House.

Schiff, S. (2010). *Cleopatra: A life*. Little, Brown and Company.

Schumacher, H. (2019, March 17). *Why more men than women die by suicide*. BBC. https://www.bbc.com/future/article/20190313-why-more-men-kill-themselves-than-women

Schwartz, B. (2004). *The paradox of choice: Why more is less*. Ecco.

Seelye, K. Q. (2013, November 24). Sticking by a murderous brother, and paying for it dearly. *The New York Times*. https://www.nytimes.com/2013/11/25/us/sticking-by-a-murderous-brother-and-paying-for-it-dearly.html

Segal, M. W. (1974). Alphabet and attraction: An unobtrusive measure of the effect of propinquity in a field setting. *Journal of Personality and Social Psychology, 30*(5), 654–657. https://doi.org/10.1037/h0037446

Seligman, M. E. P., Steen, T. A., Park, N., & Peterson, C. (2005). Positive psychology progress: Empirical validation of interventions. *American Psychologist, 60*(5), 410–421. https://doi.org/10.1037/0003-066X.60.5.410

Shakespeare, W. (1899). *The works of Shakespeare: The tragedy of Hamlet* (E. Dowden, Ed.). Methuen and Co. (Original work published circa 1599–1601)

Sheldon, K. M. (1999). Learning the lessons of tit-for-tat: Even competitors can get the message. *Journal of Personality and Social Psychology, 77*(6), 1245–1253. https://doi.org/10.1037/0022-3514.77.6.1245

Shiota, M. N., Campos, B., Oveis, C., Hertenstein, M. J., Simon-Thomas, E., & Keltner, D. (2017). Beyond happiness: Building a science of discrete positive emotions. *American Psychologist, 72*(7), 617–643. https://doi.org/10.1037/a0040456

Shiota, M. N., Neufeld, S. L., Danvers, A. F., Osborne, E. A., Sng, O., & Yee, C. I. (2014). Positive emotion differentiation: A functional approach. *Social and Personality Psychology Compass, 8*(3), 104–117. https://doi.org/10.1111/spc3.12092

Silk, J. B., Alberts, S. C., & Altmann, J. (2003). Social bonds of female baboons enhance infant survival. *Science, 302*(5648), 1231–1234. https://doi.org/10.1126/science.1088580

Simon, H. A. (1956). Rational choice and the structure of the environment. *Psychological Review, 63*(2), 129–138. https://doi.org/10.1037/h0042769

Simonton, D. K. (1994). *Greatness: Who makes history and why.* Guilford Press.

Simpson, J. A., Gangestad, S. W., & Lerma, M. (1990). Perception of physical attractiveness: Mechanisms involved in the maintenance of romantic relationships. *Journal of Personality and Social Psychology, 59*(6), 1192–1201. https://doi.org/10.1037/0022-3514.59.6.1192

Smith, E. A., Hill, K., Marlowe, F., Nolin, D., Wiessner, P., Gurven, M., Bowles, S., Mulder, M. B., Hertz, T., & Bell, A. (2010). Wealth transmission and inequality among hunter-gatherers. *Current Anthropology, 51*(1), 19–34. https://doi.org/10.1086/648530

Sohn, K. (2016). Men's revealed preferences regarding women's ages: Evidence from prostitution. *Evolution and Human Behavior, 37*(4), 272–280. https://doi.org/10.1016/j.evolhumbehav.2016.01.002

Souder, W. (2004). *Under a wild sky: John James Audubon and the making of* The Birds of America. North Point Press.

Steinfield, C., Ellison, N. B., & Lampe, C. (2008). Social capital, self-esteem, and use of online social network sites: A longitudinal analysis. *Journal of Applied Developmental Psychology, 29*(6), 434–445. https://doi.org/10.1016/j.appdev.2008.07.002

Stewart, J. B. (1992). *Den of thieves*. Simon & Schuster.

Stewart, J. B. (2005). *Disney war*. Simon & Schuster.

Strong, R. (2019). *The story of Britain: A history of the great ages: From the Romans to the present*. Pegasus Books.

Sugiyama, L. S. (2004). Illness, injury, and disability among Shiwiar forager-horticulturalists: Implications of health-risk buffering for the evolution of human life history. *American Journal of Physical Anthropology, 123*(4), 371–389. https://doi.org/10.1002/ajpa.10325

Sundie, J. M., Kenrick, D. T., Griskevicius, V., Tybur, J. M., Vohs, K. D., & Beal, D. J. (2011). Peacocks, Porsches, and Thorstein Veblen: Conspicuous consumption as a sexual signaling system. *Journal of Personality and Social Psychology, 100*(4), 664–680. https://doi.org/10.1037/a0021669

Svenson, O. (1981). Are we all less risky and more skillful than our fellow drivers? *Acta Psychologica, 47*(2), 143–148. https://doi.org/10.1016/0001-6918(81)90005-6

Swanson, A. (2015, June 23). 144 years of marriage and divorce in the United States, in one chart. *The Washington Post*. June 23, 2015. https://www.washingtonpost.com/news/wonk/wp/2015/06/23/144-years-of-marriage-and-divorce-in-the-united-states-in-one-chart/?noredirect=on&utm_term=.e87dd0f6e6b2

Tan, J. P., Buchanan, A., Flouri, E., Attar-Schwartz, S., & Griggs, J. (2010). Filling the parenting gap? Grandparent involvement with UK adolescents. *Journal of Family Issues, 31*(7), 992–1015. https://doi.org/10.1177/0192513X09360499

Taylor, S. E. (2006). Tend and befriend: Biobehavioral bases of affiliation under stress. *Current Directions in Psychological Science, 15*(6), 273–277. https://doi.org/10.1111/j.1467-8721.2006.00451.x

TED. (2009, September 14). *Misha Glenny investigates global crime networks* [Video]. YouTube. https://www.youtube.com/watch?v=XO1Me-MY-Q0

Thaler, R. H. (2015). *Misbehaving: The making of behavioral economics.* W. W. Norton & Company.

Thaler, R. H., & Sunstein, C. R. (2008). *Nudge: Improving decisions about health, wealth, and happiness.* Penguin Books.

Thomas, B. (1976). *Walt Disney: An American original.* Simon & Schuster.

Thomas, B. (1998). *Building a company: Roy O. Disney and the creation of an entertainment empire.* Hyperion.

Thomas, E. M. (1959). *The harmless people.* Alfred A. Knopf.

Tietjen, A. M. (1994). Children's social networks and social supports in cultural context. In W. J. Lonner & R. Malpass (Eds.), *Psychology and culture* (pp. 101–106). Allyn & Bacon.

Tooby, J., & Cosmides, L. (1996). Friendship and the banker's paradox: Other pathways to the evolution of adaptations for altruism. *Proceedings of the British Academy, 88*, 119–143.

Townsend, J. M., & Levy, G. D. (1990). Effects of potential partners' physical attractiveness and socioeconomic status on sexuality and partner selection. *Archives of Sexual Behavior, 19*(2), 149–164. https://doi.org/10.1007/BF01542229

Trivers, R. L. (1972). Parental investment and sexual selection. In B. Campbell (Ed.), *Sexual selection and the descent of man* (pp. 136–179). Aldine de Gruyter.

Trivers, R. L. (1974). Parent–offspring conflict. *American Zoologist, 14*(1), 249–264. https://doi.org/10.1093/icb/14.1.249

Twenge, J. M. (2017). Have smartphones destroyed a generation? *The Atlantic.* https://www.theatlantic.com/magazine/archive/2017/09/has-the-smartphone-destroyed-a-generation/534198/

Twenge, J. M., & Campbell, W. K. (2019). Media use is linked to lower psychological well-being: Evidence from three datasets. *Psychiatric Quarterly, 90*(2), 311–331. https://doi.org/10.1007/s11126-019-09630-7

Twenge, J. M., & Park, H. (2019). The decline in adult activities among U.S. adolescents, 1976–2016. *Child Development, 90*(2), 638–654. https://doi.org/10.1111/cdev.12930

United States Census Bureau. (2000). *Historical census of housing tables: Living alone.* https://www.census.gov/data/tables/time-series/dec/coh-livealone.html

United States Census Bureau. (2016, November 17). *The majority of children live with two parents.* https://www.census.gov/newsroom/press-releases/2016/cb16-192.html#:~:text=Of%20the%2011%20million%20families,to%2093%20percent%20in%201950

United States Census Bureau. (2020, December 2). *Week 19 Household Pulse Survey: November 11–November 23.* https://www.census.gov/data/tables/2020/demo/hhp/hhp19.html

U.S. Bureau of Labor Statistics. (2018). *Standard occupational classification.* https://www.bls.gov/soc/

U.S. Bureau of Labor Statistics. (2021, April 21). *Employment characteristics of families—2020* [Press Release No. USDL-21-0695]. https://www.bls.gov/news.release/pdf/famee.pdf

Vaillant, J. (2010). *The tiger: A true story of vengeance and survival.* Alfred A. Knopf.

Valdesolo, P., & DeSteno, D. (2008). The duality of virtue: Deconstructing the moral hypocrite. *Journal of Experimental Social Psychology, 44*(5), 1334–1338. https://doi.org/10.1016/j.jesp.2008.03.010

van Baaren, R. B., Holland, R. W., Steenaert, B., & van Knippenberg, A. (2003). Mimicry for money: Behavioral consequences of imitation. *Journal of Experimental Social Psychology, 39*(4), 393–398. https://doi.org/10.1016/S0022-1031(03)00014-3

Vanderveele, T. J. (2020, October 20). National well-being before and during the pandemic. *Psychology Today.* https://www.psychology-today.com/us/blog/human-flourishing/202010/national-well-being-and-during-the-pandemic

Vardi, A. (2020, September 17). He spent years forging ties with the Amazon's most isolated tribes. Then he realized his mistake. *Haaretz.* https://www.haaretz.com/world-news/.premium.MAGAZINE-he-grew-close-to-the-amazon-s-most-isolated-tribes-then-he-realized-his-mistake-1.9165808?v=1627682457073

Vasey, P. L., & VanderLaan, D. P. (2009). Materteral and avuncular tendencies in Samoa. *Human Nature, 20*(3), 269–281. https://doi.org/10.1007/s12110-009-9066-4

Verini, J. (2020, August 18). How U.S. policy turned the Sonoran Desert into a graveyard for migrants. *The New York Times.* https://www.nytimes.com/2020/08/18/magazine/border-crossing.html?searchResultPosition=1

VintagePostersNYC. (n.d.). *7 Up the fresh up family drink* [Poster]. https://www.vintagepostersnyc.com/posters/_up_the_fresh_up_family_drink_blue_border_8193.html

Visit Anaheim. (2018, March 1). *Visit Anaheim study reveals American families spend the most quality time together while on vacation*. https://www.visitanaheim.org/articles/post/visit-anaheim-study-reveals-american-families-spend-the-most-quality-time-together-while-on-vacation/

von Hippel, W. (2018). *The social leap: The new evolutionary science of who we are, where we come from, and what makes us happy*. Harper Collins Publishers.

von Rueden, C., & Van Vugt, M. (2015). Leadership in small-scale societies: Some implications for theory, research, and practice. *Leadership Quarterly, 26*(6), 978–990. https://doi.org/10.1016/j.leaqua.2015.10.004

Vouchercloud. (n.d.). *How many productive hours in a work day? Just 2 hours, 23 minutes* . . . https://www.vouchercloud.com/resources/office-worker-productivity

Walsh, P. (1983, February 2). *Admitted bigamist Giovanni Vigliotto, who named 105 wives Wednesday,. . . .* UPI. https://www.upi.com/Archives/1983/02/02/Admitted-bigamist-Giovanni-Vigliotto-who-named-105-wives-Wednesday/9996413010000/

Wang, P. (2019, May 19). Protect yourself from hidden fees. *Consumer Reports*. https://www.consumerreports.org/fees-billing/protect-your-self-from-hidden-fees/

Wansink, B., & Kim, J. (2005). Bad popcorn in big buckets: Portion size can influence intake as much as taste. *Journal of Nutrition Education and Behavior, 37*(5), 242–245. https://doi.org/10.1016/S1499-4046(06)60278-9

Waterhouse, B. (n.d.). *A sustainable future?* PBS. https://www.pbs.org/ktca/farmhouses/sustainable_future.html

Watson, D., & Humrichouse, J. (2006). Personality development in emerging adulthood: Integrating evidence from self-ratings and spouse ratings. *Journal of Personality and Social Psychology, 91*(5), 959–974. https://doi.org/10.1037/0022-3514.91.5.959

Weatherford, J. (2004). *Genghis Khan and the making of the modern world*. Broadway Books.

Williams, E. F., & Gilovich, T. (2008). Do people really believe they are above average? *Journal of Experimental Social Psychology, 44*(4), 1121–1128. https://doi.org/10.1016/j.jesp.2008.01.002

Wilson, E. O. (2014). *The meaning of human existence.* W. W. Norton & Company.

Wilson, M., & Daly, M. (1985). Competitiveness, risk taking, and violence: The young male syndrome. *Ethology and Sociobiology, 6*(1), 59–73. https://doi.org/10.1016/0162-3095(85)90041-X

Wing, R. R., & Jeffery, R. W. (1999). Benefits of recruiting participants with friends and increasing social support for weight loss and maintenance. *Journal of Consulting and Clinical Psychology, 67*(1), 132–138. https://doi.org/10.1037/0022-006X.67.1.132

World Health Organization. (n.d.). *Data and statistics: The challenge of obesity—Quick statistics.* https://www.euro.who.int/en/health-topics/noncommunicable-diseases/obesity/data-and-statistics

World Health Organization. (2021, June 9). *Obesity and overweight.* https://www.who.int/news-room/fact-sheets/detail/obesity-and-overweight

Worldometer. (n.d.). *World population by year.* https://www.worldometers.info/world-population/world-population-by-year/

Wrangham, R. (2009). *Catching fire: How cooking made us human.* Basic Books.

Wrangham, R., & Peterson, D. (1996). *Demonic males: Apes and the origins of human violence.* Houghton Mifflin Company.

Wuchty, S., Jones, B. F., & Uzzi, B. (2007). The increasing dominance of teams in production of knowledge. *Science, 316*(5827), 1036–1039. https://doi.org/10.1126/science.1136099

Zinsmeister, K. (n.d.). *Osceola McCarty.* The Philanthropy Roundtable. https://www.philanthropyroundtable.org/almanac/people/hall-of-fame/detail/oseola-mccarty

INDEX

ABOUT THE AUTHORS

Douglas T. Kenrick, PhD, is the author of *Sex, Murder, and the Meaning of Life: A Psychologist Investigates How Evolution, Cognition, and Complexity Are Revolutionizing Our View of Human Nature* (2011) and coauthor of *The Rational Animal: How Evolution Made Us Smarter Than We Think* (with Vladas Griskevicius; 2013). He has published more than 200 scientific articles, books, and book chapters, the majority applying evolutionary ideas to human behavior and thought processes. The research has been funded by the National Science Foundation and the National Institute of Mental Health, and has been published in prestigious journals, such as *Psychological Review* and *Behavioral and Brain Sciences*. Much of that research has also been covered in national and international media, including *Newsweek*, *The New York Times*, and many other newspapers and popular magazines.

Doug's paper renovating Maslow's classic pyramid of motives, which provides a central structure for this book, was the subject of two articles in *The New York Times* and articles in many other news outlets. He has edited several books on evolutionary psychology and been an author of two multiedition textbooks, including *Social Psychology: Goals in Interaction* (with Steven L. Neuberg, Robert B. Cialdini, and David E. Lundberg-Kenrick; 2020), which is now in its seventh edition and has been used by tens of thousands of students in the United States and other countries. His books have been translated into several languages, including Chinese, Korean, Italian, and Polish. Doug has appeared in several BBC and Discovery Channel documentaries on evolution and human behavior as well as on *The Oprah Winfrey Show*. He has written articles for *The New York Times* and *Scientific American* and, for *Psychology Today*, he writes a blog titled "Sex, Murder, and the Meaning of Life," which has been visited by 4.7 million readers.

David E. Lundberg-Kenrick is the media outreach director for the Department of Psychology at Arizona State University, where he is creating a new program called Psych for Life®, designed to connect psychological research to the problems we all face every day. Dave studied film production at New York University and at the University of Texas at Austin. He has worked as an animator, video editor, and video producer.

Dave has shot footage for various documentaries and television shows on the BBC, Discovery Channel, and SBS Australia networks. For the Human Behavior and Evolution Society, Dave filmed the founding members of the field of evolutionary psychology, including Steven Pinker, David Buss, Leda Cosmides, and Napoleon Chagnon. He wrote a blog for *Psychology Today* called "The Caveman Goes to Hollywood," which analyzed the connections between popular movies and the themes of evolutionary psychology. He also cohosted a popular podcast, *Zombified*, about the ways people are unwittingly manipulated by parasites from microscopic organisms to multinational corporations. Dave is coauthor of the seventh edition of *Social Psychology: Goals in Interaction* (with Douglas T. Kenrick, Steven L. Neuberg, and Robert B. Cialdini; 2020), for which he produced research videos in which active researchers from around the world, including many evolutionary psychologists, share their findings in a lively animated format.